Peter. G.

Christ Church College.

D1045201

A HUNDRED YEARS
OF EDUCATION

By the Same Author

THE FAR EAST

A
HUNDRED YEARS
OF
EDUCATION

BY

A. D. C. PETERSON

Director of the Department of Education at Oxford University.
Formerly Headmaster of
Adams' Grammar School and of Dover College.

GERALD DUCKWORTH & CO. LTD.
3 HENRIETTA STREET, LONDON, W.C.2

First published 1952
Second edition, revised 1960
All rights reserved

Printed Photo-litho in Great Britain by
Phototype Limited, London

CONTENTS

PREFACE

THIS book is meant for the general reader who wants to know something about the history of Education, but has no intention of studying any branch of it intensively. I hope it may also interest some schoolmasters and schoolmistresses who, like myself, have no time to qualify as educational experts, and perhaps even prove useful, as a very general introduction, to students of education before they get down to serious work.

It is limited to the systems of the U.S.A. and Western Europe, particularly those of England, France and Germany. Even so, the field to be covered is immense, and I have had to choose between coherent narratives, dealing with a few important issues, and a catalogue. I have chosen the former because catalogues are unreadable to the general reader and would be useless to the student; but the choice has inevitably meant a great number of omissions, and I have made no attempt whatever to include every important name or every important event in the educational history of the last hundred years. For the same reason, I have left out entirely certain topics, very closely allied to the main themes, which could certainly claim a place in a comprehensive survey of the whole field. There is, for instance, no mention of health or welfare services, and I have attempted no special treatment of the education of infants either in the nursery or the nursery school. To treat either of these subjects adequately would demand another chapter, and, since there is scarcely any human activity from the cradle to the grave which is not, in some sense, educational, there would be no end to it.

I have finished the book with a growing diffidence that it should have been undertaken by a practising schoolmaster rather than an educational expert. The disadvantages will, I fear, be obvious. I can only hope that it will have one compensating advantage. Books on education written by educational experts often seem to be written for educational experts, assuming a knowledge and employing a terminology which make them very heavy-going for the school teacher and the general reader. The fact that this one has been written in the intervals of teaching in a country grammar school will, I hope, have kept it strictly down to earth.

It could not have been written without a good deal of help from many sources, and my thanks are due particularly to my colleague Mr A. R. Hoggins and to Mr Abbott of the Shropshire Education Authority, for reading the manuscript and correcting some at least of the mistakes; perhaps I should make it clear to Mr Abbott, who did not get a look at the Epilogue, that the strictures on the administrative mind included in it are not directed against that most liberal of administrations, the Shropshire Education Authority. I am grateful, too, to the Librarians of the Shropshire County Library, the Birmingham Institute of Education and the United States Information Office, who have hunted out books for me and let me keep them far longer than I ought: to many boys and masters who have put me right: and to my wife both for moral support and valuable criticism, particularly about the education of girls. Finally, in this last respect, I would ask the reader to spare me the unreality of referring every time to "educators" and "educands", and to regard the term "schoolmistresses" as included in "schoolmasters" and "girls" in "boys" wherever the sense demands it.

A. D. C. PETERSON

Adams' Grammar School
June 1951

PREFACE TO SECOND EDITION

In so far as this edition differs from the first, which is not very much, I can no longer claim that it is written by a practising schoolmaster. The intervening years have given me a wider experience of public administration and also of the training of teachers. As a result I have re-written some of the passages on the training of teachers from what is, I hope, a more balanced understanding. I have also corrected one or two mistakes, added one or two more personal opinions, and extended a few paragraphs nearer to the present day.

What I have not done is either to "bring the book up to date" as a whole or rewrite it. It is, after all, a record of 100 years, not a picture of the contemporary scene and nothing that has happened in these last eight years has materially altered the record. Nor have I found that the experiences of the last eight years have materially altered my own opinions about it.   A.D.C.P.

CHAPTER ONE

INTRODUCTORY

THE titles of most books are more or less deceptive and this one would be no exception if it were interpreted rigidly. But while it would be impossible to confine a study of educational progress strictly to the last hundred years, it is remarkable what a good starting-point the middle decades of the nineteenth century make. The reaction after the revolutionary year of 1848 produced a break which has a real meaning in the history of state-controlled education in Europe; the Civil War is an equally important watershed in the U.S.A. In the sphere of women's education the foundation of Queen's College (1848), and in adult education that of the Working Men's College (1854), are true starting-points. In the widening of school and university curricula the middle of the century is again none too late, although of course the first moves had already been made. Only in the sphere of educational theory is it necessary to go back for a more detailed review of an earlier period, and even in this respect it was not until almost 1850 that the ideas which Pestalozzi, Froebel and Herbart developed at the beginning of the century really gained acceptance.

It will be possible, therefore, to keep more nearly than might have been expected to the last hundred years, and in each chapter except the fourth to dispense with all but the briefest résumé of earlier periods. Underlying this great educational development in the last hundred, or, at most, hundred and fifty, years has been the slow realisation that society, as represented by the State, has a duty to provide its members—and more and more of its members—with an ever-lengthening period of formal education. Roughly, until the French Revolution this duty was held to be incumbent either upon the Church or upon the parent. Our first subject of enquiry must therefore be the relations of the State, as an educational authority, with the Church and with the individual or small group of individuals. Throughout the nineteenth century the State, except possibly in Prussia and latterly the U.S.A., was mainly concerned with its duty to provide primary schools, and

9

the result of its intervention was to produce for the first time, in country after country, universal free primary education. The administrative problems involved in this expansion occupy the next two chapters.

The spread of primary education, and the fact that it was now provided from public funds, produced a growing interest in the type of education given, and for the first time educational reformers and theorists found themselves being taken seriously. In Chapter Four therefore we shall turn to consider the development of educational theory as it affects the learning process, and in Chapter Five as it affects the training of the whole character. From 1880 onwards it was becoming clearer that the processes of expansion and state control which had overtaken primary education would recur in secondary education and for very much the same reasons. In Chapter Six therefore we turn to secondary education and the changes in its nature which this development has produced, and in Chapter Seven to the later but ultimately parallel development of secondary and higher education for women. Finally, the expansion has spread to the adult members of society, and Chapters Eight and Nine therefore discuss universities and adult education.

Two chapters on separate subjects conclude the survey. The Tenth, on the training and supply of teachers, deals with what is really the key to the whole matter, for teachers matter more than schools, or administrators or educationists or equipment. In the eleventh chapter examinations are treated separately as links between the different stages of education belonging properly neither to one section nor another. The reader will see, therefore, that each chapter is more or less self-contained, and those who are not interested in the background of administration can safely skip the first three.

The purpose of this first chapter, then, is to describe the starting-point from which this hundred-year process began, and in order to avoid repetition it will be confined to primary and secondary schools, leaving the background of the other topics to the chapters which particularly concern them.

Primary Education in 1851

(a) *In England.*—Primary education in England in 1851 was a muddle and not very far from being a disgrace. Those who believed either in education or in parliamentary democracy had been urging for the last fifty years that a national system of primary education should be established. Their vehemence was not surprising, since the shortage of schools in England at the beginning of the century had been really alarming. They had been unsuccessful largely because they met with the determined opposition of both the Anglican and the Dissenting Churches; but the very necessity which the Churches conceived of opposing a state system had stimulated them to meet the obvious need themselves. The first half of the nineteenth century was marked in England by an immense effort of voluntary school-building, made chiefly by the Church of England. The support of the State for this effort was feeble, partly because direct Government activity of all kinds was contrary to the English conception of politics, and partly because the voluntary bodies would not allow to the State that measure of control without which the vote of large sums of public money could hardly be expected.

This work of the Churches had produced, by the middle of the century, results which are best summed up in the findings of the Newcastle Commission, appointed in 1858, "to enquire into the present state of education in England". The most striking change was that the proportion of school children to the total population of the country had risen from 1 in 21 in 1800 to 1 in 7 or 1 in 8. The total figures of children at school were about two and a half million, a rise of a million and a half since 1833. But even this increase was exceeded by that made in France in the same period, where, as a result of introducing a national system, numbers rose in roughly the same period from just over a million and a half to just under four million.

While the Commission considered the increase in numbers satisfactory, it was not so impressed with the schools they went to or the regularity of their attendance. More than half of them were attending private schools, neither assisted nor inspected by the Government, where there was no check on the qualifications of the teachers or the conditions of the schoolrooms. Of these it is fair to assume that the vast majority were still going to traditional "dame schools".

To keep a dame school it was not necessary to be a dame. It was not necessary, in fact, to be honest, sober, literate or free from infectious disease. There were, of course, many such schools which were run by people with a love of their pupils and a real desire and capacity to teach. The novels of the nineteenth century are full of such people, from Clym Yeobright to Bartle Massey. And it is significant how easy it was for a man like Clym Yeobright to consider starting a school as a private venture with no previous experience and no specific qualifications. The majority of dame schools, however, were simply places to which children were sent in order to get them out of the way, and the successful "dame" was the one who could pack the largest number into the small back-room that served as a school and keep them quiet. The following extracts from the report [1] give a clear general picture of conditions. They are worth comparing with the parallel description of conditions in France a generation earlier quoted on page 15.

"None are too old, too poor, too ignorant, too feeble, too sickly, too unqualified in one or every way, to regard themselves, and to be regarded by others as unfit for schoolkeeping. Nay, there are few, if any, occupations regarded as incompatible with schoolkeeping, if not as simultaneous at least as preparatory employments. Domestic servants out of place, discharged barmaids, vendors of toys or lollipops, keepers of small eating-houses, of mangles or of small lodging-houses, needlewomen who take in plain or slop work, milliners, consumptive patients in an advanced stage, cripples almost bed-ridden, persons of at least doubtful temperance, outdoor paupers, men and women of seventy or even eighty years of age, persons who spell badly (mostly women, I grieve to say), who can scarcely write and who cannot cipher at all.

"When other occupations fail for a time, a private school can be opened, with no capital beyond the cost of a ticket in the window.[2] Any room, however small and close, serves for the purpose; the children sit on the floor and bring what books they please; while the closeness of the room renders fuel superfluous and even keeps the children quiet by its narcotic effects. If the fees do not pay the rent, the school is dispersed or taken by the next tenant."

J. and B. Hammond, in *The Age of the Chartists*, paint the same picture, quoting as "probably the worst" a school in Liverpool "where a garret measuring ten feet by nine feet contained one schoolmaster, one cock, two hens, three black terriers and forty children".

What little education the children did get they consumed in

---

[1] Newcastle Report, vol. i, pp. 93–94, quoted in Curtis, *History of Education in Great Britain*.
[2] Dickens' mother tried this method, but without success.

very short gulps and very intermittently. Even in the inspected schools, attendance only averaged about seventy-five per cent. of the pupils on the rolls, and seventeen per cent. attended less than fifty days in the year. In the uninspected schools, of course, children came and went as they or their parents felt inclined, and it is probable that most of them had no more than a year's schooling. These had at least seen the inside of a school however. Another contemporary record refers to the 21,025 entirely schoolless children of Glasgow and the 17,177 of Manchester.

Once in the schools, what did the children learn? Conditions in the dame schools and voluntary schools must have differed widely, but in general it is probably fair to say that they learnt their catechisms, or some other religious formulary, by heart, reading, writing and, unless they were unlucky, a little arithmetic. In the inspected school they would be sure of this much, though the standard was often woefully low. One feature of the schools was actually remarkably good. The average number of pupils per teacher in 1860 was 37·7, and this compares well both with figures elsewhere and with figures in England to-day.

In most respects, however, English primary education at the time of the Great Exhibition was hardly worthy of a nation which claimed to be the richest and most prosperous in the world. The great American educational reformer, Horace Mann, after inspecting the schools of England, Ireland, Scotland, France, Germany and Holland in 1843, put England bottom of the list.

(b) *In Europe.*—In the more advanced European countries the situation was very different. The Iberian peninsula and Italy were even further from establishing any sort of universal school system than England herself; but in Germany, Scotland, Switzerland and the Low Countries, general systems of primary education, under the local control of the Church or the communal authorities, were already well established. In the U.S.A. there was a lively and enterprising interest in schools, but the country was too young in its development, and control too localised, for any general system to be apparent. France alone had completed a national system of secular state primary schools, and the French and Dutch schools were probably the nearest to what they have become to-day. Neither in Holland nor in France was education at any stage yet compulsory; but this is comparatively unimportant from the practical point of view. Compulsory education is meaningless unless a strongly organised state enforces it, and few states, if any, had the mechanism to impose such enforcement in the middle of the nineteenth century. Primary education had been compulsory in Denmark, for instance, since 1739, but the whole cost fell on the parishes, which had no funds to provide it, and the law was therefore a dead letter. For the same sort of reasons Matthew Arnold found that "compulsory" education in the poorer cantons of Switzerland produced no larger school attendance than "voluntary" education in the richer cantons. The fact that the principle of compulsory education had at least been recognised in Europe and actually enforced in parts of the U.S.A. was, however, of great theoretical importance.

The real clue to the establishment of a national system of education had already proved to be the provision of finance and inspection[1]; the accepted system of working through local authorities like parishes was, in fact, perfectly feasible, so long as these authorities were both enabled and compelled to carry out their task. In the eighteenth century, and particularly in the revolutionary period, it had been common enough to issue edicts establishing universal free education; but without some provision for raising the necessary money and then seeing that it was actually spent on schools, such decrees were merely what Guizot termed the French Revolution's contribution to education in France—"un déluge des mots".[2]

Since France was the one great European power which had established a national system of primary education by the middle of the century, it is worth considering the French experience in some detail.

It was Guizot's own typically bourgeois and pedestrian law

[1] France, and Europe as a whole, was very impressed by the Dutch system of inspection established early in the century.

[2] The system of school laws without schools is well illustrated in the history of some regions of Italy. A law of 1859 made the establishment of schools by all communes able to do so compulsory; a law of 1877 made attendance compulsory; a law of 1906 provided for the establishment of state schools where the communes had failed; and a law of 1911 set up provincial authorities to establish schools at the cost of the State where localities were too poor or too careless to have done so. Surely after all this the educationist in his study could safely write that primary education in Italy was universal and compulsory. Yet in 1923 when the new Fascist Government opened an enquiry it found that in Calabria less than half the children were enrolled in any school and of this minority only 32 per cent. attended regularly. And for all the new laws, if you go to Calabria to-day you will find plenty of children who have never been to school and have no intention of going.

of 1833 which really founded the French national system. Until 1833, although occasional attempts had been made in theory to organise primary education, no machinery had been set up to ensure that the theoretical decisions of the central government had any effect on actual schools or children.

Consequently normal "dame school" conditions, similar to those in England, prevailed.

"Of the 20,000 Communes provided with schools, barely one-half possessed, even in 1834, school premises of their own; in the other half the school was held in a barn, in a cellar, in a stable, in the Church porch, in the open air, in a room which served at the same time as the sole dwelling place of the schoolmaster and his family, where his meals were cooked and his children born. Where school premises existed, they were often no better than their less pretentious substitutes: they were often hovels, dilapidated, windowless, fireless, reeking with damp, where in the space of twelve feet square eighty children were crowded together; where the ravages of an epidemic swept the school every year. . . . Here the teacher was a petty tradesman, leaving his class every moment to sell tobacco to a customer; there he was a drunkard; in another he was a cripple." [1]

The law of 1833 did not sweep away these physical slum schools straight away. It first objective was to see that a school of some sort should be available in every commune, its second that the teacher should be a suitable person. To achieve the first it enacted that every commune *must* (not might or ought to) provide a school and must levy a rate not exceeding three centimes towards the cost of this. In many poor communes, of course, this did not provide nearly enough, and in such cases the department was obliged to supplement it out of a departmental rate of two centimes. Where the combined funds were insufficient the Ministry of Education in Paris made up the difference. [2]

To ensure that the teacher was a suitable person two main qualifications were required—a certificate of morality and a training in teaching. The first was a document of very doubtful value, but the second did mean that for the first time a corps of genuinely professional teachers arose. Unfortunately, the French Government made the common mistake of fixing the salary of

[1] Matthew Arnold. Mainly quoted from *Tableau de l'Instruction Primaire en France* by M. Lorain, 1837.

[2] A similar system had been introduced in Holland but without the advantage of fixing by law the proportion to be contributed by each authority.

the teachers at about the economic level previously commanded by the "dames"; and this was naturally far too low to satisfy the superior class of men whom they wanted to attract into the profession.

As a result of the new system school attendance in France rose from just over a million and a half in 1834 to just over two million in 1849; and by the time that Matthew Arnold visited France in 1869 as a *rapporteur* for the Board of Education in England the system was fully established and the school population approximately four million.

Under this system every commune in France had its school. They might not be very grand, and in country districts the schoolroom was often an old stone-floored building converted. The schoolmaster was admittedly underpaid, but he got a house and garden and was encouraged to take on such jobs as clerk to the council, which brought him in a little extra. A good schoolmaster could clearly play a large and rewarding part in the life of the village. In the big towns there were large schools of up to four hundred children, with covered playgrounds and halls where the children ate the midday meal, which they had brought with them. Guizot also saw the necessity for "higher primary" as distinct from secondary education. The higher primary schools which he founded were suppressed by the Second Republic, but their restoration constitutes one of the great positive services rendered by the Third Republic to the cause of popular education.

In all primary schools the curriculum and the method of teaching were laid down by the Ministry of Education in Paris. The weekly allocation of subjects was as follows:

Religious Instruction . . .	6 hours
Reading	4 ,,
Writing	3 ,,
French	6 ,,
Arithmetic	5 ,,
Drawing	3 ,,
Singing	3 ,,
History and Geography . . .	3 ,,

There were prayers at the beginning of the day and another break for prayers at midday. A crucifix and a bust of the Emperor Napoleon III were formally displayed in any sizable school. It will be seen therefore that a great deal of importance was attached to moral training; there was certainly some political intention behind this, since there had been much criticism of the school-masters as "revolutionary agitators" in 1848. The bust of the Emperor seems almost reminiscent of Japan, but British readers should remember that their own country has been most exceptional in its failure to use the schools for the direct encouragement of patriotic feeling.

It will not be surprising to those familiar with educational history that, apart from the low salaries of the teachers, the chief weakness of this French system was the size of the classes. In a large modern mixed school of four hundred in Paris, for instance, there were only three men teachers for the boys' side and one woman (assisted by monitresses) for the girls. In a school of four hundred, maintained by the Brethren of the Christian Schools, there were only four teachers in all—one to each class of a hundred. The "staffing ratio" fixed by law for the Dutch schools shows a better but generally similar situation [1]; and Dutch primary schools were reputed to be the best in Europe.

This meant that "teaching" consisted almost entirely of demonstration followed by copying. Part of the load was taken off the teacher in Holland, and later in Britain, by pupil-teachers, but in France at this time the only assistants were "monitors", *i.e.* senior boys or girls who passed on to their juniors by rote the lesson which they themselves had just learnt. This "Lancasterian" system had caused great controversy when first tried in France, and the "Brethren of the Christian Schools" had rejected it on the very adequate ground that it dissipated the genuine moral and educational influence of the teacher. As a result, however, the teaching brother in a large city school, with his class of a hundred, suffered so much from actual physical exhaustion that he would keep them writing on their slates most of the time in sheer self-protection. The brothers had even

---

[1] The "staffing ratio" for Dutch primary schools in the mid-nineteenth century was as follows:

```
  1- 70 boys—1 headmaster.
 70-100   ,,       ,,      +1 pupil teacher.
100-150   ,,       ,,      +1 assistant master.
150-200   ,,       ,,      +1 assistant master and 1 pupil teacher.
```

invented a sort of rattle with which all signals in class were given in order to save the teacher's voice.

By 1856 the state system had provided France with the following establishment of primary schools:

Public boys' schools	19,200
Public girls' schools	13,900
Public mixed schools . . .	17,000
Private boys' schools . . .	3,400
Private girls' schools . . .	11,600

Of the boys' schools just under ten per cent. were run by religious bodies, and of the girls' schools about seventy per cent.

This total of 65,100 schools, with an attendance of over three and three-quarter million children, compares remarkably with conditions in England. Of these children one and a quarter million were receiving their education free and the total public expenditure was £1,507,740, of which the communes found considerably more than the minimum that was imposed upon them. Matthew Arnold notes that at the same time expenditure in England amounted to just over half this amount, and that, owing to much more luxurious standards and elaborate paper records, this sum sufficed only to "aid" (not maintain) 8,461 schools. In France, he reckoned, a similar sum would have completely maintained nearly 23,000. This accusation of un-necessarily high standards at the cost of insufficient quantity is one which has been brought against English educational authorities almost as often as that of multiplying superficial courses in high school has been brought against American. At this time the only luxury enjoyed by the English system that was worth the money was probably the lower staffing ratio.

Control of the schools under the French system lay, from the moral point of view, with the Mayor and Minister of Religion of the Commune; instruction was the affair of the departmental council, and the teachers themselves were under the direct control of the Prefect of the Department, who "names, changes, repri-mands, suspends and dismisses all public primary teachers of every grade". He exercised this power, however, "on the report of the inspector", and one of the virtues of the French system was a well-organised body of primary inspectors many of whom had been primary schoolmasters themselves.

Secondary Education.

(a) *In England.*—For secondary education England was, on the whole, even worse off than for primary; but she had one very important asset. In a few great "public schools" she had already developed a model which has profoundly influenced the whole secondary education of Europe and America.

It is impossible to define exactly what is meant by a "public school" in the English sense, but in the nineteenth century even more than to-day everyone knew what the term meant—an independent secondary school for boys usually charging a comparatively high fee and intended for the education of "gentlemen". The great majority were boarding schools, and their particular virtue lay in the life of the community rather than in academic excellence. Almost all of them had, along with the universities, passed through a period of decay and degradation in the eighteenth century, from which they were rescued partly by a public opinion which refused to tolerate it any longer, and partly by the work of one or two great headmasters, notably Butler of Shrewsbury (1798–1836) and Arnold of Rugby (1828–1841).

Most people's impressions of life at one of these schools are formed from *Tom Brown's Schooldays*; and this is no bad thing. For although the period which it sets out to describe is the very beginning of Arnold's time in the 1830's, the writer is using considerable hindsight. It is also a matter-of-fact book on such subjects as fagging and sausages and football, with the result that we can get a great deal nearer to the feelings of a boy at Rugby under Arnold than we can, for instance, to those of a boy at Uppingham under Thring. And if we want to see what the inspiration of the English public schools was, for good or ill, we can hardly do better than reread *Tom Brown's Schooldays* alongside the description of a French "interne" in, for instance, *Le Grand Meaulne*, or—though this is much later—*La Pharisienne*.

Of the reforms which saved the English public school from well-merited extinction, Butler was mainly responsible for those affecting teaching methods and Arnold for those affecting "education for life".

Arnold's intentions and methods came in for a great deal of criticism in the "debunking" 1920's, and the whole value of the public school tradition must be considered much more carefully in Chapter Five; but there is no question that in 1851 these schools were considered an enormous improvement on the past, and the Clarendon Commission which inspected them in 1861 had little or no fault to find with the moral or physical conditions. They were rough, of course, and Spartan by modern standards; they were a long way from being even sanitary [1]; the food was amazingly plain except where the boys supplemented it themselves; but there was something about sausages and murphies cooked on the library fire on a November evening, something about running wild over the countryside in "hare and hounds", which no amount of free-issue milk at eleven and supervised gymnastics could replace. The Taunton Commission which followed the Clarendon Commission, and reported in 1868 on the remaining secondary schools of England, found a much more serious state of affairs and one which it is fair to assume had existed more or less unchanged throughout the first half of the century.

The supposed backbone of secondary education in England was the grammar schools, but in the length and breadth of the country the Commission found less than a thousand of these schools, and many of them had sunk to the level of inefficient primary schools. "In at least two-thirds of the places in England named as towns in the census ", they reported, "there is no public school at all above the primary schools, and in the remaining third the school is often insufficient in size or in quality." The reasons for this inadequacy are discussed in Chapter Six.

The incapacity of the grammar schools had, of course, led to the establishment of a large number of private secondary schools which lacked the grammar school endowments but which were not shackled, like the grammar schools, to an impossible curriculum. Many of the best of these had been founded by dissenting religious bodies, and the Commissioner particularly remarked on the excellence of some of the Roman Catholic schools. Private schools were not all as good as this, however, and many of them were even worse than the grammar schools. In any case they could not provide a national system of secondary education, and that was what England particularly lacked. As

---

[1] How, writing of the decline in numbers at Winchester about 1856, says: "There were several causes for this, the chief being the unhealthiness of 'New Commoners', some ten boys dying within a few years of typhoid Fever" (*Six Great Schoolmasters*).

Matthew Arnold continuously and somewhat tactlessly pointed out, her middle class was the worst educated in Europe. As far as numbers were concerned, Scotland was very much better off than England and the proportion of boys receiving secondary education was higher than in either Prussia, France or England.[1]

(b) *In Europe and America.*—In most of the other countries of Western Europe some national system of secondary education already existed, at least in embryo; and, in America, states and cities were beginning to feel their way towards the development of the high school. It was the Prussian system, however, which had developed most nearly into its modern form, and which particularly attracted the notice of other countries. It is therefore the only one which really falls outside the scope of our later enquiry and deserves a place in this preliminary survey.

The secondary schools of Prussia were divided into *Gymnasien* and *Realschule*—almost equivalent at the top to the present British conception of "classical" and "modern" sides in the grammar school. The Gymnasium had an age range of nine to eighteen, and was designed for boys who intended to proceed to the university and enter one of the liberal professions. The curriculum was the traditional classical one, modified by the addition of a certain proportion of outside subjects. Since the amount of time given to each subject was laid down by the Ministry of Education in a *Lehrplan*, which was obligatory for all gymnasia, the clearest picture can be given by quoting these regulations for 1856, the year when Matthew Arnold visited these schools on behalf of the Taunton Commission. The hours of work were from 7 A.M. to 11 A.M. in summer, and 8 A.M. to 12 NOON in winter, with afternoon school always from 2 P.M. to 4 P.M. There was one half-holiday in the middle of the week. All forms below the sixth did ten hours Latin a week, but in the sixth two of these were given to science; Greek was started in the fourth year with six hours. What would have surprised the English public school master of the time was that all classes did mathematics (four hours in the lower school, three in the middle and upper), French (two hours), German (two hours), geography and history (three hours), religious instruction, music and physical

[1] The figures were 1 in 205 in Scotland, 1 in 249 in Prussia, 1 in 570 in France, and 1 in 1300 in England (Curtis, *History of Education in Great Britain*).

training. It is remarkable how close this plan of work is to the classical side of a modern English grammar school.

The *Realschule*, which were intended for those going into trade or industry, were of varying ranks. In those of the first rank Latin was still compulsory, but the amount of time given to it was reduced in favour of more mathematics, science and modern languages. In *Realschule* of the second rank, vocational or technical subjects were introduced; and those of the third rank only accepted pupils up to the age of fifteen or sixteen. It is worth noting that *Pro-gymnasien* also existed, with an age range of nine to sixteen, and that pupils from them would go on to complete the last two years of their education at the full *Gymnasien*. This must have solved one of the difficulties which afflicts the English grammer school in country districts to-day—the impossibility of providing a full variety of sixth form courses for five or six boys. What would now be perhaps known as "multilateral" *Real-Gymnasien* were also known, but the classes were quite separate after the second year, and the combination of the two types of school was purely administrative.

Of the 66,000 boys attending these schools in 1856 approximately 40,000 were day boys, and the vast majority of the remainder lodged with private families in the town. There was, however, at least one school, Schulpforta, in Saxony, which was very like an English boarding public school. A correspondent writing to Hughes, the author of *Tom Brown's Schooldays*, describes it as "similar in antiquity and institutions to Arnold's Rugby".

Fees for day boys averaged £3 a year, and there were usually about ten per cent. of free places.

Under this system public authorities provided a first class secondary education at a reasonable cost to 66,135 pupils out of a total population of eighteen and a half million. In England, with its population of just over twenty million, Arnold calculated that not more than 15,880 were receiving secondary education at anything "which by any straining or indulgence can possibly be made to bear the title of public schools".

One weakness which would strike the modern critic is that there appear to be no grounds on which the selection for *Gymnasium* or *Realschule* at the age of nine and a half could be made. We must remember, however, that the system was devised for a society with a rigid class structure in which it could be predicted, almost from birth, which children were destined for the university and which for trade. In Germany, as elsewhere, there were, throughout the nineteenth century, two systems of education, an elementary system for the poor and a secondary system for the rich. To move from one system to the other was extremely rare.

CHAPTER TWO

CHURCH AND STATE

The State's Relations with Education

THERE is no doubt that an outstanding feature of the last hundred years has been the increased part taken by the State, that is, the central government, in the management of people's lives. This has been true both under socialist and capitalist administrations, and the extent to which it has happened has made strange reading of much classical political theory. In many respects this increasing day-to-day control by government departments has passed almost unnoticed—most people would be amazed, for instance, at the 1851 attitude towards public control of sanitation—but in the field of education each step in the increase of state control has been a battlefield; and the battle has been fought in the strong light of publicity.

The reason for this is that in attempting to manage the education of its children the State was interfering with the family in something far more controversial, and of far more intimate importance to it, than in trying to control its drains. The State was opposed, therefore, by two champions of the family, the Church and the small community. The history of educational administration over the last hundred years is largely the story of continued conflicts and compromises between the claims of the central government, the claims of the Church, the claims of the small community and the claims of the individual.

It is not my purpose in this chapter to record the details of this conflict. "Educational administration", Professor Dover Wilson has said, "is a fascinating theme." I suspect that few but "educationists" find it so, and rather than recount in detail the disputes, regulations and acts that have been recounted so often elsewhere, I shall try to sketch the broad outlines of the conflict and the various solutions that were tried.

Throughout Europe, education was originally under the control of the Church; and except in Rhode Island and Pennsylvania this principle was extended by the European settlers to

24

North America. Where the Church exercised control, much of it was delegated to the parish, and the small community was thus satisfied. By 1851, however, the Church had almost everywhere been compelled either to surrender this control to the State or to permit the establishment of private schools outside its own orbit. The question during the last hundred years has been whether the Church would retain any control at all.

The movement which ultimately led to the State securing control of education all over Europe had, of course, its origins as far back as Plato. It is clear that any theory of the State which is "positive", and which imposes upon it a general responsibility for the prosperity and welfare of its citizens, necessarily entails state control of education. The more "totalitarian" the State, the more rigid the control of education must be. Plato made this perfectly clear. It is only a State with strictly limited functions, such as Locke's, which could neglect control of education. It was, therefore, the new wave of national statism inaugurated by Rousseau and the precursors of the French Revolution which gave the impetus to state control of education, and the organised nationalism of Fichte and the Prussians which established it.

Three stages in this development can be fairly clearly traced. The first is when the State really assumes ultimate responsibility for the provision of schools, as opposed to passing general edicts encouraging someone else to provide them; the second is when the State makes attendance at these schools compulsory; and the third, following immediately from the second, is when it makes attendance free. This last stage inevitably involves the State in great expense, since the voluntary bodies which previously provided schools generally expected the parent to contribute a considerable proportion of the cost by way of fees. It is at this stage, therefore, that the State comes most strongly into conflict with the voluntary bodies, the Churches and the small community; for the supporters and officials of the State always maintain that financial responsibility must not be separated from control.

The Conflict with the Churches

The expansion of state control produced an immediate conflict with the Church, not merely because of a natural rivalry for pre-eminence, but because those States which first claimed complete control did so on grounds that were always anti-clerical, and, during the period of the French Revolution, became anti-religious. The first half of the nineteenth century, however, saw a reaction from the extreme secular position and an attempt to reach a compromise between Church and State, with now one, now the other, gaining the ascendancy.

In France, for instance, the secularisation movement, beginning with the publication of La Chalotais' famous essay on National Education, led first to the suppression of the Jesuit educational system in 1764 and then to the "Republican Cathechisms" under the Revolution. The Concordat and the subsequent return of the Bourbons ensured that religion should not be left out of French education, but as early as 1833 Guizot was trying again to establish a national secular educational system, with religious instruction left to the priests and ministers.

"It is in general desirable", he writes in a circular of that date, " that children whose families do not profess the same creed should early contract, by frequenting the same schools, those habits of reciprocal friendship and mutual tolerance which may ripen later, when they live together as grown-up citizens, into justice and harmony."

This system was overthrown in the conservative reaction after 1848, and by 1850 France had gone back to predominantly denominational schools, under an agreement by which the government inspectors were not to concern themselves with religious instruction, except to ensure that each child had an opportunity to learn the doctrines of his own family's faith.[1] And for this purpose they recognised only three faiths, Roman Catholicism, Protestantism and Judaism.

By the middle of the century the relations between Church and State on the subject of education approximated to one or other of a few standard patterns.

In countries where there were no appreciable religious minorities they had been fairly clearly settled. The Church, where it had not sufficient funds out of its own revenue to meet the increasing cost of education, was fully represented among those who controlled the machinery of state, and was therefore

---

[1] "Moral supervision" of communal schools was entrusted to the Mayor and the Minister of Religion.

content to allow the State to provide the general education and itself to concentrate upon the moral and religious side. Thus in a Protestant country like Norway, where 97 per cent. of the population are to-day Evangelical Lutherans, the general control of the bishops slowly declined, but their responsibility for the moral and religious side of the schools remained undiminished, and the schools have always been fully denominational. A similar situation existed in purely Roman Catholic countries. In Spain, for instance, the religious question was settled in 1857 by a Concordat with the Vatican under which "Public Instruction in the Universities, Colleges, Seminaries, public and private schools of every description must be at all points in harmony with the teaching of the Catholic Church."

It was in countries with large religious minorities that the really thorny problems arose. It was inconceivable that the State's claim to control education should in the long run be denied. Once compulsory education was accepted in fact instead of in theory, there was no other agency capable of raising a sufficient revenue to finance it, and finance could not be entirely separated from control. Moreover, this group of countries included France and Prussia, the two most highly centralised states in Europe, where control of all sorts of activities by the central government had long been accepted. The problems which faced such countries were:—

(*a*) How to provide a national system of primary schools which would be acceptable to Roman Catholic, Protestant and "free-thinking" families alike.

(*b*) How to secure the goodwill and co-operation of the Churches. For in many countries the Churches already controlled an educational system which the State could scarcely hope to do without.

(*c*) How to finance a state educational system without offending the tender conscience of individual taxpayers by levying upon them taxes which were used to support schools of a religious denomination repugnant to them.

The most drastic solution to the first problem is the universal and compulsory use of "common schools", in which the secular education of the children is carried out, while their religious and moral education is entrusted to the minister of their own religion at other times and in other places. This is the extreme of

27

secularism, and pleases no religious body; it certainly fails entirely to find a solution for the second problem. In its pure form it has been adopted only since the Russian revolution under purely Marxist governments, whose real, and often avowed, aim is the elimination of religion. In countries where religion was still genuinely cherished, but where a universal state system was demanded, it was, in the nineteenth century, always modified by the inclusion in the secular curriculum of some sort of "generalised" religion or even "generalised" Christianity.

The difficulty in applying this modification has been that genuinely religious people are not usually satisfied with "generalised" religion, so that it is not a full answer to the second of the three main problems. Another solution has therefore been sought by those countries which have established a national primary system, but permitted the Churches to maintain a parallel and alternative system.

The difficulty here has been that the State has usually found the Church, though initially capable of providing a parallel system, too poor to be able to keep up with the rapidly improving standards of state education, unless it receives aid from public funds; and to provide such aid is to be brought face to face immediately with the third of the three main problems.

By 1851 the two main solutions had already begun to claim their adherents, and the religious controversy had already begun to claim its victims among the schoolchildren. Matthew Arnold tells the story of a French schoolmaster of "free-thinking" views who paraded his pupils, with drums beating, to march through the town singing the "Marseillaise," until they reached the house of the Curé. On arriving there they stood for the space of some minutes shouting "Down with the Jesuits", and then, presumably, dispersed. In England he "saw with his own eyes, in a British school, aided with public money, a printed placard offering a reward of £10 to any Roman Catholic who could prove by text ten propositions, such as that we ought to adore the Virgin Mary, that we ought to pray for the dead, etc." The bitterness with which different denominations of Christians fought over the souls of the children was in fact every bit as great as that between Christians as a whole and non-believers. In England it was the main reason why a national system of primary education was delayed for nearly fifty years.

The Dutch System

Of the two main solutions attempted for this exasperating controversy that of a "generalised" religion fitted into a universal system had in the nineteenth century much the smaller following. Yet it is worth noting that the one place where it was tried, Holland, had during the period of its enforcement what was generally admitted to be the finest primary school system in Europe. In Holland, between 1820 and 1848, the teaching of "dogmatic" religions in the schools had been forbidden. Dogmatic religion was to be taught only by the ministers of the different faiths—for Holland was sharply divided between Protestants and Catholics—and outside the schools. In the schools a "general moral Christian training" was compulsory. This is clearly something not entirely unlike the present "agreed syllabus" position in English "controlled" schools under the 1944 Act. It is interesting to see the objections which were made to it in the nineteenth century. It had, of course, been considered by other educational reformers, for it seemed one obvious way of putting an end to the difficulty; and the very fact that Holland, with her much admired primary schools, made use of it was an argument in its favour.

Guizot had rejected this system in his plan for the introduction of universal common schools in France. Religious instruction, he held, "should not be a series of lessons and practices apparently capable of being used by all denominations in common. Such lessons tend to banish all positive and efficacious teaching from the schools." He preferred, therefore, to rely upon a "conscience clause"; that is, to leave the religious teaching "positive", but to allow the parent who disagreed with its bias to withdraw the child from the school during the periods when it was given. Matthew Arnold, on the other hand, objected to it on the grounds that such "generalised" or "purely moral" presentations of Christianity were a fraud, and were in fact always tinged with the doctrinal balance prevalent in the community, particularly if this was a Protestant community.

Both these objections are sound, but it is easy to see that they are mutually contradictory. Guizot, in the interests of true religion, is objecting to a jejune "ethical" approach on the grounds that it rules out all real religious training; Matthew Arnold objects on the equally valid grounds that, on the contrary, real religious training will keep creeping in. Both were probably right. No external syllabus will prevent a genuinely religious man from conveying the religion he believes in, nor enable an irreligious one to pass on what he has not got.

This Dutch system had, however, passed its zenith by the time that our period begins. From 1822 the Roman Catholics had been opposing the state monopoly of primary education and pressing for permission to open denominational schools. In 1848 the Dutch Calvinists joined them, and the government was compelled to give way. From then on Holland presents a good example of a gradual movement *towards* State support for denominational schools. From 1848 until 1888, although the scales were weighted against the denominational schools, Holland enjoyed a parallel system. The State continued to maintain the old non-denominational system, and laid it down in 1857 that its object was "to develop the reason of the young, and to train them in the exercise of all Christian and social virtues". Meanwhile the religious bodies were permitted to establish denominational schools but received no aid from public funds. In 1888 a political victory for the Church party led to a modification of the constitution, allowing the central government to subsidise denominational schools, though the local authorities were still not entitled to do so. It was not until 1917 that the principle of complete equality of financial support for denominational schools was agreed.

In thus moving away from the "generalised religion" solution to that of state aid for denominational schools, Holland was in fact coming into line with what has been one branch of normal European practice. She was undoubtedly aided in doing so by the fact that the country is mostly divided into districts which are overwhelmingly of one or the other faith. Thus internal conditions in most districts approximate to those in countries of a single religious denomination; and in such countries, as we have seen, the problem of religious education is not difficult.

The German System

The more usual European system in the mid-nineteenth century was for the State to aid denominational schools only of the faith of which it approved. An example of this was found in Germany until 1919.

Germany, it must be remembered, was not a unified country until 1871, and even then, until the drastic reforms of the Nazis, education was controlled by the individual states and not by the central "Reich" Government. This meant that it was comparatively easy to maintain a denominational system, since most states were nearly homogeneous in religious faith. Up to 1933 83 per cent. of German primary schools were denominational— Roman Catholic, for instance, in Bavaria, and Protestant in Prussia.

From 1870 onwards the preponderance of Prussia in Germany was so great that it is perhaps worth outlining the course of events in that state. An unusual feature of the Prussian school system was that state control of secondary education came long before that of primary education, and it was not until 1872 that all primary schools were made liable to state inspection. Up to that time inspection had been carried out entirely by the clergy. The law of 1872 permitted the government to revoke the licence of inspectors not appointed by the State, but this was in fact only used to eliminate the Roman Catholic clergy, and in 1919 two-thirds of the school inspectors were still Protestant ministers. The effect of state control here, therefore, was to introduce compulsorily the normal denominational system of a single-faith country for the greater part of the people. In certain areas of Prussia, as well as in certain small states where the denominations were mixed, schools of mixed denomination were either permitted or obligatory, and in these it was usual for the members of each faith to receive their religious instruction from their co-religionists. This system, like that advocated by Guizot, was generally regarded as the "liberal" solution.

When the Republic was proclaimed, the Left Wing were in favour of a universal mixed system, and the Right of retaining denominational schools. The new constitution introduced a compromise, the most important clause of which stated that parents had a right to demand elementary schools in their area, "organised in accordance with their own *Weltanschauung*" (*i.e.* "beliefs about the world"). This had the curious result that the Weimar Government paid grants to the Roman Catholic, Protestant and Marxist schools equally; and that the Nazis were able to invoke the clause to enable groups of parents (twenty-four was the minimum number) to demand neo-pagan schools. In

c 31

spite of the Concordat with the Vatican, in which the Nazi Government guaranteed the retention of Catholic schools, their numbers actually fell from 15,256 in 1931 to 9,636 in 1938.[1] It is possible to see in this progress an oscillation between the two policies of extreme statism, under which only the approved denomination is aided, and extreme liberalism, under which any *Weltanschauung* can claim the support which is granted to any other. It has been fear of these two extremes which has prompted the series of compromises adopted in England.

The French System

The movement away from state aid of denominational schools to completely parallel systems, of secular schools financed by the State (out of taxes), and denominational schools permitted by the State but financed by the Church out of endowments and fees, is best seen in France.

From 1851 to 1870 under the authoritarian régime of Napoleon III the schools were denominational, and the local clergy—predominantly Roman Catholic—had the responsibility for "moral oversight" and the selection of teachers. The collapse of the Empire and establishment of the Third Republic inaugurated a period of extremely bitter religious conflict in France; this conflict, as Professor Ducatillon has said, underlies the whole drama of modern France. When the new constitution was debated, the Catholics were solidly in favour of a restitution of the monarchy, and this solution in fact commanded a majority in the Constituent Assembly: it was only the intransigence and incompetence of the Bourbon claimant which allowed the Republicans to seize their chance. Consequently the Republic in its early years feared, and with justice, a Catholic attack on its very existence; in such circumstances it was not likely to leave control of education in Catholic hands a moment longer than it could help. The first phase of this bitter antagonism between Clericals and Republicans lasted until 1890, when the Pope gave the lead to a movement of French Catholics who were prepared to accept the Republic. From then on the causes for tension were really removed, and the bitterness began to abate, although, as so often happens, the manifestations of it reached their peak

[1] *Education and Society in Modern Germany,* R. H. Samuel and R. Hinton Thomas, p. 104.

in the years immediately following the removal of its fundamental cause. By 1906 it was beginning to be true to say that the anti-Republican Catholics were a dwindling minority and the anti-clerical Republicans a diehard core. As far as it affected the schools, the course of the feud was therefore very nearly parallel in time to that between the Nonconformists and Anglicans in England, and the decisions were taken at the same moment and in exactly the opposite sense to those taken in Holland.

The three stages by which the Republic freed state education from any vestige of influence by the Church were the laws of 1881 and 1882, which established free secular education and made school attendance compulsory; the law of 1886, which excluded clergy from the state teaching body; and the law of 1904, which suppressed the great teaching orders. This lay system of education did not, of course, admit to any intention of banishing religion from the instruction of the young: its guiding principle was that this was the concern of the family, not of the State, and for this purpose there was no school session on Thursdays, so that parents might arrange on that day whatever form of religious instruction they chose. Those who have seen the attitude of schoolboys to instruction that takes place on an official holiday can gauge the effect. The law of 1904 also only suppressed what we should perhaps call monastic schools; it did not forbid lay brothers from teaching, so that in fact a parallel system of Catholic schools was still permitted, though these received no form of aid from the State.

In spite of the fact that denominational schools were thus penalised, only four-fifths of the children educated in primary schools in 1930 were attending the free secular state schools. This high proportion of children still attending the Church schools probably indicates a more anomalous position than appears at first sight, since the strong Catholic feeling was very much localised in districts like Brittany and La Vendée. Even in these, every commune or group of communes was compelled to maintain a secular state school, and a Catholic priest has told me of one case at least where the only boy attending the state school was the schoolmaster's son. It is worth noting that when Alsace-Lorraine was recovered in 1919, the French government found the denominational system established by the Germans so popular that in spite of strong pressure from anti-clericals they were compelled to let it go on. The brief reactionary régime of Vichy introduced compulsory religious instruction into the state schools and extended state support to the Catholic schools; but after the Liberation, France reverted to the system established at the beginning of the century. To-day the question of government support for Church schools is again a burning political issue.

The Religious Dispute in England

In 1851, as we have already seen, England was very backward in education; and she owed this backwardness largely to the religious dispute. At first sight this appears a most improbable situation. England was at that time a predominantly Protestant country with no considerable minority, either of Roman Catholics or free-thinkers. In theory it should have been comparatively easy to establish a national system of Protestant schools; and if only the British government, and of course ultimately the British people, had been prepared to accept, as the French did, no more than three religious categories, Catholic, Protestant and Jew, this could have been done. Unfortunately the Protestants of England were divided, and the rivalry between the Church of England and the Nonconformists was quite as acute as any existing elsewhere between Protestants and Roman Catholics, or Christians and free-thinkers. Unfortunately, also, the division coincided, as in France, with a political division, the Church of England being on the whole supported by the Tories and the Nonconformist Churches by the Radicals.

The violence of this dispute is difficult for modern readers to imagine. It did not really begin to reach its bitterest in the educational sphere until there seemed some genuine likelihood that the State would establish a comprehensive system of schools. The nearer this got, the more intransigent the two parties became in their demands, just as the Muslims and Hindus in India became increasingly more intransigent the more they realised that independence was really coming. This is seen very clearly in the period immediately before 1851. In the report of the Royal Commission of 1818 it is made clear that the "national" schools (denominational schools of the Church of England) were in fact adopting that positive yet liberal attitude which Guizot later wished to introduce in France. "The Church catechism is only taught and attendance at the established place of worship only required", it reads, "of those whose parents belong to the establishment; due assurance being obtained that the children of sectaries shall learn the principles and attend the ordinance of religion according to the doctrines and forms to which their families are attached." [1]

Yet when, in 1820, Brougham introduced the first of many Education Bills attempting to set up a comprehensive primary school system, it was thrown out by the combined efforts of Church of England and Nonconformist supporters. The Church of England opposed it on Guizot's grounds, that the teaching was to be "undenominational" and therefore vapid; the Nonconformists because of a provision, designed to placate the Church, that the schoolmasters were to be members of the Church of England.

From this time onward every move towards establishing a universal "undenominational" school system increased the determination of the Church of England to maintain and increase its own schools; while every suggestion of aiding such schools out of taxation enhanced the determination of the Nonconformists to oppose their creation. The watchword of the Church of England was "a Church system or none"; that of the Nonconformists "rather none than a Church system".

This bitterness had three results. First, it prevented any national system at all for approximately fifty years; second, it combined with the influence of the Oxford Movement to bring to an end the original liberal policy of the Church schools; and, third, it led to a tremendous effort of school-building by the Church of England. The establishment in 1839 of the first governmental body concerning itself with education, the Committee of Council, was met by this new rigidity on the part of the Church. No longer were the national schools to educate all children, allowing those who belonged to Nonconformist families to withdraw from religious instruction under a "conscience clause". On the contrary, Archdeacon Denison, the leader of the High Church party, said: "Under no circumstances whatsoever could I consent to admit a single child to a school of which I have the control and management, without insisting most

---

[1] Hansard, 1820, vol. 11, col. 6, quoted in S. J. Curtis, *History of Education in Great Britain*.

positively and strictly on the learning of the catechism and attendance at church on Sunday."

This extremely rigorous view was not, of course, adopted in all Church schools, but it was reasonably common, and Matthew Arnold quotes another inspector as saying: "I heard of an English national school aided by public money, the only school in the place, which had for one of its regulations that no child of dissenting parents should be admitted unless he consented to be re-baptised."

By 1851 the position, was serious. Another Education Bill had been thrown out in 1843, and England still had no national school system and no public control of education. The only right which the Committee of Council possessed was that of inspecting those schools among which it distributed its small grants. Even here the inspectors of Church schools had to be nominated by the Church authorities. On the other hand, the quarrel between Church and Chapel had at last stirred the free-thinkers into action, and a movement was started in the North in favour of a purely secular system. This was a development quite contrary to the spirit of the nation and one which neither Church nor Chapel had expected. It did not at first have very much success, but it drew what strength it had from the exasperation caused to those primarily concerned with education by the intransigence of the religious bodies. The temptation to cry "a plague on both your houses" was strong, and by 1869 the secular Birmingham Education League, of which Joseph Chamberlain was vice-chairman, was strong enough to be one of the forces which induced the clerical parties to accept the famous compromise of 1870.

In 1852 the Committee of Council felt strong enough to take at least one step towards dissolving the rigidity of the religious antagonisms: it ruled that no grant would be paid to any school unless a "conscience clause" were included in the constitution of the school. This was a fairly bold move considering that virtually all the efficient primary schools of the country belonged to one or other of the religious foundations. It was not, of course, anything like universally effective, for the grant still played a comparatively unimportant part in the finances of the school, but it is interesting from the point of view of administration, as being one of the first uses of a typically English method of exercising control by the central government over independent school authorities. The withholding of grant was to become the main weapon in the hands of the Board of Education, and it is still the chief way in which the Ministry of Education controls the procedure of individual local education authorities.

The conflicting Protestant bodies may have become rather angry and over-combative during this period, but at least such rivalry stirred them, as men are often stirred even by inter-departmental jealousy, to vigorous action. England owes a great deal to the tremendous voluntary effort put into education by the religious bodies—predominantly by the Church of England.

By 1851 there were 17,015 Church of England schools with 955,865 pupils, and 1500 Nonconformist schools with 225,000 pupils. The disparity in size apparent in the figures is mainly due to the fact that the Church of England schools were often built in small country villages, while the "British" or Non-conformist schools were almost entirely concentrated in the towns. Nor were these Church schools at that time in any way behind the standard which a state system could have demanded. We often find in present-day educational reform that there is quite a question whether these out-dated Church of England schools should be scrapped or remodelled; but the very fact that many of them have served for a hundred years is an indication of a fairly high building standard when they were first put up. Indeed, it was one of Matthew Arnold's main complaints against the English system in the 1850's, as opposed to the French, that the money was squandered on too high a standard of building, when the same expenditure, if controlled by the State, could have provided far more school places in more austere school-houses.

"These schools", he writes of the French village school-houses, "would look humble enough beside an Elizabethan normal college in England, or the elaborate Gothic edifice with which the liberality of the Committee of Council enables our English rector to adorn his village."

It is only in comparatively recent times that the Churches have been unable to keep up with the building standards demanded by the Board or Ministry; and one wonders what devotees of plain living and high thinking, like Matthew Arnold, would think of the present accepted building cost per pupil.

The appointment and report of the Newcastle Commission

(report issued 1861) left the religious position unchanged. Grant was still to be paid by the central government to any privately provided school which was not actually insanitary, without taking its religious denomination into account; but no machinery was devised by which schools could be set up at public expense. It was not until the Education Act of 1870 that any workable solution to the religious problem in England was found. The administrative importance of this Act will be treated later in this chapter; its religious solution was to secure agreement to the provision of schools out of public funds by banishing from them any positive religious teaching without even insisting, as the Dutch had done, on some sort of generalised Christianity. The famous Cowper-Temple clause, which has been in spite of many attacks the key to the English position ever since, reads:

"No religious catechisms or religious formulary which is distinctive of any particular denomination shall be taught in the school."

A further clause laid it down that neither attendance at a place of worship nor at religious instruction of any sort should be made a condition of entry.

It must not be thought that this extremely secular Act did in fact banish religion from English schools. In the first place, it referred only to the schools provided by the School Boards, and for many years these were far outnumbered by the Church of England schools. The latter were allowed to continue their denominational teaching, provided that parents who wished to do so could withdraw their children under a "conscience clause". Secondly, although the Act did not stipulate that any non-denominational religious instruction should be given, it raised no barrier to the individual School Boards making such regulations as they saw fit; and the number of Boards which opted in favour of completely secular schools was very small. The effect of the Act of 1870 in practice, therefore, was to initiate a dual system in England:

(*a*) Of public primary schools, most of which included generalised Christianity.

(*b*) Of denominational schools, aided by public funds, but with a conscience clause.

The Cowper-Temple solution of 1870 was attacked from the first. In 1886 the majority report of the Cross Commission voted for its abolition; in 1896 the Conservatives brought in an Education Bill which included its repeal; but it remained in force because nothing else would satisfy the Nonconformists. By the end of the century the number of children in primary schools provided from public funds at last exceeded those in Church schools; a complete reorganisation was necessary and was carried out by the Act of 1902. The religious settlement of 1870 was not disturbed, except in so far as the aid granted to voluntary denominational schools now came from the local rates and not from central government funds. In spite of this, it was the Nonconformists who now fought the Bill more strongly than ever. Although two clauses were put into the Act to prevent the religious teaching at a denominational school from offending local feeling, a number of Nonconformists refused to obey it when it had become law. As they also refused to pay the fines imposed by the courts, their goods were occasionally seized in distraint with every circumstance of publicity. They were, however, the extremists of the cause, and although the Liberal (and therefore largely Nonconformist) ministry which came into power in 1906 made two attempts to repeal its religious provisions, the essential justice of the Act was beginning to be recognised and the amending Bills were both withdrawn.

This was the last blaze of the long religious controversy between the Nonconformists and the Church of England. It is difficult to recover the feelings which inspired it. It could only have happened between Christians who were so assured of the essential acceptance of the Christian faith that they could afford to quarrel bitterly over secondary points. Dr Micklem, the Principal of Mansfield College, has recently pointed out that "those Nonconformists who in 1902 favoured even a 'secular solution' as the only way to escape from sectarian controversy did so because they lived, or thought they lived, *in mundo Christiano*. It was assumed that the general atmosphere of the schools would be Christian, and especially that Christian moral principles would everywhere be inculcated." The logic of their position is difficult to see. They objected to paying rates which went in part towards the support of Church of England schools, but Matthew Arnold had pointed out in the 1860's that there is no justification for any group in society refusing to pay taxes for the support of an institution which the country as a whole has decided to support, unless they find it actively immoral. Even though his words went unheeded, the Nonconformists had in fact long ago submitted to the principle of paying taxes which were used by the central government to make grants towards denominational schools. The only change in 1902 was that the money was raised and the grants made locally: no new principle was involved, but the whole transaction was easier to observe and therefore raised greater passion.

The period between 1902 and 1944 was one of continual discussion rather than conflict or change. The gradual abolition of fees in public elementary schools, which was completed in 1918, meant that the cost of maintaining schools continually rose. Since the Churches could not hope to meet these costs themselves, the proportion met from grants grew bigger, until in most cases virtually the whole running cost of the school was met from public funds. This of course lent force to the secularist argument that he who paid the piper should call the tune, that complete support from public funds should entail complete public control. This was most strongly urged in districts where there was only one primary school available—usually one which had been built in the first place by the Church of England, but was now financed from public funds.

The comprehensive Education Act of 1944 tried to find a permanent settlement of the religious question by its division of "voluntary" schools into "aided" and "controlled", and by the regulation which made religious instruction in accordance with an "agreed syllabus" compulsory in county schools. This appears at first sight to confirm that combination of the two methods adopted in the nineteenth century which had been initiated in 1870—licence to the Church to maintain a parallel system and the inclusion, now officially enforced, of "generalised" Christianity in the state system. Examination shows, however, that in both halves of the scheme the Churches have got more favourable treatment than any "secular" reformer a hundred years ago would have prophesied as possible. It is true that the enormous improvement in standards demanded by the Act meant that almost every one of the "elaborate Gothic edifices" was condemned as uninhabitable; and the cost of rebuilding or adaptation was far more than the Churches in these times of high taxation for social services could hope to raise by voluntary effort.

On the other hand, the conditions under which the State was prepared to allow schools to remain under denominational control were really very generous. All that was demanded of the controlling religious or other body was that it should demonstrate its willingness and ability to meet half the cost of the improvements required in the school buildings, and their subsequent maintenance; all other expenses of the school were guaranteed from public funds. On the other side, the "generalised religion", included for the first time by law in the state schools, turned out to be much more specifically Christian than the vague ethics which Guizot had distrusted. A glance at the "approved syllabus" of any English education authority will show that it differs very little from the syllabus which any Protestant church would have recommended. The experience of those who have been concerned in drawing up these syllabuses has almost always been that far more agreement can be reached than would have seemed possible during the struggles of 1902. This may be partly due to a lessening in the political tension between denominations, but it is also a result of a change in teaching methods which has meant far less insistence on the dogmatic presentation of facts in any subject in the curriculum. It was hoped that the 1944 Act would really produce a permanent settlement, but the dispute seems perennial and already in 1949 it was being questioned, openly by the Roman Catholic hierarchy and tacitly by economic pressure. The Roman Catholics have in principle reverted to the Continental claim, accepted in Scotland and the Netherlands, that where Roman Catholic schools exist the State should treat them on an equal footing with state schools as far as financial aid is concerned, but that the Church should retain control over the religious teaching and the appointment of teachers. They maintain that otherwise the Roman Catholic parent, if he sends his children to an independent Catholic school or gives financial aid to an "aided" one, is being penalised by having to pay for education twice—once when he pays for his share of the state school and once when he supports Catholic education. This argument is, of course, much stronger in countries where no state aid is given to denominational schools, and it is difficult to see how the State could yield to it in England without provoking immediate demands, for instance, from the Church of England and the Nonconformist Churches.

One new solution has been suggested in the last few years which seems at least to have equity on its side. This is that those who prefer to withdraw their children from the state system of education on religious grounds and educate them at their own cost at schools which are certified by the State as efficient, should be relieved of that proportion of taxation which represents the cost of each child's education. There are obvious administrative difficulties in the way of this, but it would have the advantage of removing what at any rate seems to many to be an injustice, and would free a certain amount of resources for the support of denominational religion. For there is no doubt that the chief reason for the decline in voluntary and charitable support for education is that much of what was given voluntarily in the past is now collected in taxation.

Church and State in America

The American scene can now be dismissed in a few words. The founders of the new nation adopted many of the advanced notions current in the Europe of their time, and from the point of view of this issue the dominating factor has been the separation of Church and State which has existed since the time of the American Revolution. The public school system was from the first conscientiously secular, and religious instruction was not given in schools provided from public funds, apart from the non-doctrinal study of the Scriptures—and even this is forbidden by some authorities. As in France, denominational schools have been permitted parallel with the public system, and, as in France, many such schools have been provided by the Roman Catholic community. The majority of American Catholics are educated in them and not in the public schools. Possibly because education is such a local affair in America, there has been no serious demand for financial support for these schools from public funds.

CHAPTER THREE

PUBLIC SUPERVISION AND ADMINISTRATION

THE problems with which the last chapter dealt were largely political. The more purely administrative and educational difficulties arose from the conflict between the centralised State and the individual school or small community.

In the eighteenth and early nineteenth centuries the State was usually in favour of education and occasionally interested in its content, but only too pleased to leave its actual provision and administration to the small community. When the statesmen decided, for instance, that universal education would be a good thing, their normal reaction was to pass a law saying that everybody must be educated and then leave it to someone else, usually the parishes, to provide the schools. Since the parishes had no funds for this purpose and no means of raising them, the law remained a pious wish—like the American ordinance of 1787, that "schools and means of education shall forever be encouraged", or the Danish compulsory school attendance law of 1739, which (as we saw in Chapter One) produced universal education in the statute book and nowhere else. The centralised State did not begin to come into serious conflict with the local communities therefore until it determined to make education really universal by making it free; and this it did in country after country during the nineteenth century.

Here again almost every type of solution from the extreme decentralisation of the U.S.A. to the extreme centralisation of France or Japan has been tried in the last hundred years.

It will be convenient in considering these various solutions to distinguish between control of teaching and control of administration. This distinction was always made in the Prussian system, which deeply influenced much of Western European educational practice, and a chronologically excellent starting-point for the history of the last hundred years is provided by the article

43

of the Prussian constitution of 1850, which stated:

> "For the education of the young, sufficient provision is to be made by the provision of public schools. Everyone is free to impart instruction when he has proved to the proper State authorities that he has the moral, scientific and technical qualifications requisite. All public and private establishments are under the supervision of the State."

This only reiterates in slightly more liberal language the article in the 1794 constitution which stated more bluntly: "The teachers in the Gymnasien and other higher schools have the character of State functionaries."

The public control of education which was thus laid down was strictly divided into "supervision" and "administration"; "supervision" meaning the control of teaching, and "administration" the control of finance, buildings, and all the mechanism required to bring teacher and class together in the classroom. Supervision was a function, in Prussia, of the State Department of Education; administration of the local authority. I shall use these two terms throughout this chapter in the sense given them here, and deal with supervision first.

Public Supervision: (a) *General*

In general it is true to say that supervision by the central government has been comparatively rigid in Japan, Germany, France, Russia and Sweden; hardly apparent in England and Norway; and non-existent in the U.S.A. In its extreme form it means not only the prescription of all text-books by the State, but the control by the State of the amount of time allotted to each subject, the hour at which each subject will be studied, and the proportion of the rigidly fixed curriculum that should be covered in each lesson. It has often been repeated that a certain Minister of Public Instruction in France once remarked with pride, as he glanced at his watch, that he could tell not only what book every schoolboy in France was reading at that moment, but also which page he had got to. We shall see later that, whether he made it or not, it would have been no very extravagant boast.

The advantages of supervision are threefold. It ensures that all schools are providing a curriculum which is educationally the best that the government experts can devise. In this respect

44

its purpose is to act as a diffusing agent, so that all schools shall benefit from the educational researches which they themselves could not hope to carry out. Secondly, it increases the equality of opportunity between all children attending state schools, for if the State cannot ensure that all teachers shall be equally competent as teachers, at least it can see that they all teach the same things at the same time and by the same methods. And this also means that movement from one school to another is made very simple. Thirdly, it enables the State to use the educational system for training the young as citizens—citizens of whatever mould the State in being at the time may require. Rousseau, in *Emile*, maintained that you have got to choose between educating men and educating citizens, and if the State prefers citizens it is by means of supervision that it must try to produce them.

It may seem strange that with all these advantages before them the educational leaders of Britain and America should have been so chary of supervision. They were liberal enough, perhaps, to prefer that boys should grow into men before they became citizens, but what of the great advantages to be gained under the first two heads? Alas, they bring with them grave disadvantages also. In the first place, it is very difficult for a teacher to remain spontaneous and lively if he is working strictly to a curriculum not merely worked out with his own headmaster but imposed by an impersonal government department. The State may try to "vitalise" from above, as the French Instruction of 1923 does, but this is an unnatural task.

Secondly, educational theory changes with extreme rapidity. The curriculum and methods approved by our experts to-day may be under strong criticism in 1960, abandoned as an outworn shibboleth from 1970 to 1990, and reintroduced as the latest discovery of the Institute of Paedagogics at Verkhoyansk in 1995. Government departments, however, do not act so swiftly; something approaching a vested interest in text-books and methods grows up, and soon the schools which were endowed with a brand new system are repeating, with inward tedium and contempt, the same fare which was offered to the children's fathers. The fact that the fathers are usually in favour of this is no consolation to the teachers or children. It does not always follow, of course, that the old methods and content are bad or that the new methods and content are any better; but unless the state system is free to accept the stimulus of new methods and content, much of the liveliness and spontaneity goes out of education. The progress of educational thought may be a spiral or even circular, but much of the most fruitful work is often done under the stimulus of what is imagined, however fondly, to be a new discovery. Its followers have the enthusiasm of pioneers, and enthusiasm counts for a great deal in making the difference between good teachers and bad.

It is not surprising therefore that, in general, supervision has been adopted either by states which wished to use it for training a special type of citizen or by those which placed more emphasis on the content of education than the process.

(b) *The Supervised Countries : Prussia and France*

Supervision by the State began in Prussia with the secondary schools, probably because it was felt that the primary schools were already adequately supervised by the State Church. By the middle of the century it was well established and carried out by means of a careful control of curricula, text-books and the training of teachers. The subjects to be studied and the number of hours to be allotted to each had been laid down by the State since the inauguration of the system by von Humboldt in 1806. Control of teacher training and of text-books came a little later, but already by 1844 a decree laid it down that inspectors were to check the books at the disposal of teachers in training at the normal schools. The usual German arrangement with regard to text-books was that only those approved by the State might be used in public schools; and for the convenience of teachers a list of these was kept at the Ministry of Education. All this was quite easy, and gave rise to little professional or political controversy as long as the subjects studied were confined to the ancient classics and mathematics. Between 1880 and 1890, however, the balance of the *Gymnasium* curriculum became a hotly contested political issue, and with the increase in the teaching of modern history the possibilities of using supervision for political indoctrination were vastly increased. In 1889, for instance, the Imperial Government issued instructions that more attention was to be paid to modern German history, "in order to show that the power of the State can alone protect the individual: how Prussia's kings have exerted themselves to raise the conditions of the workers: and how considerably and constantly in this country the wages and conditions of the working classes have improved under this monarchic protection." At this stage it is clear that Prussia has embarked on a career of using supervision to produce the type of citizen required by the State.

A similar system of supervision was adopted in the reform of French education after the defeat of 1870, though the philosophy behind it was by no means the same. Nevertheless, the Prussian influence was very strong. Europe as a whole, and France in particular, believed that the war of 1870 had been won in the German schools; German schoolmasters were accustomed to regard themselves as the real architects of Sadowa and Sedan; and France was determined that the next war should not go the same way. The decision of Japan about this time to model her educational system on the new French code, as she modelled her Navy on the British, was another indirect tribute to the military efficiency of Prussia.

Even without the Prussian model, however, supervision and centralisation came very naturally to a people with the French regard for reason and tradition. The French conception of primary education also, as the acquisition of a limited quantity of essential knowledge, has always favoured a fixed curriculum. It would be false therefore to the true genius of French education to attribute the main lines of Jules Ferry's educational reforms entirely to a determination to copy the victor's methods.

After his establishment of free primary education for all in 1881, the whole French system was codified in 1886 and a general "Statement of Instructions for the Conduct of Primary Schools" issued in 1887. This Instruction was not changed until 1923— a good example of the conservatism of supervisory methods—and even then, if one reads the introduction to the new Instruction, it is clear that it is only a modification of the old. "What demand does the reform meet?" say the authors of the new Instruction. "Has the system drafted by the authors of our School Laws revealed itself as defective? By no means. Each time that one reads over the statement in the Instructions of 1887, one is filled with admiration. In reforming the institution, we intend to remain faithful to the principles of the founders. But experience has proved that, in order to obtain a better application of these principles, there was need of a definite statement on the proper use of the time allowed, of simplifying and graduating

D 47

the programmes, of vitalising the methods, and co-ordinating the subjects. To define, to simplify, to graduate, to vitalise and to co-ordinate, such has been our aim."

The two Instructions of 1887 and 1923 should therefore be regarded as expositions of a single doctrine. If we look at supervision in France as exemplified in them, two things become immediately clear: that it is a much more logical system than anything evolved in Germany, and that it is far more concerned with truth and learning and less with national policy.

State supervision in Germany combined with local administration produced a confusion of authority and overlapping of officials which was only brought to an end when the Nazi Government liquidated the old German States. In the French system, on the other hand, both supervision and administration were combined in the hands of the State, to such an extent that the almost functionless local committees frequently died of inanition. In the sphere of content, the new system, being the creation of an established, reasonable and confident culture, could afford to take the line that, in the teaching of history for instance, French patriotism required nothing more than the presentation of the truth. If we wish to examine supervision in its finest and most developed form, therefore, we cannot find a better example than the French system as laid down in these two Instructions.

In the first place, they prescribed, as usual, the subjects to be studied and the allocation of time to each subject. They also laid down that the "exercises requiring most effort of attention" should be done in the morning. Apart from that, the head of the school could draw up his own time-table, but he had to submit it for approval to the primary inspector. The method of teaching, to which all teachers were expected to adhere, was laid down in manuals; it consisted of exposition and discussion leading to crystallisation of what had been learnt in the lesson, which the pupil must write down in his notebook. Article 15 of the Instruction of 1887 will probably interest teachers who have never worked under a system of complete supervision:

"Each pupil at the time of his admission to the school will receive a special notebook which he must preserve during the entire duration of his course of study. The first exercise each month, following the order of each study, will be written in this book, in class and without outside help, so that all these written exercises considered

48

as a whole may give an idea of the progress of the pupil during the year. This notebook will be kept at the school."

The most notable features about the control of the content were the extremely detailed instructions given to teachers and the high proportion of time devoted to revision. Revision seems, of course, of great importance where the main emphasis in education is laid on acquiring a minimum stock of factual knowledge: and there is no doubt that it was, at first, overemphasised in France. The 1923 Instruction sees the danger: "But if it is desired that the child should study with pleasure and profit", wrote the authors, "the monotony of repetition and distaste for what has been already studied should be avoided." Nevertheless, it still lays down that three months out of the ten in the second year of history should be devoted to revising what was learnt in the first.

The extent of detail into which the Instructions went can best be illustrated by direct quotations taken at random. Here, then, are the Instructions of 1923 on "Distribution of Subjects: Geography, Middle Course. May, First Week: Western Africa—Senegal, Guinea, Sudan. Cities: Dakar, St Louis. Products: groundnuts, cattle. Equatorial Africa: rubber. The Cameroons: timber. Second Week: Indo-China—extent, relief, rivers, coasts, etc." Of course the introductory statement makes it clear that these are not to be regarded as limiting the content, "but rather as a simple statement of the principal features and characteristics which it would be regrettable to omit". Nevertheless, the control of content is fairly rigid and all schools would be doing Dakar in the same week. Finally, let me quote the rather charming curriculum in moral and civic instruction, for the elementary course, first year, November:

(1) Grandparents. They are old and suffer from being less strong and active. Respect and tenderness which they need.

(2) The elder sister or brother. Duty of watching over the little ones. The good example.

(3) The younger sister or brother. Need of confidence in their elders. Ask them for advice and protection.

(4) Mother's birthday. When one greets her. Why? What should one do?

Those who have tried it know that one of the most difficult teaching problems is to gauge whether "moral instruction" is having any effect. The uniformity of the French system does seem to offer some scope here to the educational research worker. It is surely time that some aspirant to a Ph.D. in Education discovered for us whether there is a marked increase in respect and tenderness towards grandparents among six-year-old French children in the weeks immediately following the first of November: and whether mothers whose birthdays fall in the last week of November do noticeably better than others in the matter of presents.

Control of content and method were of course reinforced by control of text-books. Here the system seems at the same time more spontaneous and more rigid than the Prussian: more spontaneous, because the list of books was in the first instance suggested by the teachers themselves; more rigid because the actual number and types of books to be used were prescribed by law (decree of 1890).[1] The books suggested by the teachers were considered first by the inspector for their area, then by a departmental committee, and finally by the Rector of the "Academy" responsible for the district. If he disapproved, the dispute was referred to the Minister. Finally, the results, both of individual pupils and of schools, were measured by an external examination for which the pupils in primary schools could present themselves as soon as they reached the age of twelve. The examination was drawn up by the District Inspector, on a syllabus supplied by the Ministry, and held in the cantonal capital. On the result of it the Inspector issued a *certificat d'études primaires* to each successful student and made a report to the Ministry on the results achieved by the schools.

Both in France and Germany care was taken to see that this system of supervision was really effective through a strict control of the normal schools where teachers were trained, and of the appointment of teachers. Once the teacher was appointed he was kept to a strict observance of the Instructions by a well-organised corps of inspectors.

Supervised systems of this kind continued in force in both countries with no important modification until the war of 1914–18.

---

[1] *E.g.* for the middle course: a Reader, an Elementary Grammar with Exercises, an Arithmetic, a History of France, and a small Atlas.

This had an effect in Germany similar to that produced in France by the defeat of 1870, but much weaker. In the first place, the Weimar Republic proposed a general Reich Law of Education which should be valid throughout the individual states much as the French Instructions were. Secondly, it introduced, administratively and compulsorily, many of the features of "progressive" and "liberal" schools elsewhere, imitating in this the British and American victors rather than the French. The English phraseology was adopted and instead of "instructions" to teachers the Ministry of Education issued "suggestions". This liberalising tendency, however, ran counter to the general spirit of the people and, it must be admitted, of the teaching profession. The Reich Law of Education was never enacted, the liberal reforms forced on the schools for the most part failed and were tacitly dropped, while the teachers as a whole ignored the liberal and international suggestions from Weimar in favour of more nationalist inspiration from elsewhere. Weimar, for instance, issued suggestions forbidding "the glorification of war or false interpretation of the World War and its causes", and recommending that all pupils should receive instructions in the "nature, duties and aims of the League of Nations". Most of the teachers, however, seem to have ignored the suggestions of the central government and preferred to follow the more nationalistic line taken by the Prussian Ministry of Education.

In France the post-war reaction in favour of greater freedom produced the revised Instructions of 1923, which, as we have seen, tried to vitalise the old system by introducing a greater flexibility without seriously modifying it.

It was left to the Nazis to complete the system of supervision in Germany. By the abolition of the semi-independent states they did what the Weimar Government had failed to do and brought the whole control of education under the Reich Minister. The elimination of these overlapping authorities was followed, however, by a new confusion: as in all other spheres of German life, it became difficult to distinguish between the functions of the party and those of the government. The extreme of supervision, the introduction of Nazi propaganda into every type of school-work was in fact more the function of the National Socialist Teachers League than of the Minister, good Nazi though he was. It is worth quoting perhaps, from *Education and Society in Modern*

Germany, one example of the lengths to which this propaganda went. History was, of course, again entirely perverted, but it was a new development to include in arithmetic books "a table giving the sum of money paid annually by the State for elementary and secondary school children and for lunatics, in order to prove that a lunatic is an expensive liability; the child is then told that there are 200,000 lunatics in Germany, and he is required to estimate how much they cost the State each year and how many marriage loans could be made with the money thus used. Other problems to be worked out deal with the Jews and military events." Remembering the ultimate fate of the Jews and lunatics at the hands of those who were brought up on these arithmetic books, it is difficult not to accord to them pride of place in any educational Chamber of Horrors.

(c) *Unsupervised Countries*

The contrast between these uniform systems and the immense variety to be found in England and the U.S.A., the most important unsupervised countries, is very marked. There is, however, a great difference between the types of academic freedom enjoyed by English and American schools. Both countries were heirs to the tradition of Locke, who, in his *Thoughts Concerning Education*, had emphasised the need for freedom and variety in teaching methods, and actually urged parents "to consult their own reason rather than rely wholly on old custom". Both, during the nineteenth century, were bred on the principles of J. S. Mill, who, in his *Essay on Liberty*, wrote:

"A general state education is merely a contrivance for moulding people to be exactly like one another, and as the mould in which it casts them is that which pleases the predominant power in the government . . . it establishes a despotism over the mind, leading by natural tendency to one over the body."

In England, however, the manifest disadvantages from which the educational system suffered in comparison with that of Prussia or France in the mid-nineteenth century led to a short period of half-hearted supervision; while, in America, the refusal of the Federal Government to accept responsibility for education at all, allowed for a considerable degree, varying it is true, but occasionally onerous, of supervision by state and local authorities.

In England it was the fear of what Mill called a "general state education", almost as much as the religious controversy, which thwarted Matthew Arnold's early attempts to secure acceptance for a reasoned and national system of education; nevertheless, under the "Revised Code" introduced in 1862, England was probably nearer to the supervised state than at any other time.

The Revised Code was intended to deal with two failings in those primary schools which were then being aided by government grants—irregular attendance and inefficient instruction in what would now be called the "basic skills"—reading, writing and arithmetic. Its method was to link the grant paid to the number of satisfactory pupils in the school; and this was calculated on the average number of attendances during the year and the number of pupils who passed an annual examination, conducted by the Education Department's inspectors and graded according to the pupil's age. The Code was widely condemned when it was introduced in 1862 and has been ever since, mainly on the grounds that it was inhuman to the children and that it estranged inspectors from schoolmasters; for, since the financial position of the school now depended on the results of the inspection of its registers and the examination of its pupils, the temptation to fake the one and cram the other must have been considerable; and the inspector came to be regarded partly as a suspicious auditor, and partly as an antagonist through whose mesh as many of the children as possible were to be forced. It is significant that the inspectorate were not consulted in the deliberations which led to its introduction.

The factors which were supervised in England under this system were the subjects taught and the standards to be achieved each year, for unless a subject was "grant-earning" there was every temptation to omit it. No detailed curricula were imposed, and the whole system, of course, had no force of law behind it, since it depended entirely on the competition for grant, and any school which did without grant escaped the Code altogether. Nevertheless, few schools could afford to do this, and the effect of the examination on the method and content of teaching was considerable. Kay-Shuttleworth, in his report on elementary schools for 1869, says: "Unless a rigorous effort is made to infuse more intelligence into its teaching, Government arithmetic will soon be known as a modification of the science peculiar to inspected schools, and remarkable chiefly for its meagreness and sterility." The opposition of Kay Shuttleworth and Matthew Arnold shows in fact how far England was in spirit from accepting supervision even at this time. It is doubtful whether the Code would have run even as long as it did, if England also had not been, at least in part, bewitched by the vision of those Prussian schoolmasters basking in the glory of Sadowa and Sedan.

The Revised Code dragged out a continually watered-down existence until 1897, but when, in 1902, the whole English educational system was revised, the new Board of Education "Code for Public Elementary Schools" abandoned supervision altogether. There was no longer any published list of suitable or unsuitable subjects, or instructions on method. The only guide issued to teachers has become famous from the liberality of its title, and from the clear and unequivocal way in which it states the anti-supervisionist point of view. It was called *A Handbook of Suggestions for the Consideration of Teachers and others engaged in the Work of the Public Elementary Schools*; and it stated in the preface that "The only uniformity of practice that the Board of Education desire to see in the teaching of Public Elementary Schools is that each teacher shall think for himself and work out for himself such methods of teaching as may use his powers to the best advantage and be best suited to the particular needs and condition of the school. Uniformity in practice . . . is not desirable even if it were attainable. But freedom implies a corresponding responsibility in its use." This extremely liberal attitude on the part of the Board of Education was transmitted with all the authority of the Board to the L.E.A.s (local education authorities), so that in England since 1902 the school itself has retained the greatest share in deciding both content and method. It would be hard to find examples of either political or theoretical interference in the practice of individual schools. On the political side, for instance, it was even possible in 1949 for the headmaster of a large controlled secondary school to be an avowed and prominent Communist; while, on the theoretical side, experimental techniques in education are almost always encouraged rather than repressed. The intervention of the State has been, in fact, concentrated mainly on welfare: "school meals", for instance, began in 1906 and medical inspections in 1907.

The course of events in the U.S.A. has been very different. From the first the Federal Government in Washington disclaimed any supervision whatever of education; but the constitutional effect of this was only to relegate the possibility to the state governments. At first most states were too busy to concern themselves seriously with the content of education, but as the machinery of democratic administration developed, a possibly unexpected result of this local control became apparent. Whereas supervision on Prussian lines by a central government in Washington would have been even more abhorrent to Americans than to Englishmen, the very American faith in local democracy inclined the people of states and cities to the view that the voter ought to control what was taught in "our" schools. If L.E.A.s had attempted any such control in England, the Board of Education could always have stepped in and, by withholding grant, enforced its own more liberal view. In the U.S.A. there was no such counterbalancing authority, and the years following 1870 saw a considerable amount of state (but no federal) supervision, often initiated on trivial or vote-catching grounds. Professor I. J. Kandel [1] has listed the subjects on which state supervisory legislation was passed as:

(1) The teaching of nationalism (flag display and flag exercises, teaching of patriotism and patriotic songs, prohibition of foreign languages as languages of instruction, teaching of the history of the United States and of the State, and the observance of special days).

(2) The teaching of health and Prohibition.

(3) Conservation of life and property.

(4) Special practical or cultural subjects including agriculture, drawing, music, domestic science, industrial arts, book-keeping, exhibitions of school work, cotton grading and art.

(5) Humaneness—*i.e.* humane treatment of animals, prohibition of vivisection, etc.

(6) Fundamental subjects, such as arithmetic, English, geography, penmanship, reading, spelling.

(7) Religious and ethical subjects, sectarian doctrine, Bible reading, ethical conduct, etc.

[1] *Comparative Education*, p. 324.

(8) Miscellaneous subjects, elementary science, algebra, metric system, forestry and plant life, use of dictionaries, Darwinism and the reading of survey maps.

These subjects divide pretty clearly into those which were introduced by educational enthusiasts—"we will see to it that every school in this state is compelled by law to teach algebra"—and those which were introduced to catch votes—"vote for me and I will see to it that our schools teach useful subjects; why there isn't a youngster coming out nowadays who can write a decent hand".

The movement probably reached its peak in the famous "Monkey Trial", when two school teachers in Dayton were prosecuted and condemned for teaching Darwin's theory of evolution, in defiance of a state law forbidding it. Since that time the trend on the whole, particularly in the more developed areas, has been to withdraw education from "politics"—that is, from the influence of popular schemes to catch votes—and to rely more on the views of the educational expert. The fact remains, however, that although the U.S.A. has absolutely no national supervision of her education, the mechanism of her educational administration makes local supervision easy and tempting; and the tyranny of the "expert" might be worse than that of the voter.

Much more effective in fact than legal supervision by state authorities has been the influence of the great schools of education, such as Teachers College at Columbia, and of the educational publishing houses. It has often surprised European observers that in America, where there is so little legal supervision, there is often actually more uniformity of practice than there is in Europe. This uniformity, in respect of content and method, is the result of the very large measure of agreement on educational theory reached by the training colleges for teachers, and of the use on a very wide scale of identical text-books, not because they are imposed by an outside authority but because the teaching profession has accepted them for the moment as the most up-to-date. In respect of administration a similar uniformity has resulted from the practice, started in 1909, of publishing "School Surveys", by means of which any new device for increasing the economy or efficiency of administration is quickly publicised throughout the

United States.[1] In the secondary sphere an additional voluntary feature making for uniformity is the influence of the "accrediting agencies",[2] which is always exerted to raise the standards of all "accredited" schools to each new level of excellence achieved by the best.

Public Administration: (a) General

The control of administration has taken as many forms as the supervision of teaching. The State, as we have seen, never found itself with a clear field in setting up a system of primary education. Either the Churches or else the small communities, or both, had anticipated it. The administrative problems facing the central government were therefore:

(i) Was administration to be financed and controlled by the central government or by local bodies?

(ii) If by local bodies, by what bodies and what aid should they receive?

(a) *Centralised Countries: France and Prussia.*—In the answers given to this problem the western countries fall into the same two groups; but in this respect it was France which led the way in swallowing up the functions of the local body, while Germany, owing to her decentralised political structure, followed only half-heartedly in 1919 and finally caught up in 1934.

The immediate concern of parents for their own children, and the fact that local schools already existed, made it inevitable that lip-service, at least, would be paid to the method of working through local bodies. Departmental and communal councils did in fact form part of the French educational system introduced in 1886, but their functions were purely advisory, and only in the communal council were there any popularly elected members. Moreover, the functions of these communal councils are—for the system has been preserved unchanged in this respect—so trivial, and their powers so limited, that it has often been difficult to get anyone to serve on them or to attend meetings when appointed. The effective local authorities for education in France have been since 1886, the local representatives of the central Ministry of Public Instruction (including the Prefect of

---

[1] The very full and discursive report of H.M.I.'s in the period before the Revised Code had much the same effect in England.

[2] See Chapter Six.

the Department who, on educational matters, reports to this Ministry).

The administrative position in Germany up to 1934 was not unlike that of the U.S.A., apart from the great preponderance of Prussia. Educational administration remained the business of the individual states, and therefore differed quite considerably from one to another, but Prussia was so much more important than any of the others that in this instance also it is reasonable to treat the Prussian as the German system. It was based, as we have noticed, on the distinction between supervision and administration, and while supervision was carried out by or for the central government, administration was largely delegated to town or country-district "school deputations". The legal powers of these deputations, drawn from the elected local councillors with the addition ultimately of teachers' representatives, were small; for their actions required to be confirmed by the county school boards which were appointed by the State Ministry of Education. In practice, however, such restrictions are often less important than they seem on paper, and in most cases the proposals of the school deputations were accepted. In general, it would be fair to say that whereas in France the balance of effective control was weighted so heavily in favour of the Ministry that there was nothing worth doing left for the locally appointed committee, in Prussia the real work was so evenly shared that neither body felt itself impotent.

The first attempt to administer the German educational system as a whole was made by the Weimar Republic from 1919 to 1934, but the only effective change introduced by Reich Law was the general establishment of the common primary school (the *Grundschule*) and even this did not become effectively compulsory until the advent of the Nazis. The Nazis took education out of the hands of the individual states in 1934, and organised their own substitute throughout the country, the Reich Ministry legislating for all states but leaving the execution to the individual state authorities.

(b) *Decentralised Countries*: (1) *The English Administrative System.*—In England and America the fear of a "general state education", and the belief in local control as a method of stimulating the voluntary effort of the community, ensured that some sort of decentralised system would be retained.

In England the first problem was that in 1850 no local authorities comparable to the French Communes or Prussian *Kreis* existed; the religious controversy made it impossible that education should be delegated to the parishes, and there were no other authorities, comparable to the modern Urban, Borough and County Councils, in existence. The method of distributing state aid which was tried in the first half of the century—that is, the subsidising of any voluntary body which provided schools, by augmenting its public subscriptions—seemed morally well designed as a reward for meritorious communities, but did little to improve the distribution of education. For it was just those poor neighbourhoods, which could find no wealthy patron or rich subscribers, who most needed help from the state. So that what the nation got was "elaborate gothic edifices" erected by the squire or rector in small country parishes, and no schools at all in the slums of Liverpool.

It was clear by 1870 that, since no local authority capable of supervising education existed, England would have to do what France and Prussia had done early in the century and create special authorities for this purpose. These were the "School Boards" created by the Act of 1870 which, as we have already seen, marks the beginning of a national system in England. In setting up a local authority to control education there are two types to choose from, the expert specialist committee elected or appointed to deal with education only, and the sub-committee of whatever local body is responsible for water, drains, roads and so forth. The advantage of the first method is that the members of the committee are people genuinely interested in education and often experts in particular fields. Its disadvantage is that education has to be carried out in the first place by teachers in schools, and secondly by permanent officials. A specialist body may easily go beyond the consideration of general lines of policy, and, if it contains too many educational experts, start conducting the business of the permanent officials, or, even worse, of the individual schools. The English school boards were at first of the specialist type. In the big towns where there had long been a frustrated desire for education, they very soon got to work. In the country districts their progress was much slower. The reason for this was that school boards were set up only where local enterprise had not already provided the necessary schools, and we have already seen that religious rivalry had led to a great effort of building, very largely concentrated in country districts. The Government still believed so profoundly in private enterprise that it much preferred this method to the school board, and gave the voluntary societies six months grace to provide schools themselves before a school board was set up. It usually turned out, therefore, that in country districts school boards were only required if the squire and the rector were so little interested in education, that they had failed to provide an adequate school in the past; and where the squire and the rector were of this frame of mind it was often difficult to find any other educated man to sit on the school board. One inspector is quoted who, receiving no answer to his letter to the school board, found that: "There was not a man on the board who could read and write, and they had to take all their correspondence to the market town to get the advice of the clerk to the Guardians before they could reply." [1]

School boards were empowered to make attendance compulsory, but as fees were still charged it was difficult to do so, and many of them decided not to use their powers. It was not until 1880 that they were compelled to make regulations for compulsory attendance, and not until 1893 that the school-leaving age was raised to eleven. Thus laws which, in the centralised countries, were introduced at a single moment for the whole country were, in England, the result of piecemeal local advances and gradual change. The abolition of fees for primary education proceeded, for instance, partly by individual local authorities abolishing them, partly by a general enactment in 1891 that parents who could not afford to pay them had a right to demand free places. It was actually not until 1918 that they were entirely abolished.

In 1902 a genuinely national, though still decentralised, system of administration was introduced for the first time. The school boards were dissolved, and local control of education was entrusted throughout the country to the new units of local government, the County, County Borough, and Urban District Councils. Since the new education committees now consisted of sub-committees of these "general purpose" councils, this was a tacit reversal of the decision made in 1870 in favour of specialist committees. The new authorities, however, co-opted a few

[1] Quoted in Curtis: *History of Education in Great Britain.*

outside members who had special educational experience, and in most cases included, as in Germany, a number of teachers' representatives.

The system of administration introduced in 1902 remained basically unchanged until the act of 1944. Under it the Board of Education was primarily a mechanism for inspection and advice, and for the allocation of grants. Schools which did not seek the latter were under no obligation to accept the former, although by 1944 all the great independent public schools had already done so voluntarily. It was the duty of the local authorities to plan and finance from rates and grant the educational system for their area —subject to the national laws affecting school attendance. The Board was there to see that their provisions were satisfactory, and where they failed to come up to its standards, to enforce its views by withholding grant, a course of action very rarely taken. The method of calculating these grants was at first complicated, but in 1918 it was changed to a block grant covering not less than half the approved expenditure of the local body. It is easy to see that financial help on such a scale meant that no local authority could carry on at all without the support of the Board.

The Act of 1944 would have pleased Matthew Arnold, and in many ways brought England more into line with European practice. The President of the Board of Education became, at last, a Minister of Education. His functions became more positive, for instead of inspecting and allocating grant, he was enjoined to "promote the education of the people of England and Wales". He can therefore compel local education authorities more directly than could his predecessors. The local authorities themselves were also commanded to provide many facilities (*e.g.* nursery schools) which they had only been "permitted" to provide before. Finally, in the Central Advisory Councils which the Act set up, one can see something like the French and Italian Higher Councils of Public Instruction, and for the first time an official body in England who might take the initiative in "supervising" the content of education.

To those who still fear a "general state education" this may prove a serious flaw in the new system. No ministerial order supervising content has yet been issued, but the fixed age-limit imposed on candidates for external examinations—whatever its merits—was clearly a step in this direction. On the side of administration, the degree of forward planning and consultation demanded from local authorities has undoubtedly increased the power and influence of the central government. On the whole, however, the decentralised system established in England in the nineteenth century remains essentially unchanged.

(2) *The American Administrative System.*—The extreme example of decentralisation is found in the United States. The Federal Government has played virtually no part in, education, compared with the central government of any European state; but even the State Governments have considerably less control of education within each State than a European central government would have. In the English decentralised system it was the provision of funds which gave the central authorities their influence, and it is significant to note, therefore, that in the U.S.A. between the two wars the contribution to the total cost of education made by the Federal Government was less than 1 per cent., and that made by the State Governments less than 17 per cent. The rest was found by local school boards.

The administrative problems which this extreme decentralisation produced have probably sprung in part at least from the natural conservatism of a young and democratic nation. The educational unit of the country's heroic youth was the local school board with its "little red school-house"—just as the social unit was the log-cabin; and this heroic youth is so recent that any attempt at change has met the vehement opposition of those who were actually educated in it themselves. Quite apart from the extremely good educational record of local bodies in America, the little red school-house has become to many people a legend and a symbol, and it is defended with all the emotional force that symbols command.

As we have seen, the Federal Government hardly touches education at all and the State Governments, though ready occasionally to pass frivolous laws in favour of compulsory spelling lessons, have been chary of the fierce passions which would be aroused by removing control of educational administration from the small local bodies. As a result, education was administered until very recently by about 150,000 different and independent school boards, each raising its own funds and providing the services which its own people demanded. This extreme variety had, of course, one great advantage, which was noticed by an English inspector who visited America at the beginning of the twentieth century. It meant that every form of educational experiment got a chance, and that there was real and very valuable competition and imitation among the best schools in the richer districts.

In poorer districts, however, the effect has not been so good. There is one great difficulty in working entirely through local bodies, which is that some of them are inevitably too poor to provide from their own funds education of the standard required. If the central government then intervenes to the extent of equalising the funds available by means of large grants in aid of poor neighbourhoods, the burden of finance begins to fall, not on the local ratepayers, but on the whole body of taxpayers. When this happens there will always be a party who consider it unjust that what is mainly paid for by taxes—let us say, of city folk—should be controlled by a local body of country folk. Even if they do not think it unjust, they are apt to think that the small village will probably control it inefficiently. Even where this argument does not triumph, it often proves in fact that the small country neighbourhood has too few children to fill a school of the minimum "efficient" size. Thus a movement develops not only for taking the control of educational administration out of the hands of small rural bodies, but for actually removing the children in buses to larger and more "efficient" schools in the towns. And then the champions of rural life come in and complain that the countryside is being bled white, and that good young countrymen are being educated as mediocre townsfolk.

Something of this kind has been happening in the last twenty years in America. The variety of practice in different states makes it impossible to avoid rough generalisations, but the main lines of controversy have been the same all over the country. It was not until well into the twentieth century that any movement for state control as opposed to district control of administration began to make headway, and even then it progressed so slowly that by 1933 there were still six states which had not developed any state education authority at all. Where state authorities do exist, the cities and, in the South, the counties are still almost always independent. They pay the piper and can therefore call the tune.

Even if the states dare to intervene with public funds and level up the expenditure (and therefore the quality of education) in the different districts, there are such vast differences in the revenues of the states themselves that the biggest discrepancies are scarcely touched. The Harvard *Report on General Education in a Free Society* puts very clearly the effect of this economic division into rich and poor states, particularly on secondary education:

"The educational effect of this mighty change (*i.e.* the change leading to secondary education for all) has been equally great, though different, on city and on country. Of the two, the country has fared far the less well, and because education is a state and local responsibility, those states which are largely rural, less industrialised and less wealthy have been at a great disadvantage in comparison with their richer and more urban neighbours. Mississippi, for instance, is able to spend only a fifth as much per pupil as New York and to pay its teachers and principals an average annual salary of $559 against New York's $2604. Ten states annually spend less than $50 per pupil, whereas eight spend more than $100. The birth-rate being higher in the country than in the city, the poorer states face the further disadvantage of having a relatively higher proportion of children to educate. South Carolina, for instance, has twice the proportion of children to adults of Los Angeles County; yet Los Angeles has five times the wealth available for education. Indeed, if South Carolina spent its entire state budget for education, it would still be spending less per pupil than do several states."

It is clear, therefore, that over and above the case for incr sed state aid to level up the differences between districts there is a very strong case for Federal aid to level up the difference between states. Without it, equality of opportunity for children in different states is a manifest impossibility.

The movement, on the other hand, for combining this with a concentration of country children in central city schools appears to be on the wane in America, just when it is being seriously taken up in some parts of England.

CHAPTER FOUR

DEVELOPMENTS IN THEORY AND TECHNIQUE OF TEACHING

THE principal theme of this chapter will be the changes which have taken place in the last hundred years in the theory of teaching; and the emphasis will be mainly on those changes which were due to new theories of psychology and particularly of the act of learning.

Early Theory and Technique of Teaching

The generally practised technique of teaching up to the middle of the nineteenth century was that which had endured more or less unchanged since Sumerian times. Recently deciphered clay tablets from that remote past tell the story of a schoolboy who got as many as nine beatings in one day for such faults as not having learnt his letters; and much the same, on a reduced scale, might have happened to any eighteenth- or early nineteenth-century child.

During the four or five thousand years in which this system had lasted there had, of course, been a succession of warm-hearted critics, like Montaigne, who condemned it as both illiberal and ineffective. Individual teachers, too, often broke away from it, employing systems of their own which produced startling results. But the system itself continued, gradually softened perhaps in humanitarian periods, but essentially unimpaired by the actions and words of a few eccentrics.

This traditional practice of education had nowhere been explicitly formulated as a theory, partly because each generation accepted it as inevitable, partly because the whole conception of education as a "science" had yet to be developed. The theory can be deduced, however, from the practice, and it is to the practice that we must therefore look first.

This was, in general, for the teacher to break down the subject into what, to his adult mind, appeared to be its elements; and then to compel the pupil to learn these by heart. Only a small minority of the population received any formal education at all, and of these the majority went on to what we should now call the secondary stage, so that most primary education consisted of learning by heart those elements which would later be useful for secondary education. In learning to read, for instance, children since Roman times had learnt first the letters, then syllables, then short words, then longer words—without any consideration of whether the words they learnt meant anything, much less whether they meant anything to a child. In writing they had learnt first to make lines and shapes neatly (pothooks), then individual letters, and finally a cursive hand.

When we come to the secondary education for which this was a prelude we find that it consisted almost entirely of a thorough instruction in the classical languages, predominantly Latin. The reason for this is clear enough. Education was, throughout the Middle Ages, a function and a privilege of the Church, whose language was Latin. Since none but the clergy were educated, Latin was not only the common language of the undivided Western Church, but also the common language of science, art and diplomacy. As late as the seventeenth century, Milton was Latin Secretary in what we should now call the Foreign Office.

So complete was this concentration on the classical languages that a famous judgment of Lord Eldon (Lord Chancellor of England in 1805) ruled that a "grammar school" was an institution "for teaching grammatically the learned languages", and that therefore the introduction of mathematics into the curriculum was contrary to the statutes and illegal. Americans as well as British will remember that in the early nineteenth century the "Latin School" was often a synonym for the secondary school, though in America "Classical English Schools" grew up alongside the Latin Schools, unhampered by legal judgments.

Traditionally, it took a child ten years to acquire a mastery of Latin and Greek, and children were expected to begin the study of these languages at the age of six or seven. Again, the system was to begin with the elements, the grammatical forms, including innumerable rare exceptions, and to learn them by heart. After some years of this, those pupils who had mastered them went on to read more and more Latin authors, to compose Latin verses, and even to such refinements as "transposing odes of Horace and Pindar into other metres". But the greater part of school life, and for some boys the whole of it, was devoted to studying unrelated elements. R. H. Quick, writing in 1880, points out that the subject of instruction in the schoolroom had come to be "not the classics, but the classical languages". The classics were used as school books, but the only meaning thought of was the meaning of the detached word, or at best of the detached sentence. "You ask a child learning to read if he understands what he is reading about, and he says: 'I can't think of the meaning because I am thinking of the words.' The same thing has happened to the schoolboys' classics." This judgment was not true, perhaps, of the sixth forms at the very best schools, but as a general criticism both of primary and secondary teaching it is just and unanswerable.

The disadvantages of such a system of teaching seem obvious to us nowadays, and it could only be defended on the grounds that, if it was *necessary* to master the grammatical obscurities of the classical languages at some stage, childhood was the best stage to devote to it.

The great disadvantage, of course, was that very few, if any, children could be expected to take to it willingly, or to show any natural interest in Greek roots. It was a fact empirically recognised, however, long before Herbart formulated it as a theory, that no learning is possible without "interest"—that is, that neither man nor child will learn anything unless he has an interest in learning it, or in later terminology a motive for learning it. Since therefore the traditional teacher could hardly hope that his subject-matter would be interesting in itself, he had to supply an interest or motive from outside. The child must be given an interest in learning, either to please his parents or teacher, or to avoid punishment—in common language, by the use of the "carrot" or the "stick". Exceptionally skilled parents or teachers were able to stimulate interest even in this unattractive curriculum mainly by the use of the carrot; but this was really beyond the powers of the majority, who naturally fell back on the stick. And thus was perpetuated the time-honoured system by which the young learnt their meaningless and disconnected "lessons", and their elders flogged them for forgetfulness, laziness and stupidity. Quick records again that he saw "a little fellow of not more than ten" caned, because, although he had answered that *proficiscor* was a "deponent verb", he could not explain what a deponent verb meant. In our concern, nowadays, about the use of corporal punishment for moral offences, we are apt to forget that for the first five thousand years of our history it was used mainly to stimulate intellectual activity.[1]

The literary opponents of the grammar-and-birch school were usually, like Montaigne, people with a vast interest in life and literature themselves, who scarcely saw that for the average child some form of outside stimulus was necessary as long as the subject-matter of his studies and the method of teaching remained unchanged and uninteresting.

Practical teachers, on the other hand, concentrated on finding a less repellent and more effective form of outside stimulus. Far the most important of the attempts to do this was the introduction of rivalry as an incentive. Everyone knows that children immediately find interest in any activity when it involves competition with other children, and it was soon seen that the passion to achieve the position of "dux", or top of the form, might stimulate the quicker minds, and the fear of a dunce's cap the slower ones, quite as much as fear of the birch. This form of internal competition was the main driving force of the eighteenth-century Jesuit schools in France, where each boy had his appointed "rival"; and in Europe it has remained to this day the chief outside incentive to interest. In England it was, by the middle of the nineteenth century, gradually gaining favour, as the birch lost it—though Dr Johnson had been opposed to it on the grounds that whatever harm flogging did was less than that done by the "introduction of emulation between brothers and sisters". Its greatest supporter in England was probably Dr Butler, the great headmaster of Shrewsbury, who really introduced into English schools the complicated system of "marks" which they have retained ever since.[2]

The second great objection to the whole traditional system was that, even with the introduction of interest by external means,

---

[1] Professor Cubberley (*History of Education*) quotes a statistically-minded German teacher who worked out the total number of punishments he had inflicted in a teaching career of just over fifty years. These included over 900,000 strokes of the cane, of which 800,000 were for "Latin words".

[2] Butler also introduced the curious Shrewsbury custom of "merit money", *i.e.* direct payment for good work—since abandoned but in some ways a better idea.

only a small proportion of those educated under it ever reached the final years of classical learning, for which the whole of the rest of education was a preparation. To them their education gave a priceless and lasting gift, the confident freedom of the whole literature and civilisation of Greece and Rome. We have only to read the lives and letters of the really educated men of the seventeenth and eighteenth centuries to see what this meant. To them it was perhaps worth all the gerund-grinding and the floggings—indeed one may assume that such pupils got their gerund-grinding finished early and escaped equally quickly the range of the birch.

For the majority, however, who never could master Cicero, however many times they were flogged, education was largely torment, and what they learnt largely useless, either as knowledge or training. That this was not more clearly recognised seems strange and was probably due to a combination of causes: first, that the leaders of thought in Europe were, in the main, those who had successfully absorbed the classical education, and for them it had been well worth while; secondly, that for the dullards the rosy hues of reminiscence clouded the memory of their miseries, and the fact that they had gone through the same mill as the great ones filled them with a vicarious pride. A classical education, even if all that was left of it was a few Latin tags, was the hall-mark of a small class. It would have been an instance of remarkable human sympathy if those few leaders who had profited by it themselves, had been able to see how useless it was to the majority, at a time when the majority were still its stoutest supporters. As soon as education ceased to be the privilege of this small class the old system was exposed and collapsed. We have seen that its practitioners never had to justify it theoretically against the attack that the "interest" on which it depended was always something outside the actual learning process. If they had had to do so, they would, I suppose, have adopted much the same line as the supporters of the pure milk of the classics at the end of the nineteenth century—that since education is preparation for life, and since in practical life a great many jobs which are not interesting in themselves have to be done either to avoid external penalties or to secure external rewards, it is as well to train the mind early to this unpleasant process. That, it will be noticed, is a social and not an educational argument, but it is a question how far "education" has a right to the place, which is sometimes claimed for it, outside the social framework.

Development of Educational Theory in England in the Nineteenth Century

The first attempts at mass education in England show clearly how the traditional methods of logical analysis into elements and learning by rote, with the outside interest supplied by emulation or the stick, were preserved unchallenged. The "monitorial system" by which, in the 1820's, Bell and Lancaster proudly proposed to extend education at a minimum cost to the whole mass of the English people, was entirely based on this conception. Under Bell's and Lancaster's system a number of senior pupils, called monitors, were first taught a "lesson", *i.e.*, a number of elementary facts or words to be spelled, by heart. Each of these then assembled in the great hall a group of other children to whom he taught, in turn, what he had just learnt. The schoolmaster stood on a raised platform, like a master of galley slaves transported to Waterloo Station, and conducted the whole business. Lancaster claimed that by this method one schoolmaster could teach as many as a thousand boys.

Where no provision was made even for understanding what was learnt, interest had of course to be supplied from outside. The reformers—for they were genuinely enthusiastic and humane men—chose emulation rather than the stick. No boy was whipped in a monitorial school, though at first in the Lancasterian schools a boy who was "going up" in class would wring the ears of all whom he superseded. Disgrace attended the failures, however, and promotion the successes. "Untidy, talking or idle boys had to wear a disgrace mark. Dirty boys were sentenced to have their faces and hands washed before the whole school and to be confined for half an hour."[1]

Such was the first attempt at general education of the masses in England. On the assumption that education consisted of getting by heart a number of elementary facts in their logical order, there seemed no reason why it should not work. It never seems to have occurred to Bell or Lancaster that education could be anything but this, and Bell actually visited Pestalozzi, but

---

[1] It is interesting to note that this confinement could be bought off by the acquisition of merit tickets—a cheaper device than Butler's merit money.

thought nothing of him. It was left to Kay Shuttleworth to demonstrate that it did not work even at its own level, and to propose that the shortage of teachers should be met not by monitors but by "pupil-teachers".

Even the substitution of pupil-teachers for monitors, which dates from the 1850's, began with an unquestioning acceptance of the traditional methods of teaching. Though Kay Shuttleworth saw clearly that any expansion of education demanded a great increase in the number of trained teachers, it was the subject-matter of their "lessons", not the art of teaching, in which he wished to train them. The whole movement was first designed, in fact, to eliminate the illiterate dame school type of teacher; the *method* of teaching was left to be conveyed by the older generation of schoolmasters to their pupils, without any serious consideration of the possibility that the old method might be itself at fault.

While this necessary but pedestrian progress was being made in the actual training and practice of teachers, the very fact that the establishment of universal education was a political issue in England during the last quarter of the century was leading many speculative minds to consider for the first time what this education should be; and a few even began to study again the first principles of educational theory in the works of those "eccentrics" who had protested in vain against the accepted system of the last three hundred years. Thus we find in England a generation where great progress is made at the two ends of the scale, in philosophic speculation by the few, and in raising the intellectual and moral standards of the mass of primary school teachers. It was not till nearly the turn of the century that the two trends fused, the views of the philosophers being applied to practical teaching and the first serious attempts made to treat education as an applied science. The title of one of the most influential books published in England during this latter period illustrates the new attitude towards education. It was Sir John Adams' *Herbartian Psychology Applied to Education*, published in 1904 —the first attempt in this country to put the new psychological theories into a form that would be useful to the practical teacher.

What was new in England, however, was already a common-place elsewhere. We have seen that English education in the nineteenth century was in some ways singularly backward, and this backwardness was just as apparent in theory as in administration. Apart from the "Public School Code" (the unspoken principles on which the great private boarding schools were based, and which are described in the next chapter), England contributed nothing to the newly arising art or science of education; and where she was ignorant herself she was extraordinarily slow to borrow. The true line of theoretical advance in this century derives from the work of Rousseau, Pestalozzi and Froebel; and the vast mass of English teachers or educationists were totally ignorant of it. R. H. Quick, in the preface to his *Essays on Educational Reformers* (1868), writes: "Good books are in German, Professor Seeley says. I have found that on the history of education not only good books, but *all* books, are in German or some other foreign language." Although his own *Essays* were for a long time the only English text-book on the history of education, no more than five hundred copies of the first edition were printed in England, and no second edition was called for until 1890. By then it had been "pirated" with enthusiasm no less than three times in the United States.

This little bit of publishing history epitomises the international reaction to educational theory in its broad outlines. It was in Germany that the theories of Pestalozzi, Froebel and Herbart were first accepted, put into practice and further developed. The Americans, with an enthusiasm for education unmatched in Europe, borrowed and tried out each new European idea as it became known: but they soon abandoned the monitorial system of Bell and Lancaster and accepted Pestalozzi and Froebel as their masters. It is from America rather than Germany that the new theories of education have reached England.[1] In turning to them we are turning to the main current of nineteenth-century educational reform.

Influence of Pestalozzi and Froebel

To understand the educational theory and technique of the reforming party in the mid-nineteenth century it is necessary to go back at least to their masters, Pestalozzi and Froebel. Neither of these two were profound thinkers; and where Froebel was

---

[1] It is an interesting speculation, whether the fact that educational theory reached us from Germany via America is not the explanation of the unfamiliar English in which so much of it is written.

original he was usually talking transcendental nonsense. In the practical affairs of life they were both incompetent, Pestalozzi unusually so. Yet their influence on education has been incalculable and almost entirely for good. To see what it was we must look at it in its contemporary setting.

Pestalozzi lived in Switzerland and taught from 1798–1828. His contribution to educational theory has been summed up by his biographer, Morf, under twelve headings, most of which are different ways of saying the same thing, that education consists of training a child, not of imparting a collection of factual knowledge, and that it must therefore proceed by stimulating the child's mind to such activities as are suitable to the stage of development which it has reached. Some of them are very suggestive of later theories, but there is really nothing in them that had not been said before by Montaigne, Locke or Rousseau.

What, then, is the secret of Pestalozzi's immense influence? Partly, I think, it lies in Morf's tenth point that "the exchange between teacher and pupil, and particularly school discipline must be based on love". As a man Pestalozzi seems to have been something approaching a saint, and as a teacher something approaching a genius. Whatever fantastic muddles developed in his various educational institutes, he had only to go back to teaching a group of small children himself and his greatness as a teacher became immediately obvious again. Secondly, the world, which had been unprepared for the educational views of Montaigne and Locke, was ready for those of Pestalozzi. What he said was not new—it almost seems as if nothing good in educational theory ever is—but for the first time people paid attention to it. The age of Pestalozzi and Froebel was the age of the great liberal and rationalist movement in Germany. It was an age when for the first time men were seriously considering the possibility of universal education, and new systems were being tried with enthusiasm everywhere. Bell's in England and Jacotot's in France came to nothing because they were ill-founded. Pestalozzi's survived to give its direction to the following century, not because it was profoundly original, but because it restated the ancient truths, and because through his own devotion he made it work, attracting at the same time, by the beauty of his own character, disciples who saw it working.

Stripped of certain queer fancies which he seems to have

owed to German Masonic-mystic thought, Froebel's theory is a continuation of Pestalozzi's (whose pupil he was) with two main additions:

(a) Froebel emphasised above all the importance of the years of infancy. It was he who first took schools for very young children seriously, and his name for them, *Kindergarten*, is still maintained even where strictly Froebelian methods are no longer used.

(b) He laid even greater emphasis than Pestalozzi had on the activity of the child. In his insistence that we "learn by doing" he was the father of modern "activity" methods.

It should be noticed that both Pestalozzi and Froebel were concerned with the education of children of what we should now call primary age or even younger. It is possible that Pestalozzi actually failed as a teacher when he tried with boys from ten to sixteen, though the evidence is doubtful. It would not have been surprising, in any case, since boys of that age need to acquire learning as well as to be educated, and Pestalozzi was a singularly ignorant man.

It is possible that the derivation of so much modern educational theory from the work of these two men may, therefore, be responsible for some of the heated and misinformed controversy which goes on about "modern" methods. Those teachers who attack them are often opposing their introduction to the selective secondary grammar school—of which Pestalozzi knew nothing, and for which they were certainly not designed and may well be unsuitable; those who support them are commonly thinking of their use in the primary schools, for which they were designed and where they have long proved their value; "armchair educationists" tend to write of them without specifying what range of age or ability they have in mind.[1]

The practical effects of the work of Pestalozzi and Froebel fall almost entirely within the period covered by this book, although their theoretical influence was already widely spread in the first half of the nineteenth century both in Germany and America. In America, for instance, Warren Colburn's *First*

[1] William James, in his *Talks to Teachers on Psychology*, pointed out this danger as long ago as 1899. "Our modern reformers in their text-books", he writes, "write too exclusively of the earliest years of the pupil."

THEORY AND TECHNIQUE OF TEACHING

Lessons in Arithmetic on the Plan of Pestalozzi (1821) was for a long time the most popular arithmetical text-book at a time when scarcely any teacher in England had heard of the new methods.[1]

In Germany itself the first phase of Pestalozzian influence was brought to an end by the Conservative reaction after 1848, which led to an edict of the Prussian Minister of Education in 1851, forbidding the establishment of schools "after the principles of Friedrich and Karl Froebel". The edict was really directed against Froebel's nephew Karl, but it remained in force until 1862 and the whole feeling of German officialdom was certainly hostile to new ideas of any sort during these years.

1862, the year of the lifting of the edict, has a double significance, for it marks also the acceptance of a system of education based on the views of Pestalozzi and Froebel by the Education Board of Oswego, New York State. From Oswego the new methods spread rapidly through the North and West of the United States, and what had been an intellectual curiosity soon became the basis of actual teaching methods in all the more advanced schools. In Germany also there was a rapid revival among the followers of Pestalozzi, and in 1872 a congress, at which more than ten thousand German elementary teachers were represented, petitioned the Prussian government for "the organisation of training schools in accordance with the paedagogic principles of Pestalozzi, which formerly enjoyed so much favour in Prussia and so richly contributed to the regeneration of the country". Froebelianism, however, never recovered the degree of acceptance in Germany which it enjoyed during the latter half of the nineteenth century in England and America.

The subsequent history of the school of Pestalozzi and Froebel illustrates an almost inevitable development in the teaching of any educational pioneer. Their ideas first stimulated a number of teachers to greatly improved practice. Then, largely in order that they might be taught in training colleges, they were systematised; and in this process the outward forms remained while much of the spirit was lost. Finally, this new "dead formalism" was attacked by the next generation of reformers, in the name of the very principles on which it had originally been established, and cast out neck and crop.

[1] Though Mr Squeers, it will be remembered, had got hold of the Froebelian idea of "learning by doing".

For instance, one of the basic principles, both of Pestalozzi and Froebel, was that young children should learn from actual contact with physical objects around them, and not from lists of names given in books. When systematised by the training colleges this admirable principle gave rise to the arid "object lessons" which were fashionable in primary schools in the second half of the nineteenth century. It is hardly surprising that Herbert Spencer attacked these as "well conceived but ill conducted", if many of them were like the example quoted below. Yet this is taken from the Oswego system as finally developed, and is almost certainly no worse than many given by teachers all over Europe and America who fondly imagined they were following in the footsteps of Pestalozzi:

Lesson on Shells

Given to a C class, primary; ages of children 5 to 6 years

Object of the lesson was to lead the children to observe the parts of the shell, also to perceive the appropriateness of the names given to the parts.

The teacher, holding up a shell before the class, told them that an animal once lived in that shell, and then asked, "What do you live in?"

Children. "Houses."

T. "This was the house of an animal. Now I want you to look at it, and see if you can find different parts of this shell. James may point to some part of it."

The boy touched the small point at one end. The teacher said: "This part is called the apex of the shell. Now point to the apex of this cone; of the pyramid." The word apex was now printed on the blackboard.

"Mary may touch some other part of the shell." She put her finger upon the largest part, or body of it; and the teacher said, "This is called the body of the shell," and printed the word on the board.

Pointing to the whorl on the shell, the teacher said: "Look at this; see how it winds around the shell; this part looks as if it whirled around, so we call it the whorl." This word was also printed on the board.

The opening of the shell was pointed at, and the children asked to give it a name. No one replied, and the teacher requested a boy to open his mouth, and the other children to look at it, upon which several of them suggested the word mouth as a good name for the opening of the shell. This was printed on the board, and the children told that it is the name for that part of the shell.

Next the edges of the shell were pointed at, and the children referred to parts of their own mouths for a name. Lips was readily given, and printed on the board.

The groove leading to the mouth was pointed at, and the children were told to call it a canal. The word was then printed.

The attention of the children was directed to the lower part of the shell, containing the canal, and the children asked if they had ever seen any part of a bird that resembled it in shape. " The bird's beak "? was the reply. "That is right; and we will call this the beak of the shell," said the teacher. This word was also printed on the board.

A child was now called to take the shell and point out the parts as the children named them. The teacher pointed out the parts, and the children named them.

Quoted from Barnard's *Pestalozzi and his Educational System* in S. G. Noble's *History of American Education*.

Teaching of this type was soon abandoned along with Froebel's cones, cylinders and spheres, but the real doctrines of Pestalozzi and Froebel are still honoured in all our educational theory. "The essential principle of education is not teaching, it is love", said Pestalozzi; and we owe it to him above all that in the education of young children we think now first of the child and its development, and not, as the eighteenth-century schoolmasters used to, of the subject-matter which it has to learn. If Pestalozzi had not succeeded where others failed, in turning the attention of teachers away from the subject to the child, the whole development of modern educational thought could never have started. We owe to him directly the substitution of oral for book work, the use of the child's own environment (*Heimatkunde*) and the whole idea of child-centred education. Froebel carried on Pestalozzi's work, and the success of his kindergarten and of the parallel he drew between the teacher and the gardener helped people to see, what had indeed been stated before, that no one learns except through his own activity and that there is, strictly speaking, no such art as teaching—only the art of helping people to learn. The restatement of these great principles is all that is left in modern educational theory of the work of Pestalozzi and Froebel. Their idiosyncrasies have been forgotten like the idiosyncrasies of all great innovators, but the genuine acceptance at last of these principles and the memory of Pestalozzi's life were legacy enough.

Influence of Herbart

The effect of German thought on educational theory was

continued by the work of J. F. Herbart (1776–1841) who had probably more influence than any other writer on the educationists of the late nineteenth century. Herbart started as a romantic German idealist of the school of Herder and Schiller. He strove for a regeneration of German youth by bringing them back to the ideals of the ancient world. Specifically this meant teaching the literature and history of Greece and Rome as well as the linguistics. There were others, notably in England, who were not behind him in this.

The great advance made by Herbart—and its importance can hardly be exaggerated—is that he based his educational views on a new and fully worked out psychology. He is therefore the founder of the whole subsequent school of educational reformers who have held that their first requirement was an independent study of the workings of the human mind. One possible confusion of thought must be avoided however. Herbart's psychology was not "scientific" in the modern sense—that is, based on measurement and statistics. It would, no doubt, be condemned by a modern laboratory psychologist as being just as "metaphysical" as the psychology of Locke, which, in educational matters, it replaced. It was not even, in its main outlines, original, for it is little more than a careful working out, in the educational sphere, of Hume's theory of the association of ideas. What makes Herbart so important in the history of educational theory, apart from the fact that he maintained a school himself and was often right in practice, is that for the first time an educational prophet saw the necessity of deriving his theories from a coherent psychology.

The disciples of Herbart were therefore able to claim for the first time that their educational theory was scientific; and this was very important particularly in Germany, and particularly in the latter half of the nineteenth century. It fitted in also very well with the needs of the new training colleges and education departments in the universities. The second half of the nineteenth century saw a wide acceptance of the view that teachers, like engineers, ought to be trained; but until "education" had been raised to the level of an organised science with its own terminology (and perhaps a little jargon), the colleges, and even the university education departments, were looking round anxiously for something sufficiently advanced and abstruse which future teachers could be set to study. In such a situation "Herbartianism" came as a godsend. Even his vices were "scientific".

The essence of Herbart's psychology was Hume's view that the mind is not active at all, but that consciousness and thought consist of the association of ideas. He expresses this by saying that what happens when we think is that "an idea rises above the threshold of consciousness". Once an idea has entered the consciousness, it forms, by "fusion" or "complication" with other ideas, an "apperception mass". Ideas which are rich in their associations are, of course, readily absorbed into such apperception masses and held in the consciousness; those which have few or no associations with our other ideas "mean nothing to us" and so quickly "fall below the threshold of consciousness". Ideas therefore differ in their "presentative activity" according to their vividness for different minds, and this vividness depends on the extent to which they are attachable to already existing apperception masses. The main difference between his view and Hume's therefore was that Herbart thought of ideas, not as dead pictures arranged in patterns, but as dynamic entities struggling for admission to the consciousness.

It is interesting to note, in view of the later developments of psychoanalysis, that Herbart recognised two "thresholds of consciousness", the statical and the dynamical. He believed that an idea which had fallen below the dynamical threshold could still affect us, though we were no longer conscious of it; an idea below the statical threshold did not, for us, exist as an idea at all. This conception and the whole "dynamic" treatment of ideas foreshadows, the work of Freud, who acknowledged his debt.

Finally, Herbart applied to these conclusions, intuitively reached, an elaborate mathematical organisation, unjustified in view of the material on which he was working, but foreshadowing again the statistical work of later psychologists.

The acceptance of such a psychology as Herbart's could not fail to have a profound effect on educational theory. In the first place it commits its holder fully to the side of Helvétius in the great controversy between heredity and environment, since the mind of every child at birth must be presumed to be a complete and equal blank, all subsequent differences being due to the different ideas which rise to consciousness and form apperception masses. Herbart in fact held that ideas make the man. Secondly,

F

by denying to the mind any activity, it denies the existence of those separate faculties of the mind, memory, imagination, constructive logic, etc., which had been accepted from the psychology of Locke and whose "training" formed the staple of current educational theory. It condemned, for instance, the study of Latin in order to "train the memory", or of geometry in order to "train the faculty of logical reasoning".

To the Herbartian the teacher's function was not to train non-existent faculties, but to feed the soul with those ideas which would build up in it the right apperception masses; and this he could do only by increasing their "presentative activity", *i.e.* relating them to what was already known. Since, therefore, no place seemed left for the will of the pupil, any more than for the constructive activity of the mind, everything depended on the subject-matter being presented to the pupil in such a way that it would rise vividly into his consciousness and, linking with ideas already there, form new apperception masses. In common terms this meant that the ideas must be so presented as to secure the pupil's interest and attention. Interest and attention were, according to Herbart, the permanent condition of the mind, and the teacher's function was therefore to inhibit interest in other ideas, so that it would be centred on those which he was introducing to the pupil.

There is obviously a great deal in this that is true, and in some directions the influence of Herbart was altogether excellent. In particular, his destruction of the "faculty doctrine" freed educational psychology from a dangerous false system, and preceded by more than half a century the practical demonstrations of such psychologists as Thorndike. His "scientific" explanation of the importance of securing the pupil's interest was also a valuable aid to those who had already begun to work on this assumption from practical experience. On the other hand, the purely negative psychology of Herbart conflicts not only with the main trend of philosophy since Hume, but with our common experience of life. We do not in fact feel that in order to stimulate interest in an idea or group of ideas we have simply to inhibit interest in all other groups of ideas. And in this feeling we are surely right. Nor do we find in fact that men consist simply of those groups of ideas on which their previous life has been organised. "That a great poet at maturity may become a great warrior or mathematician the

Herbartian would emphatically deny", says one of his admirers.[1] Writers and painters like Mr Churchill, mathematician-statesmen like M. Poincaré, and all the host of scholars who in the second world war appeared in new guise as exceptionally efficient soldiers, give the lie to this extreme associationist theory. It is not true that "l'éducation peut tout" nor that a man is simply the sum of all the ideas which have been fed into him since birth. Herbart was in fact a brilliant psychologist, a man of real practical experience in teaching and the founder of all modern educational psychology; if anything, he is perhaps underrated at the moment; but the theoretical basis of his psychology suffers from the fact that he accepted the conclusions of the English philosophical school which culminated in Hume and James Mill, and seems to have neglected the work of Kant, whereas subsequent psychology has in the main followed the Kantian line.

The influence of Herbart in Germany, America and England in the latter half of the nineteenth century probably did more good to education than it did to Herbart's reputation. In America a National Herbart Society was formed, and it was not until 1895 that, as a result of Dewey's criticisms of Herbartianism, it changed its name to the National Society for the Study of Education. In England, as we have seen, Sir John Adams' *Herbartian Psychology applied to Education* was still an immensely influential book, although published as late as 1904. The damage to Herbart's reputation was due to the usual factors, the inflated importance given to an unessential piece of theorising generally known as the "culture epoch" theory, and the attempt to systematise the results of his psychology into "rules for the conduct of lessons". The "culture epoch" theory held that the process of mental growth in each child reproduced the process of mental growth in the human race since the dawn of prehistory, just as the development of the individual embryo reproduces that of the species since the dawn of life. It was a fascinating speculation—for eleven-year-old boys are indeed very like Red Indians—but it was based on insufficient evidence to be used, as in practice it was, to determine the content of the school curriculum at each age-level. The systematisation led to the establishment of five formal steps in the presentation of any new idea to be taught; and like all formal schemes of that kind which neglect the individual nature of the

[1] Sir John Adams, *op. cit.*

teacher, the pupils and the material to be taught, it produced a crop of empty and pretentious jargon which was exposed by the first sincere and enquiring mind to give it serious consideration.

Experimental Psychology

Since Herbart was so extreme an exponent of the environmental theory of training, it was not inappropriate that the next great advance should have come from the leader of the "heredity" school, Sir Francis Galton. Galton's *Enquiries into Human Faculty*, published in 1883, is a work quite as important in the history of educational theory as any of Herbart's or Froebel's. It introduced for the first time statistical methods which made valid experimental results possible. Herbart had built up an elaborate mathematical system of psychology on the basis of what were, in the first place, unchecked introspective intuitions about the working of the human mind. He did this largely because he believed that it was impossible to get any more certain empirical data to work on. Galton showed that by applying statistical methods to information collected from a sufficiently large number of tests, carried out in something approximating to "laboratory" conditions, such as Wundt in Germany had already established in 1878, it was possible to found psychology on a genuinely experimental basis. His work was immediately taken up in America by Cattell and his more celebrated pupil, Thorndike, whose first study of the subject, *The Theory of Mental and Social Measurements*, was published in 1904. A great deal of interesting but unco-ordinated "child study" had been going on in America for some years, and Galton's statistical approach seemed to provide the means by which all this eager research could be so directed as to produce valuable results. It is worth stressing, however, that these results, as usually happens with new steps forward in educational theory, only confirmed in the main what the great men of the past had always said. The great importance of the new method was that the conclusions were now demonstrable.

One of the first conclusions to be published by Thorndike as a result of experimental measurements was a complete confirmation of the Herbartian attack on the "faculty" doctrine. Measured experiments seemed to show conclusively, for instance, that "training" of the "memory" by learning poetry or Latin voca-

82

bularies did not in fact improve any general faculty of memory at all; it only produced increased skill in learning poetry or Latin vocabularies. Some of the original experiments failed to eliminate possible causes of error, and it is generally admitted that the conclusions were at first too confidently stated. The accepted view now is that "transfer" of training from one "subject" to another does often take place, but only to a very limited extent, and only in so far as the two subjects have identical factors and the pupil is aware of these factors. This rather complicated question can best be explained by an example.

The exponents of formal faculty training, attacked in the nineteenth century by Herbart and in the twentieth by Thorndike, believed that the study of geometry trained the faculty of logical thought, and that this trained faculty would then be just, or nearly, as strong if turned to a problem in law as if turned to another problem in geometry. The first reactions to the published work of Thorndike were that the study of geometry trained the mind in geometry and in nothing else. The view accepted at present is that if, in the study of geometry, pupils are taught to use consciously a technique of logical deduction, and then turn to some other study in which this technique is shown to be valuable, they can to some extent apply their training in technique to the new subject. That is to say, that once they have seen the old subject-matter in relation to the technique, they can, if presented with the new subject-matter, educe for themselves the potential new relationship between it and the technique they have acquired. If, on the other hand, they have been taught geometry without understanding the mental processes they are using, then, as was at first believed, there will be no transfer whatever and their training will remain confined to geometry.

The practical effect of these experiments in the "transfer" of training was of course immense, but must be left to Chapter Six. They destroyed for ever the main argument on which the supporters of the old curriculum had taken their stand. Since, on the other hand, it now appeared to progressive educationists, for a moment at least, as if all subjects must have equal value for "training" (because their effects were non-transferable), curricula in many American schools ran wild.

The new technique of experiment on isolated types of mental activity combined perfectly with the increasing accuracy in statistical methods of measuring the result. It would be outside the scope of this book to attempt either a detailed description of the technique of the psychological laboratory or a list of all the results of such work. In general, it would be fair to say that the laboratory technique consists of isolating and then measuring or timing certain activities of the mind—in which there are often significant connections with the neurologist's investigations of the brain—and applying to the results the statistical techniques of "correlation". Again, it will be easiest to illustrate the new approach by taking an example.

The question of the relative parts played in learning by "reason" and "memory" was one which the old kind of "metaphysical" psychologist would discuss at length, but to which he could provide no demonstrable answer. The experimental psychologist has by now demonstrated what Herbart proved logically, that there is no such thing as an undifferentiated faculty of memory. If he wants to determine the difference between learning by rote and learning by logical connection, he will conduct some such experiment as this (based on Experiment XVIII of Professor Valentine's *Introduction to Experimental Psychology*):

The following list of words is read out to a number of students at the rate of one second for each word:

> "Strict, cot, pan, gate, friend, table, paper, bird, flower, bite, walk, piano, ship, glass, photo, bucket."

At the end of the list they are asked to write it down as well as they remember. The experiment is then repeated with this second list:

> "Christmas, plum-pudding, mistletoe, parties, dancing, games, children, snowball, ice, skating, hole, danger, ducking, cold, bed, doctor."

Naturally, a far greater proportion of the second list will be remembered, and this proportion can be expressed mathematically. This is, of course, an extremely simple experiment, but it will serve to illustrate the method. First, its result, as suggested before, is only to confirm what all good teachers knew already; but it is valuable because it demonstrates what could only be stated before as an opinion. Second, it requires, as all such experiments require, that great care should be taken to isolate the one factor under consideration. For instance, the students might have done better on the second list partly because it *was* the second and because they had gained some practice on the first; the experiment would therefore have to be repeated an equal number of times with the logical list taken first. Then part of their improved performance on the Christmas list might be because of an emotional stimulus conveyed by such pleasant associations, and therefore a second experiment would be done in which one list consisted of words with strong emotional appeal but unconnected, and the other of words logically connected but dull. All such questions the psychologist must consider carefully before he draws any conclusions from his results. The danger in using the results lies always in the possibility either that some other factor than the one which it is intended to measure has influenced them, or in the assumption that they are valid for a type of mental activity similar to the one tested but not exactly the same. It would not be permissible, for instance, to assume that the results derived from the experiment just described would necessarily hold good for *retention* in the memory, since all that was tested was immediate recall.

We can use the same example to illustrate the vital statistical technique of "correlation". Let us suppose that the investigator is trying to find out whether the feeble-minded are exceptionally good at rote memory. We must assume that he can try the lists on a great number of subjects who have been certified as feeble-minded, as well as on his normal students. The simplest type of correlation technique will then be this: let a score of above average in the rote memory test be represented by A and a score of below average by B; let feeble-mindedness be represented by X and normal-mindedness by Y. What we wish to discover is whether there is any significant connection between A and X and between B and Y. A very simple, diagram will illustrate a method of doing this:

	B	A
X	31	69
Y	78	22

Suppose that 200 people are tested. In the top right-hand corner we enter those who have A and X, in the top left-hand

B and X, in the bottom right-hand A and Y, and so forth. Now by adding the diagonals (the sections whose correlation is to be tested) we get the following sum $\dfrac{69 + 78 - 22 - 31}{200} = \cdot 47$ and this may be taken as the coefficient of correlation (usually symbolised as ρ).

This, of course, is an extremely simplified form of correlation, where we are assuming that there are no degrees either of feeble-mindedness or use of rote memory. In practice we usually want to investigate the *degree* to which possession of one quality is correlated with possession of another. In that case the same diagram can be used, and the position of each person tested must be plotted in his quadrant in accordance with the degree to which he varies from the average. For this it is necessary, of course, that the quality should be measurable on an arithmetical scale. The diagram, for instance, would now look something like this on a much larger scale:

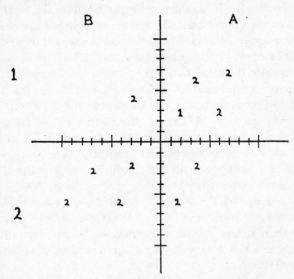

A person who showed three degrees above average feeble-mindedness and two above average of rote memory would be plotted at 1. The "2's" represent plottings of other subjects tested. The whole then produces what is called a "scatter diagram". The practised statistician can tell fairly accurately from the shape of this diagram what the coefficient of correlation will be—a roughly circular "spread", for instance, clearly indicates that there is no significant correlation. The mathematical formula required to establish the exact coefficient is not our concern.

Two essential features about correlation should be noted. Like all mathematical processes it works on the data given; if insufficient care was taken to exclude irrelevant factors in the original test, the correlation process will give what looks like a definite result, but it will be quite worthless. This is particularly worth remembering in view of the fact that to employ it at all assumes, in the first place, that the quality we are investigating can be measured arithmetically. Secondly, in any investigation a certain degree of correlation may easily result from sheer chance: unless the result is very definite, it is rash to assume that an investigation shows either a negative or a positive correlation. Not long ago someone who mistrusted the significance being attached to comparatively low positive correlations in the distribution of birds was able to show that he could get correlations equally high between the distribution of chaffinches and that of telegraph poles. This probability of error due to chance can also be calculated mathematically, however, and due allowance made.

We can now turn to the main accepted results to which the new techniques have led educational theory. The most important modifications of the Herbartian psychology have been in the reintroduction of the mind as an active factor in interpreting its own experience; and in this respect, as was noted above, modern psychology has followed the line of Kant rather than of Hume. The exponents of the school known as Gestalt psychology pointed out that Herbart's individual "ideas" were in fact unwarrantable abstractions themselves and that sense data are never experienced as separate individual presentations; moreover, the mind, they held, is always active in organising its experience in accordance with some intelligible "scheme" of its own. In this process of ordering, the mind is capable of "educing" new knowledge, and this knowledge is always a knowledge of relations. The most widely accepted view of this process of educing new knowledge (noegenesis) is that of Professor Spearman, who is also responsible for introducing the detailed mathematical technique of correlation.   According to Spearman:

(a) Any experience involves both perception and self-consciousness.

(b) Any experience tends to evoke perception of relations within the whole scheme of sense-data of which the mind is conscious.

(c) Any experience tends to evoke memory of related experiences.

He therefore distinguishes three steps in "noegenesis":

(a) Apprehension of experience.

(b) The eduction of relations.

(c) The eduction of correlates (a correlate being another idea not present in consciousness, but related to some idea that is present).

He sees in the eduction of correlates the type of "thinking" by which all really new knowledge is acquired, and therefore the highest type of mental activity. It is for this reason that in "Intelligence Tests" based on Spearman's conclusions the student will constantly find the question framed like this:

"Army is to Navy as soldier is to . . . . . ."

In that case the correlate to be educed is "sailor".

With regard to the nature of mental activity, Spearman suggests the existence of a general factor, which he calls "g" and which is much more general than the old "faculties" of memory, logical reasoning, etc.; allied with this he finds specific factors which he calls "s", and which are much more specific than the old general faculties. Thus, we should not now say that X had a good memory or that "Kim's Game" trained the memory, but rather that X had a good visual memory and that "Kim's Game" trained immediate recall of objects visually memorised. "g" (for it is so general that any word used for it would define and limit it too far) seems to be a sort of mental energy or awareness; it is held to be innate and inherited, and to reach its full development by the age of sixteen or before. Some psychologists doubt whether it may not turn out, like the ether, to have been a useful working conception of something which does not exist. It is to the "s" factors that we owe our skill in particular forms of mental operation: they, too, are to a certain extent innate, but unlike "g" they can be trained by the special forms of education that exercise each particular factor.

The most recent researches of the scientific educational psychologists have had their effect more upon the testing of children for suitability for different types of education than on teaching methods. For the basis of changed techniques in the school, such as "projects" and "activity methods", we must turn in the next chapter to a more philosophical school, in full accordance with the principles of Pestalozzi, who are more concerned with the emotional and psychological life of the child than with the purely mental act of learning. It is important to realise, however, that it is the Gestalt psychologists who have provided a reputable theoretical basis for their views.

CHAPTER FIVE

EDUCATION FOR LIFE

The Position in the Early Nineteenth Century

EDUCATION to-day claims to be much more than the mere communication of a certain body of knowledge and skills—more even than the training of the mind. That this was so was always the view of the great teachers and educational philosophers of the past, from Plato onwards; throughout the Far East it has never been questioned; but in Europe at the beginning of the nineteenth century it had almost been forgotten. Schools were supposed to exist for the instruction of the young in certain specified skills and for handing on a specified body of knowledge. That was all.

We have only to consider the philosophy underlying Bell's and Lancaster's monitorial system to see that it assumed this limited view of education. The conditions of the great English public schools indicated their agreement with it, for once lessons were finished the boys were free to go poaching, drinking and fighting with the town roughs to their heart's content. At Eton they locked the boys—of all ages—up for the night at 8 P.M., and no master entered the building, much less the dormitory, until next morning. What happened to the boys "out of school" was in fact nobody's business; the very use of the phrase "out of school", meaning "after the end of fixed classes", and used even in boarding schools where the boys scarcely ever leave the premises, has come down to us from that period.

It might be thought that the influence of the Churches would have produced a broader conception of the nature of education; but although they laid great emphasis on religious training, just as moral training was included in the various French and Dutch codes, this was treated simply as another subject to be learnt in class. Children learnt their catechisms, their sectarian doctrines or their moral aphorisms just as they learnt multiplication tables and spelling—in an adult form and with a view to knowledge, from which it was assumed that behaviour would follow. The only training in behaviour which was given was in the maintenance of the particular form of drilled discipline which the teacher considered necessary for the orderly conduct of a class—silence and immobility as far as possible, broken only by replies, occasionally chanted in unison, or the shuffling of one pupil as he "went up three" above his neighbours.

Thomas Arnold and "The Public School System"

The first great change in this attitude came from the English public schools and is rightly attributed to Thomas Arnold (headmaster of Rugby 1828–42).[1] What this change meant is perfectly illustrated by Squire Brown's soliloquy on sending his son to school at Rugby: "I won't tell him to read his Bible and love and serve God; if he don't do that for his mother's sake and teaching, he won't for mine. Shall I go into the sort of temptations he'll meet with? No, I can't do that. Never do for an old fellow to go into such things with a boy. He won't understand me. Do him more harm than good, ten to one. Shall I tell him to mind his work, and say he's sent to school to make himself a good scholar? Well, but he isn't sent to school for that—at any rate, not for that mainly. I don't care a straw for Greek particles, or the digamma—no more does his mother. What is he sent to school for? Well, partly because he wanted so to go. If he'll only turn out a brave, helpful, truth-telling Englishman, and a gentleman, and a Christian, that's all I want."[2]

In modern parlance the Squire would be said to hold that the function of the school was to transmit the heritage of the community, and that its main purpose was "education for life"; and Arnold's method of education for life was to "learn by doing", *i.e.* to learn to live as a member of a community by living as a member of a community. Of course Hughes in this passage, written after Arnold's death, is projecting backwards in time an attitude which was mainly due to Arnold's own work. No one would have thought of sending their son to the average public

[1] A distorted portrait of this great man may be found in Lytton Strachey's *Eminent Victorians*, and a sympathetic one in Professor Basil Willey's *Nineteenth-Century Studies*.

[2] *Tom Brown's Schooldays.*

school with such a purpose as this in 1810, for instance, when Sydney Smith was describing them as "a system of premature debauchery that only prevents men from being corrupted by the world by corrupting them before their entry into the world". Nor was the work of reform entirely due to Arnold; Butler and Kennedy, at Shrewsbury, probably did more for teaching methods and curriculum, and Arnold's predecessor at Rugby, Dr James, had rooted out many abuses before he came. His own contemporaries were probably right, however, in regarding Arnold as the founder of the English public school system.

Arnold's reforms had a profound effect on all other public schools in England. These public schools, in their turn, have affected the whole secondary system of Britain, the U.S.A. and the British Dominions, and even primary education, far more than is commonly realised. To take a single instance, it was extremely rare for a headmaster before Arnold to take the slightest interest in the boys' games or athletics [1]; it was indeed rare for any games or athletics to be organised in the school at all. Some people with an eye on the semi-professional athletic threat to American education may wish things had not gone so far; but no one can deny that the change is one of profound importance, and not confined either to England or to public schools.

Arnold's work was effective and important because it embodied a widely held and consistent view of the nature of education. He believed strongly that education did not consist simply of book learning; he would assuredly have agreed that it must "educate for life", and above all that his boys must be educated to be good adult members of the community—"Christian gentlemen", Squire Brown would have called them. But he also believed strongly that schoolboys were incapable of acting as adults, and that he could not expect from them the same response as he would expect from a mature mind. "I can train them when they are boys so that they will grow into good Christian men", he said; "I cannot make them into Christian boys." Now this may display a misunderstanding of what a Christian boy is, but it shows a real understanding of youth; and it is the basis of Arnold's method. Just as in the intellectual sphere it took the reforms of Pestalozzi

---

[1] Dr Moss (headmaster of Shrewsbury 1868–1906) could still affect such ignorance of cricket that when, on arriving at a school match with a guest, he heard the umpire cry "over", he called his guest away with regrets that play was finished.

and Froebel to show that the material of knowledge must be presented to children in a childish and not an adult way, so Arnold insisted that the material of conduct and character must be presented to adolescents in an adolescent and not an adult way. There are, in fact, two streams of development present in the modern movement for "education for life"; one is Arnold's, based on the view that if a boy is a good schoolboy at school he will grow into a good citizen in the world; the other, which derived its early inspiration from the work of Dewey, is based on the belief that the schoolboy is a citizen already, and that he should have, at least to some extent, the interests and the moral responses of the responsible adult citizen even when at school. This second theory is, however, of much later date and we must first consider that on which Arnold worked at Rugby, and which is still the guiding principle of the English public school and all its derivatives.

Arnold saw much in the behaviour of Rugby boys which he considered unChristian; but he also saw, or believed he saw, that it sprang from inevitable impulses of the immature adolescent mind. He tried therefore not simply to abolish abuses, but to find legitimate outlets for the impulses which had produced those abuses. His object was to make Rugby a community where boys would not so much repress their boyish instincts as learn to control and use them right. It was to be a community with its own schoolboy standards, the highest of which schoolboys were then capable—but definitely not adult standards. And by living in this community, boys were to learn those qualities of character, courage, kindness, self-reliance, obedience, industry and intellectual honesty which would enable them later to live as good members of the greater community. They were to learn government and administration as well as obedience and self-restraint, but it was to be boys' government and administration of boys by boys' standards. If Dr Arnold had heard that one of his pupils had attended a Youth Conference in London and advised the Chancellor of the Exchequer on his Budget, he would probably have expelled him on the spot for intolerable presumption.

Some Controversial Elements of the Public School System

Many of the typically public school practices which Arnold either introduced or encouraged are now among those most frequently accepted by traditional English schools and attacked by progressive educationists, so that it is worth considering them in some detail. Let us take four of the most controversial—organised games, prefects and "fagging", the "house" system and corporal punishment.

(a) *Organised Games.*—Organised games have spread from the English public school to secondary schools in almost every part of the world. In fact, the spread of "sport", which is scarcely ever mentioned in educational text-books, is possibly the most widespread educational revolution in the last hundred years. Arnold himself regarded organised games not as admirable in themselves, but as a much preferable substitute for the continual fights with "louts", poaching and rowdyism which went on at school in his day. They have been accepted since, partly on his own principle that they provide a comparatively social outlet to an adolescent impulse for physical dexterity and violence; partly because a later generation of physical educationists have held that they are much more valuable to physical development than the scientific but soulless "Swedish drill" preferred by their early critics; and partly because many people have seen in them an opportunity for adolescents to exercise, and therefore train, the virtues of physical courage, endurance, quickness of decision, command and obedience which are so valuable in life, but so difficult to "learn by doing" in an artificial situation. The critics of games have concentrated mainly on their abuse rather than their use. They have objected, for instance, that games take up too much time and that skill in games acquires far too high a value in public opinion. Here, in so far as they are deploring the type of *schoolmaster* who places too high a value on them and so leads his pupils backwards instead of forwards, they may have some justification; but if they are objecting to the boys' natural standards, then they make the mistake of asserting that boys ought to be men—and unusually intellectual men at that, as the normal adult value set on sport clearly shows. If the average adolescent boy did not admire the captain of cricket he would go back to admiring the "cock of the fifth" who "licked four town cads in one afternoon". It is a fallacy to suppose that he would transfer his support to the best physicist or violinist in the community. The standard of values of the games-playing schoolboy in the Arnold tradition may not be high, but it has every chance of being higher—and usually is higher—than that of the displaced urban adolescent without games or playing fields.

Secondly, there was, from 1920 onwards, a strong reaction against *compulsory* games. Particularly in *avant garde* literature it became fashionable to inveigh against "this hellish hockey" and to describe the torments of a sensitive and poetic youth, or even a keen naturalist, compelled to spend his afternoons playing cricket or Rugby football. The attack was directed mainly against the "public" boarding schools in England, because their imitators, the day grammar schools, had never found it possible to enforce games playing to nearly the same extent; while compulsion in America seems mainly to have been applied by public opinion, and to have extended to watching rather than playing. The attack on compulsory games was very largely successful and there must be very few schools now where compulsion means more than the compulsion to take some form of exercise, out of a fairly wide choice. Compulsory watching of school games is also very greatly diminished.

In the U.S.A. the problem of school games and athletics is rather different. The interest of the outside public in this side of school life has become so strong that there is a serious danger of semi-professionalism among schoolboys, and the adulation from which good athletes suffer is not that of little boys in their own school but of the local press. It is nothing unusual for a high school basket-ball team to "make the headlines" in a daily paper. This is tending to produce a situation where the school gets all the worst and none of the best out of a games-playing tradition. In the school the proportion of watchers to players, and of practices to games, rises steadily, and instead of nearly every boy benefiting from the physical and moral training of the game, a small élite suffer all the temptations of stardom.

(b) *Prefects and "Fagging"*.—The establishment of the prefectorial system as an essential part of school life is of almost equal importance. Something like it had, of course, existed before—notably at Winchester—but it was Arnold who elevated it to a conscious system, to be imitated and adopted by schools all over the world. In Arnold's time the comparison which would have occurred to students of comparative education, had such people existed, would have been with the pupil-teachers

G

and monitors already well known all over Europe: and they would have noticed that Arnold's system was new because it had nothing to do with school "lessons" and was not in any way designed to eke out the shortage of teachers. The prefects—Arnold's "sixth form"—were expected to exercise a moral influence and to control the behaviour, not the studies, of the younger boys. In doing this they were not acting as substitutes for teachers, for it was quite a new idea that even teachers should concern themselves with such things. The great virtue of the prefectorial system was that it bridged the gap between masters and boys, and made possible the building up of a strong moral influence among the boys from inside rather than from outside. Of course this moral system—call it "school tradition" if you prefer—was not the expression of a pure and spontaneous virtue by each individual boy; neither Rugby, nor any other school since based on the English public school tradition, has been or attempted to be a community of saints. The prefects were as authoritarian in their imposition of a moral code on the juniors as any teachers could have been—often more authoritarian; but they were boys, and their rule was therefore, if not democracy, at least self-government. A secondary virtue of the system was that it gave to a boy, who went right through it from top to bottom, experience in all the degrees of ruling and being ruled. They "learnt by doing" what it felt like to be at both ends of an authoritarian scale, and they gained an experience in command and administration that was in most cases of great value.[1]

The principle on which this system was based was again that of recognising and using the existing facts. Arnold found that in a community of boys the younger were naturally ruled by the elder, and looked up to them. The tyranny of "fag-masters" and the bullying which were a detestable feature of the English public schools in the first half of the nineteenth century resulted from leaving this situation in its natural condition. Arnold determined, therefore, not to change human nature, but to use this natural impulse through the medium of the sixth form, to

[1] One of the curious results of the extension of the system until the present day is that the "privileged" boy in England, who goes to an expensive public school, is often expected to endure in his first years there a degree of physical hardship and personal subordination that the boy of middle-class parents, educated within the State system, does not experience until he does his military service.

influence the mass of the school in a way in which he could not possibly have influenced it direct.

The system of "fagging" which has been publicly countenanced at almost all English public schools since Arnold's time is an offshoot of this decision. It is not infrequently attacked on the grounds that it is cruel or degrading to a small boy to inflict on him the task of cleaning the captain of football's boots, and bad for the captain of football to have little slaves to clean his boots for him. The defence is that in such a community it will be natural for the bigger boys to expect respect and service from the little ones, and—what is perhaps more important— natural for the little ones to wish and expect to give it. Small boys will always worship their heroes, and there will always be someone who actually regards it as a privilege to clean the captain of football's boots. In accordance with Arnold's method, therefore, many schools have thought it better to regulate this interchange and, by making it official, ensure that it is not abused: under all fagging systems the fag has his rights, privileges and sanctuaries. Moreover, it did men no harm to learn early what it felt like to be a servant and how to treat servants.

In some schools in the twentieth century a further development has been tried, with the idea of using this instinct for social training, by diverting fagging from the service of the individual to the service of the community as a whole. Whether this proves successful or not, it is a good example of the way in which school training may be used actually to modify the traditions of society as well as to hand them on.[1]

(c) *The "House" System.*—The "house" system developed at the English public schools as a natural result of physical conditions in boarding schools. Particularly in the newer and growing schools it was at first accepted that any assistant master might take boys to board with him and attend the school. This was a private financial arrangement between him and the boys' parents. As long as the assistant masters were commonly men "of private means" it had its advantages and there were undoubtedly some who spent more on their boys than they ever got out of them in board money. As the moneyed middle class died

---

[1] We shall see later that, as early as 1899, Dewey noted that the freedom from "domestic chores" of the modern American boy left a gap in his experience which required filling. "Fagging" is no more than doing domestic chores.

out, it became clear that a man could not be expected to combine the professions of teacher and hotel-keeper: in the first quarter of the twentieth century, therefore, almost all boarding schools went over to the plan of the school collecting the fees and paying the housemaster a salary. The system had established a division of the school, however, into more or less self-contained units, called houses, containing boys of all ages and numbering between 30 and 50. The excessive devotion to games which undoubtedly existed in the last years of the nineteenth and first years of the twentieth century—the period of "the flannelled fool at the wicket and the muddied oaf in the goal"—created a fierce rivalry and sense of exclusiveness in these houses: and this has been attacked as a flaw in the system. The disadvantages are clear enough, but it is only fair to mention some of the compensations: a small unit gives the master in charge a far greater chance of personal contact with his boys, so that a good house in a bad school is often a better place than a bad house in a good school; and in the conflicts of loyalty between house and school which do arise—and which inexperienced boys often wish to decide wrongly—there is an admirable opportunity for learning young, and by experience, how to take one of the most difficult types of decision. This system, too, has been copied from the original schools by most day secondary schools in England, and decentralisation of some sort is clearly necessary as schools grow larger and larger. As practised in the day secondary schools it is very like the "home room" system of American High Schools.

(d) *Corporal Punishment.*—The last and most vexed of all English public school practices is corporal punishment. Arnold beat his boys, and he expected his prefects to beat them. Almost without exception, British schools have maintained the tradition, and, on the whole, the rest of the world has professed to regard it as a barbarity.

Historically there is no doubt that even in Britain corporal punishment has been used less and less during the last hundred years: in particular, it was, throughout the nineteenth century, gradually abandoned as a penalty first for ignorance and then for idleness. The old practice of beating a child for "wilful ignorance" of something he often could not understand had been completely discountenanced, and very largely abandoned, by the end of the century; even as a penalty for offences against morals and order it seems to be dying out and is officially countenanced in schools scarcely anywhere but in Britain.

It should be emphasised first, perhaps, that where the British are eccentric is not in practising it but in publicly authorising its use by schoolmasters. Parents continue to employ it in almost every form of society, and Stuart Chase (*The Proper Study of Mankind*, 1949) records a wonderfully typical "poll" taken in the U.S.A., in which, after 100 per cent. of parents had answered that they were "opposed to corporal punishment", 80 per cent. of the same group answered that they "spanked junior" when he needed it.[1]

Secondly, the controversy should be separated from the general objection to all punishment. There are some educational theorists who hold that the whole system of character training by means of rewarding social and punishing anti-social acts is wrong. This is a genuinely revolutionary view, in the sense that it proposes to change a feature of human life which has been almost universally accepted since the dawn of history. This extreme form of "free discipline" received some support in the early part of the twentieth century from a misinterpretation of the conclusions of psycho-analysis—the assumption that *all* repression was harmful, but its genuine supporters are now so few, that it need hardly be considered here.

Once it is accepted that punishment is to be used as a method of moral training, whether that punishment takes the form of a caning or the withdrawal of the teacher's approval, we are in a position to consider rationally the objection to corporal punishment in schools. This objection is based almost entirely on the view that physical pain is so intimately connected with sex instincts, both in the mind of the sufferer and the inflictor, that it is psychologically too dangerous to use as a deterrent. Those who would abolish it claim that almost inevitably it feeds the sadistic impulse in the master and the masochistic in the boy; since the time of Quintilian they have pointed—and there seems little doubt that their evidence is genuine—to boys whose emotional lives have been profoundly disturbed by such punishments; they point also to occasional schoolmasters whose instincts

---

[1] I know from personal experience, or enquiry, also, that in at least three countries where it is officially abolished assistant masters use it regularly in the privacy of the classroom.

have undoubtedly been perverted; and they demand that in the schools at least, where public control can be exercised, the practice should be forbidden by law. That is the rational argument for the prosecution and it has undoubted force.

The opponents of corporal punishment grew in number during the first half of the twentieth century, though it is possible that within the last few years the tide has begun to turn. On the whole, they seem to have adopted the naïve view that those who advocated its retention—and in this country these included the vast majority of the most experienced and successful teachers of adolescent boys [1]—had never seriously considered their arguments, and that there was no genuine case for disagreement.

This is not true. The opposition case admits all that has been mentioned above, but holds that, before altering a system which has so long a history, the reformers must show not merely that the system is open to abuse, but that the proposed alternatives would remedy that abuse without introducing others equally great. Corporal punishment, after all, was employed by the great majority of men of sense for the first nineteen hundred years of the Christian era. The great Pestalozzi himself, in spite of the widely held assumption to the contrary, was on the side of the stick, and writes, in a way that would horrify some modern critics: "My punishments never produced obstinacy; the children I had beaten were quite satisfied if a moment afterwards I gave them my hand and kissed them, and I could read in their eyes that the final effect of my blows was really joy." The same acceptance of this method of punishment among children themselves is a commonplace among the boys of the English public schools. In this sense corporal punishment has some claim to being at least as "child-centred" as the various substitutes. And it is as well to remember that in matters affecting the human heart there is not the same reason that there is in the measurable sciences to assume that the most recently accepted view is the right one.

For the main contention of those who support corporal punishment is that the substitutes are equally open to abuse and often even more dangerous, largely because the children understand them less. They hold that once training of behaviour and

---

[1] The headmasterships of the great public schools are the recognised "plums" of the teaching profession and, by and large, attract the ablest men. Very few headmasters have abandoned corporal punishment.

character by punishment is accepted, then mental sadism is at least as dangerous as physical: that the bad headmistress, who prides herself on being able to reduce any girl in the school to tears simply by a "talk", is quite as dangerous as the bad headmaster of the old days who relied on the salutary effect of frequent public canings.[1] It is even suggested that the excessive fuss made about physical pain, while mental suffering is treated as if it did not matter, fosters an entirely wrong sense of values. Those who hold such views believe that since punishment must, by definition, hurt, something which is simple, quick and physical is better understood by the victim and less likely to harm him than any psychological deprivation—whether of long periods of leisure and activity (keeping in), membership of the group (sending out or expulsion), or the teacher's sympathy ("lectures", "black marks", etc.).

In practice the extent to which the cane is used has steadily decreased, and it is almost universally recognised that there are certain psychological types for whom, if they are to be punished at all, some other type of punishment must be found; and that no school can fulfil its purpose whose discipline is based on a pervading consciousness of the cane.

Subsequent Development of the Public School System

Since this typically English system was based not on any philosophical theory of human nature nor on a "science of education", but on a pragmatic treatment of existing boy-communities, it has steadily evolved during the hundred years since Arnold's death. Two aspects of this change are worth brief consideration. The first is the slow melting of the barrier between masters and boys. When Arnold came to Rugby, the boys' world was a world of their own, and the masters only entered it to conduct classes: it is not accidental that Tom Brown's last scene at school shows him chatting freely with Arthur and a young master, as all three of them watch a cricket match. Even so, there was still much progress in this direction to be made after Arnold's death. Readers of *Tom Brown* will again remember the strict code by which it was inconceivable that any boy, however weak and small, and however ill-treated, should apply to a master for help. By the time that Thring

[1] A recent Swedish film *Frenzy* was a vivid study of this problem.

(headmaster of Uppingham) was writing on the public schools in the 1880's he could attack this custom as outworn nonsense; and though it still lingers on with regard to certain offences, it has long ceased to command the support of the leaders in the great majority of schools. Indeed, from Arnold's time to the present day, each successive generation of boys has amazed, and sometimes shocked, their fathers by the familiarity with which they treat their teachers.

The second change has been in the broadening of the schools' interests. Lytton Strachey in his essay on Arnold writes: "Was he to improve the character of his pupils by gradually spreading round them an atmosphere of cultivation and intelligence? By bringing them into close and friendly contact with civilised men, and even perhaps with civilised women? By introducing into the life of his school all that he could of the humane, enlightened and progressive elements in the life of the community? On the whole he thought not." There is, of course, no evidence that Arnold ever considered surrounding the sons of his nineteenth-century squires with that "atmosphere of cultivation and intelligence" which twentieth-century Bloomsbury found so improving to the character; on the other hand, he did introduce into the school all that he could of the humane, the enlightened and the Christian virtues—while "progressive" was not, in his days of real progress, quite the password that it has become in this uncertain age. There is, however, this much truth in the gibe, that Arnold was not a man of great artistic sensibility and did not live in an era when the arts and crafts flourished in England. In the first public schools, organised on Arnold's model, there was undoubtedly a concentration on work, games and religion which left a large part of adolescent nature unsatisfied. The great pioneer in extending the interest of the school to all forms of art and craftsmanship was Thring, headmaster of Uppingham from 1853; and in the twentieth century the second stream of social development, which owes so much to Dewey, began to influence these schools also, so that now the danger to the most intelligent youth from too many interests seems almost as great as the old danger from too few.[1]

---

[1] The Fleming Report (1942) confirms the general view that the defects produced in the nineteenth century by excessive athleticism had been virtually eliminated by 1939.

The English public school system presented, therefore, a typically Platonic answer to the great question of the aim of education. It did not maintain that the sole purpose of education was the spiritual development of the individual; nor, on the other hand, that it was the moulding of a socially valuable type. Starting from its confidence in its own ultimate values, it simply asserted that the two aims were synonymous and that the individual, reaching his true spiritual development—the Christian gentleman —was in fact the type which society required. This was peculiarly the legacy of Arnold, who of all nineteenth-century social thinkers was the most passionate believer in a genuinely lay, but Christian, society. If he had not been quite sure what he wanted to produce, he could never have changed the face of education as he did.

By the end of the nineteenth century it was firmly established in England, not merely in the public schools, but in the accepted national principles of education. T. Raymont, in *The Principles of Education* (1904), writes:

"When intellectual ability, not to speak of mere learning, is made the sole measure of scholastic success, no words of condemnation can be too severe. The greatest English schoolmasters of recent times are just those who have seen most clearly the dangers attending "knowledge worship and the lust of the head" and have had the courage to defy the application of purely intellectual standards."

The "Public School Type" and the Individualist Reaction

This English method of "training for living" was known as such in Germany in the latter half of the nineteenth century and favourably compared with the "dry pedantry" of the German *Gymnasium* by such critics as Kessler.[1] It was in fact in Germany, apart from the British Commonwealth and U.S.A., that the most direct imitations of the English public school were established. The Germans had of course, in Schulpforta, an indigenous school which had grown up on very similar lines, but it was to a somewhat eccentric member of the genuine English public school line, Abbotsholme, that Hermann Lietz turned for a model in the foundation of Haubinda (1901) and Bieberstein (1904).

In nineteenth-century France, on the other hand, English ideas of secondary education found little favour. The intellectual

[1] Samuel and Hinton Thomas, *op, cit.*

standard of the *lycées* in the nineteenth century was immeasurably higher than that of the English schools, and the French conception of education as almost wholly an intellectual process made it unlikely that they would be attracted by English ideas. In their anxiety to cultivate the purely intellectual side of the *lycée* they had separated the actual teaching from the supervision and control of the pupils, the first being the function of the *Professeur* and the second that of the *répétiteur*. This meant, of course, a great economy in the time and nervous energy employed by the *Professeurs*, but it prevented that close personal contact between master and boy which developed in the English schools, and an English critic has described the *répétitorat* as "the curse of French education". The same concern for intellectual excellence first led the French to establish their boarding schools, not as the English did in the open country where the boys could get the maximum of fresh air and exercise and grow up as an isolated community, but in the largest towns where they could get the advantage of the most eminent teachers. The existence of the staff of *répétiteurs* and the fact that the schools were placed in large towns were perhaps partly responsible for the very much more rigid supervision of *internes* (boarders) and for the fact that there was no development of internal self-government on the lines of the English prefects. Even in France, however, many English ideas were being adopted by the twentieth century, and the degree to which the main principles of the public schools were admired in Europe is sometimes surprising to English educationists. It is, for instance, quite a shock to find José Ortega y Gasset (*The Mission of the University*, 1930) writing: "Even granted that English secondary education and German higher education are perfect, they would not be transferable, for the institutions are only part of a larger entity." The compliment paid to English secondary education is the more overwhelming when one remembers the awe with which German universities had long been regarded throughout Europe.

In the nineteenth century, however, acceptance in Germany and rejection in France had also a more sinister moral. Many of the attacks on "over-intellectualism" and "outworn curricula" made in Prussia, though justifiable enough on grounds of pure education, were in fact mere disguised chauvinism. And Arnold's system was admired, not for the type of boy and man which it produced, but simply because it was a system for producing types—and was therefore corruptible to such totalitarian uses as Rousseau, in his practical rather than Emilian mood, had proposed for the Polish educational system. Supposing Arnold was wrong and there *was* a cleavage between the spiritual development of the individual and the production of socially desirable types. The English system was clearly the one, which in practice had produced "the public school type" and from which any nation bent on educating an officer class could learn. Substitute Führer-worship for Christianity, and the system could be adapted almost without change, as Hitler in fact tried to do.

In England itself the opposition to the public school system on these very grounds was growing by the beginning of the twentieth century. It became a platitude to say that it crushed individuality for the sake of producing the "public school type". The difference in the climate of thought can be gauged by the following quotation from Sir Percy Nunn's *Education, its Data and First Principles*, which was first published in 1920 and has probably had more influence than any other English work of educational theory written during this century.

"Educational efforts must, it would seem, be limited to securing for everyone the conditions under which individuality is most completely developed—that is, enabling him to make his original contribution to the variegated whole of human life, etc."

Although this is not the cult of extreme idiosyncrasy that it might appear at first, since the exclusive value placed on "individuality" is later modified by the operation of "moral imperatives", it is a long way from the "moulding" of character in accordance with an ideal which was the basis of Arnold's system. This change in the English conception of "education for life" was, of course, part of that vast reaction against Victorian certainty and authoritarianism which affected every sphere of English thought and conduct, as the nineteenth century drew to its close. In the specifically educational world, however, it was considerably influenced by the "progressive education" movement in America.

This American influence, which from now onwards becomes by far the most important factor in the development of educational theory throughout the West, produced, as its first result in England, a typical compromise. Arnold and his immediate followers, as we have seen, admitted no problem in balancing the educational needs of society and those of the individual, for they held that the Christian gentleman was the answer to both demands. The writers at the turn of the century seem to have been the first to take refuge in such definitions of the purpose of education as Raymont's: "To help the individual to seek his own perfection in and by seeking the good of the community." This form of words and others like it have frequently been repeated since, usually with more acclamation than they seem to deserve. For they may mean anything. Everything depends on whether the writer thinks that there is any conflict between the perfection of the individual and the good of the community, and, if so, which should be sacrificed in each specific case and to what extent. As it stands, the definition could have served equally well to justify the systems of Sparta, Athens, Soviet Russia, Nazi Germany, Japan and the U.S.A. To tell us that we should all strive for our own good and at the same time for the good of the community would hardly be accepted after 2500 years as a useful restatement of ethical truth. And there is no reason why education should lag behind ethics in the discipline of meaning. Arnold at least was saying something positive when he affirmed that it was his business so to train his boys that they would grow into Christian men— for by implication he meant that if their "individuality" was aggressive, proud, uncharitable or cynical, it was his purpose to educate them out of it.

John Dewey and the "Progressive" Movement

In turning to the history of the Progressive Movement in America which produced this solvent effect on English educational thought, we are first faced with a problem of names. "Education for life", like "child-centred education" or "the integrated curriculum", is itself a "progressive" phrase. Moreover, the very word "progressive" needs some justification. Can it describe anything definite, and if it does, is it not a vast begging of the question to use it? Theoretically there are so many possible lines of educational advance that it seems meaningless to describe any plan or theory simply as "progressive"—for it would mean no more than that its supporters considered it better than other plans, which would be self-evident. In practice, however, it refers to a general body of educational thought, not

clearly defined but sufficiently distinctive for the title it claims
to have a definite meaning; the believers in this general body of
thought in America came together in 1918 and formed themselves
into the Progressive Education Association. It is the sort of
views which they and their supporters hold that are, for convenience, termed "progressive"; and the use of the title no more
implies acceptance of any claim to superiority than the recognition
of a "Liberal" party in politics implies a conviction that their
policies are in fact more liberal than those of their rivals. As to
"education for life" being itself a progressive theory of education,
it must already be clear that what the progressive writers have
here invented is new words rather than new thoughts.

The progressive movement towards education for life owes a
great deal to John Dewey, and the publication of his first important
work, *School and Society*, in 1899 may conveniently be taken as
a starting-point. The title itself suggests what has been one of
the main purposes of the movement ever since—that is, to break
down the barriers between the school as a place of education and
the world outside. There were two quite separate motives
behind this, and both are, to some extent, expressed in *School
and Society*.

(a) *Individuality and Free Activity.*—The first is a straight-
forward development of the accepted Herbartian doctrine of
interest and of the German emphasis on *Heimatkunde* (*i.e.* study
originating in the child's own environment). Dewey, like many
others, was impressed with the ease and pleasure with which
children learn what they want to learn, particularly the things
that are part of their home life, compared with their apparent
dullness at "lessons". He found that, in spite of the enthusiasm
with which educationists had accepted the teaching of Pestalozzi,
Froebel and Herbart, the actual practice of schools was still
predominantly intellectual and paid insufficient attention to the
natural motives and activity of the child. Since motive and
activity appeared to be essential to learning, and since in the great
majority of human beings the intellectual interest was not
dominant, it was not surprising that many children who were
bright at home seemed dull at school. And Dewey found this
particularly true where industrialisation and urbanisation meant
the end of the home as a productive community. In the interests
of the learning process therefore, he proposed three principles

which have been generally accepted by progressive educationists ever since:

(*a*) That the child must become the centre round which the appliances of education revolve.

(*b*) That the ideal school is the expansion of the ideal home; and that as genuinely educational activities are less practised in the home, so the school should accept increasing responsibility for them.

(*c*) That the child must be given enough opportunity for personal activity to balance what he gets from books, and that this activity must be so conducted as to provide a motive for acquiring the basic skills.

Those who are familiar with educational writing will notice two phrases, "activity" and "child-centred", which have become a great deal more than familiar in subsequent discussion. Two other extremely fruitful conceptions—the "integrated curriculum" and the single or "common" school—are sketched out in Dewey's remarkable little book, but their development really belongs to our next chapter.

It must have been clear at once that the individualism implied above would not only conflict with Arnold's conception of educating a type, but would be extremely difficult to put into practice. The difference between the school and the home, for instance, is not simply one of size, in which case expansion might have been easy, but, among other things, of the ratio of adults to children. It is equally obvious that the "Copernican revolution" demanded in the change from organisation round a single centre— the work in hand—to organisation round thirty-five or forty centres is going to impose a very considerable strain on the organiser, or teacher. Finally, it is easy to praise, or introduce into a school, "activity"; but not so easy to "conduct it in such a way as to provide a motive for acquiring the basic skills". The first practical difficulty about progressive methods of education in fact, is that they demand a higher quality of teacher and a lower pupil-teacher ratio than society in many cases has yet been prepared to pay for.

The doctrine of "activity" was accepted with such enthusiasm no doubt partly because of its real merits, particularly for younger children, and partly because it fitted so well the accepted psychology of Froebel and Herbart; but it was also in line with a less healthy phenomenon. The transference of value from the acquisition of objective truth to the subjective activity of the learner, the cult of individuality rather than conformity, the abandonment of much of the discipline of learning, all fitted in with the neo-romantic and anti-rationalist movement which was spreading throughout the western world. For a combination of reasons, therefore, "free activity" schools sprang up all over Europe and America, and the conscientiously progressive Weimar Republic actually made "civic training and activity methods" compulsory by law.

The acceptance of this doctrine meant, of course, a changed attitude towards the function of the teacher which was easily exaggerated, so that to some people the idea of a progressive school is still of one where the pupils do exactly as they like, and the teachers dare not interfere for fear of thwarting their individuality. The cult of activity was, in fact, pursued by some progressives with so little judgment that Dewey himself was compelled to point out (*Experience and Education*, 1938) that physical activity was not an end in itself but a means towards developing freedom of intelligence, and that in this sphere also "it may be a loss rather than a gain to escape from the control of another person only to find one's conduct dictated by immediate whim and caprice".

Such a warning would not have been necessary if the new movement had not, like so many new movements, quickly proceeded to extremes. How far the free activity view of the teacher's functions, even in dealing with adolescents, had gone by the beginning of the second world war may be seen from a pamphlet by Nils Hjelmtveit (Norwegian Minister of Education 1935–45), describing for English readers the educational system of Norway. Some allowance must be made for propaganda at a time when we were at war with an authoritarian state, but in general it sets out a view which derives legitimately from Froebel and the "activity" school, which is akin to the method successfully employed by Madame Montessori in the education of infants, but which many progressives accepted then and might accept to-day as a general principle of education: "The teachers are not allowed to try to mould the children in their own image or to make them think or feel alike, or to believe in the same ideas." And again: "Sometimes—speaking to bodies of teachers—I have tried to illustrate this point by telling the old story of Alexander the Great's visit to Diogenes. At the end of the conversation Alexander asked the old philosopher if he wanted to ask a favour of him, now master of the world. Diogenes answered: "I have only one wish: stand aside so that the light and warmth of the sun's rays may stream down on me." Every teacher should be able to imagine the pupil saying to him: "Don't stand in the light. Let the great truths and experience which have been gleaned through the centuries of man's life and struggles and sufferings and hopes, and which have been given expression in the works of great men, shine upon me without any colouring from you." [1]

It is, of course, unfair to the old-fashioned teacher to suggest that he was consciously engaged in anything so blasphemous as an attempt to "mould pupils in his own image"; he was, if he was a good teacher, trying to mould them in the image of an accepted ideal to which he himself was also trying to conform. But he would certainly have admitted that he was trying to make them think and feel alike—think clearly what was true and feel strongly what was good. To this extent there is a real clash between the two conceptions of education for life; and if the progressives, working from a pragmatist philosophy, claimed, on the whole, the support of psychology, anthropology was surely on the side of idealism and the traditionalists.

(b) *The function of the School in Society: Education for Citizenship.*—The extreme development of free activity and individuality was at first pursued by the progressives in conjunction with the second or "social" strain of Dewey's teaching. "Civic training *and* activity methods" were enjoined by the new constitution of the Weimar Republic (Article 148). But a conflict between the two is in fact inevitable if they are pushed to their logical conclusion.

The social side of Dewey's influence derives from two fundamental conceptions which reflect his pragmatist philosophy. The first of these is perhaps best expressed in his own words from *School and Society*: "All that Society has accomplished for itself is put, through the agency of the school, at the disposal of

---

[1] It is doubtful how far this attitude is "child-centred" and how far it projects into the child desirable adult attitudes. It certainly requires an extraordinary effort of imagination in the teacher. I have never, personally, been able to imagine any pupil saying anything remotely resembling it. My pupils, as a whole, have been either lamentably uninterested in the great truths or else, as soon as they are interested, only too anxious to hear their teachers' views about them.

its future members. All its better thoughts of itself it hopes to realise through the new possibilities thus opened to its future self." And again: "The modification going on in the method and curriculum of education is as much a product of the changed social situation, and as much an effort to meet the needs of the new society that is forming, as are changes in the modes of industry and commerce." Stripped of personifications, this seems to mean that those who control the schools ("Society") intend to use them in order to bring about those changes in the social system which they consider desirable ("to realise the new possibilities thus opened to its future self"). This view would no doubt be generally accepted nowadays in many quarters without much hesitation, but it is very different from the more Platonic view of education which lies behind the Arnold tradition. It had long been an accepted function of schools to pass on to a new generation the established social culture of their fathers; Dewey here suggests —and it is a most important and far-reaching suggestion—that they should train the young for the new culture of the future; and from that it is an easy step—since no one is very clear what this new culture will be—to claim for the schools an increasing part in moulding the new forms which it will take.

How clearly some of his modern followers have realised this implication is well exemplified in the view expressed by my predecessor in the Department of Education at Oxford: "Salvation is not to be found either in a remote philosophy or in a divided Church or in an irresponsible science: perhaps it may be found (as Quintilian hoped it might be found) in an educated people." [1] Stripped again of personifications, this must surely mean that neither the philosophers nor the divines nor the scientists, but the school-teachers (and, of course, the educationists, though in practice the school-teachers would do most of the deciding) are to play the chief part in deciding how the new society is to be remoulded. They are thrown on their own resources without the help of philosophy, science or religion, but "with these rivals dead", Mr Jacks goes on, "education comes to life".

Dewey himself does not take this further step, and so remains in this respect more in line with Arnold and his predecessors than he is with some of his own followers. In his last major work,

[1] M. L. Jacks, *Modern Trends in Education*, P.9.

Education and Experience, he makes it clear that his reason for valuing experience in a wide social environment is simply that it helps the young mind to develop a flexibility and capacity for further experience, which is in fact his only criterion of education. He never specifies who the abstraction referred to above as "Society" really comprises. Many of his followers, however, have accepted the challenge in the spirit of the quotation from Mr M. L. Jacks. They agree in fostering the closest possible integration of the school children with adult society, which means, in practice, visits to factories, foreign travel, current affairs talks, youth forums and so forth; but their intention is by this means not merely to increase their capacity for experience but to train them as good citizens. This training in good citizenship has two sides: it is to be achieved partly by accustoming the child to take an interest, and if possible a part, in public affairs, and partly by giving him the necessary knowledge about public affairs. It has become a truism with such later advocates of the social side of progressive education to say that the schools must not merely avoid lagging behind but must actually be "in advance of society".[1] They are sometimes called the "crystallisation point" where, in each generation, a new conception of democracy takes shape.

It is clear that this concept of education is to some extent in conflict with the liberal and individualist strain in Dewey's work, stemming from Froebel and represented by the quotation from Nils Hjelmtveit. In the first place, education for citizenship on these lines is not child-centred. The average adolescent himself will not, if left undisturbed, display much concern about public affairs.[2] They are too far outside the range of his natural interests

[1] In considering such a proposal the sceptic is bound to question whether that abstraction "the schools" is in any position to know in which direction society is going; and secondly, whether it is a valid assumption that this is necessarily the right direction. If by any chance the schools—deprived of the aid of science, religion and philosophy—should take the wrong road, it will not profit them to have set off in advance of the rest.

[2] A distinction should be drawn here between the organisation of discussion groups, conferences and so forth for sixth formers and the teaching of "Current Affairs" as a general school subject. The former represents nothing new. It is merely a more highly organised version of the long-standing and calculated willingness of sixth-form teachers to digress, and, in the intervals of Cicero, discuss with their pupils anything from Correggio to Communism. Pupils of seventeen and eighteen are often naturally interested in a host of "current" affairs and it has long been recognised that the school should encourage and, where possible, guide this interest. The only new development is the publicity given to such discussions and the exaggerated attention paid to the views expressed: and this seems a pity. The introduction of current

and understanding. Hence the amount of enthusiastic encouragement which teachers have to contribute if interest is not to flag. Moreover, much of the teaching about such subjects is about as unrealistic as anything could be. The old-fashioned devotion to the Wars of the Roses has been attacked, and with some justification, by one branch of progressive educators; but, in point of interest, this sort of course, with its accounts of battles and marches, is much nearer to the natural play instincts of small boys than the explanations of the Marshall Plan or the Town Rating System which are sometimes pushed down their throats by the followers of the "social" branch of progressive thought. In this sense much education for citizenship is conducted in a way that is technically not progressive at all, the only progressive part about it being the content and social intention. The danger inherent here is pointed out in the Report of the English Secondary Schools' Examinations Council (1941): "Nothing but harm can result, in our opinion, from attempts to interest pupils prematurely in matters which imply the experience of an adult—immediate harm to the pupil from forcing of interest, harm in the long run to the purpose in view from his unfavourable reaction." There is in fact, in this emphasis on the social intention, yet another conflict between different theories often lumped together as progressive: for since the publication of Rousseau's *Emile* it has been completely contrary to progressive theory in other spheres to teach anything *because it will be useful at a later stage.* Yet this is surely the main reason for explaining to children the problems of U.N.O.—for there is nothing whatever that they can do about it at the time, and it is doubtful how far it can really be regarded as educative to acquire a habit of forming judgments on current issues from inadequate evidence and experience.

Secondly, such education is not "designed to enable each child to make his unique contribution, etc." The teacher is again—just as in Arnold's time—concerned, and avowedly concerned, with producing the socially desirable adult. This, combined with the view that the schools themselves are to be the judges of what is socially desirable, throws a very heavy political responsibility on the teacher. Arnold could claim, and

affairs into the curriculum of younger and less intellectual pupils, on the other hand, is a new educational development and one of the main features of progressive theory. It is with the second, not the first, phenomenon that we are concerned above.

the early twentieth-century individualists could claim, that the schools stood outside politics and should be free from political interference. Once subscribe to the view that the schools are moulding the society of the future and this claim must be abandoned. To take a concrete instance, it was not uncommon in the 1930's to find progressive teachers in England enthusiastically organising branches of the League of Nations Union, who would have regarded the formation of a branch of the Royal Empire Society as a gross case of political indoctrination in the schools. Yet the decision that support of the League of Nations was more important than support of the Empire was clearly a political one. To educate children in the principles of collective security, or on the assumption that the time has come when world citzenship should replace national loyalties, may be a step on the road that will lead the world from chaos; but it is just as certainly a political decision as a decision to educate them in a narrow nationalism would be; and those educationists who claim the right to make it cannot simultaneously claim that education should be free from control by other politicians for their political ends.

This branch of progressive thought has therefore returned to something much nearer Arnold's idea of education but with these differences: where Arnold thought that boys must be educated in a boy's way and through membership of a boy's world, they believe in introducing them at the earliest possible age to adult problems and an adult world; and where Arnold believed that the good society for which they were being fitted was already established as the Church of Christ, the progressive thinks that the good society will be some new form of social organisation, better than the present one, more Christian perhaps, but which the pupils themselves, as they grow to maturity, will create.

It is not surprising, therefore, that even where both schools of thought agree, as in the view that social conduct should be learnt by living as members of a school community, Arnold should have worked through the type of school community that evolved spontaneously from the boy's nature, while the progressives insist that the community should be "democratic", because that is the type of adult community which they wish the next generation to build up. It is largely a difference of view on the "transfer" of social training. Arnold and his successors believed that there were certain fundamental Christian virtues which could be learnt by boys only at a boyish level and through life in a community which corresponded to a boy's stage in social development; the progressives seem, on the whole, to believe that there are certain modes of democratic social organisation which, if boys practise as boys, they will find easy and attractive as men. It is doubtful whether such forms of social organisation are natural to adolescents, and there is therefore a tendency to establish them "over the boys' heads". In some parts of Germany, for instance, school democracy was made legally compulsory after the 1914–18 war. Experience seems to show that such social imposition from above is only successful where it is inspired by the influence of an exceptionally strong personality. The German attempt to introduce it administratively was a failure.

(c) *The School as a Productive Community.*—The second effective strain in Dewey's social teaching has been his insistence on the value of the school being as far as possible a productive community. To some extent this is a natural conclusion from the importance he attaches to motive and interest in the learning process; but it also springs from a realisation that even in 1899 the American social structure was changing, and that if the virtues of the pioneering generations were to be reproduced in their grandchildren, then some other institution must take the place of the log cabin. At the very beginning of *School and Society* Dewey points out that children no longer shear sheep, card and spin wool, weave or make candles for the household; and he believes that this communal productive effort must now be reproduced by the school. Since the family no longer initiated the child into life as a productive member of society, the school must take over the job.

It is clear immediately that here also "civic training" is in conflict with "free activity"; there is, undoubtedly, a strong romantic tendency in Dewey's thought as a whole, but when *School and Society* was written, the log-cabin existence was still too recent for anyone to suppose that the children had done these chores in a spirit of free activity. They may have enjoyed them— it is more likely still that in retrospect the middle-aged imagined that they enjoyed them—but what is certain is that they did them under compulsion and evaded them when they could. The comparison between Dewey's proposals and the fagging system of the English public schools has been noted already, and it is not as absurd as some readers may imagine; more than one boy has spoken to me of the sense of achievement he got from producing, for his prefect's tea, exquisitely-cut sandwiches or well-browned toast. Such an experience is certainly as close to that of the log-cabin as is that of the child who is persuaded by an emotional appeal from teacher that she really wants to make raffia mats for the school dining-hall. If Dewey was right in thinking that children derive benefit and satisfaction from communal work of this kind, it does not necessarily follow that they will freely choose to undertake it. Most attempts to combine communal work with free activity have also depended on the moral influence of a strong personality, as Homer Lane's "Little Commonwealth" did.

One development which could hardly have been foreseen when *School and Society* was published has greatly increased the importance of this side of social training. This is the vast expansion of secondary education. As long as the youth left school and became in fact a productive member of society at the age of thirteen or so, the social necessity of this kind of training was not so obvious. Now that an increasing number of British and American youth are growing almost to manhood at school, the movement for including such training in the work of the schools has received great encouragement. This doctrine of Dewey's is therefore of very great importance and the extent to which it is still in the forefront of progressive thought may be judged from the following extract from *Teach Them to Live* by Mr James Hemming (1950):

> "Training for life was, until about fifty years ago, adequately supplied for the majority of the population not at school but by life itself, and in the most natural way of all—by offering examples of skill and action for the young to imitate. To ride a horse, to handle an axe, to make and follow a map; planting and reaping; [1] to hunt and cook; and much other equipment for living was picked up as a matter of course, in the same way that a baby learns to speak. Daily life was educational in the best sense."

This is almost exactly what Dewey said in 1899, and by 1949 the romantic element in it has become more obvious. The proportion of children who learnt to make and follow a map as part

---

[1] It is a curious anomaly that, on the whole, those who hold these views about "planting and reaping" protest most strongly when children are let out of school to plant or lift potatoes, or when they do something productive like helping with a milk or paper round.

of their daily life in America or England in 1899 must have been infinitesimal, and far smaller than now learn it in the Boy Scouts. Moreover, it is hard to see any realistic reason why it should be more "educational in the best sense" to learn to ride a horse and handle an axe than it is to learn to ride a motor bicycle and handle the interior of a radio set. Dewey's original view had in fact something in it of the romantic nostalgia for the log cabin which is so potent a feature in American mythology; and this seems to have infected subsequent expressions of a theory which could well have stood on its own merits, as soon as it became clear that the new generation of adolescents were to be cut off from that participation in common production which had been the lot of their fathers at a similar age. Putting all the romanticism aside, it is clear that if the whole nation, and not an academic minority only, are to receive secondary education, this principle must play a large part in their education.

(d) *Co-operation between School and Society.*—It was clear that if the school was to take over what had been the function of the home, the fields and the workshop, the closest possible co-operation would have to be established between parents and teachers and between school and society. Both of these were strongly advocated by Dewey from the first and have become part of the standard programme of progressive educationists. The close connection between school and society has usually been sought by urging the teachers to acquire a wide knowledge of the social and economic structure of their own neighbourhood and use this in their presentation of their teaching material. This is to be supplemented by visits, wherever possible, to places of interest outside the school. It is clear again that this demands a high quality of teacher, for it is not an easy or superficial thing to acquire a wide knowledge of the social and economic structure of one's neighbourhood; and school visits—though they seem in the minds of some people to have acquired a sort of transcendental value of their own—serve no useful purpose unless they are well conducted and form part of an intelligent plan of instruction.

Co-operation between parents and teachers has usually been sought by the establishment of parent-teacher associations. These have been most successful in the U.S.A., where the pride of a small community in its schools is often quite surprising to the European, accustomed only too often to apathy or even opposition from the tax- or ratepayer. They have been slower to find acceptance in England, partly from conservatism and partly from a suspicion on the part of headmasters that only the least desirable parents would join them.[1]

In Germany this side of progressive education was welcomed with the usual enthusiasm by the Weimar Republic, and for a short time parent-teacher associations as well as school democracy were made legally compulsory in some areas. The associations soon got involved in politics, however (which is an inevitable danger), and some of the democracies degenerated into complete anarchy, so that the reforms were tacitly abandoned.

On the whole, France remained until 1939 relatively impervious to American, just as she had been to British, influence; and education for life as a general theory raised little interest. Moral training continued to be given in intellectual form in the primary schools, and at the secondary level the academic and technical "streams" maintained their own separate high standards. The school continued to be regarded as a place where a child or youth learnt facts and skills, and the established culture of France; it was emphatically not a "crystallisation point for a new form of democracy" or an "experiment in living" or even a "community of youth", nor was it a substitute for the home; it was indeed a French educator who coined the expressive, if tautologous, aphorism "*L'école est l'école*". Even in France, however, the influence of the progressive movement has made itself felt since the war, particularly in the organisation of the Classes Nouvelles.

Pragmatist Basis of Progressive Education

It is not often that the founder of a great educational movement is in a position to sum up, forty years later, those beliefs

---

[1] The conservatism is a natural product of the nineteenth-century system; as long as it was assumed that the schools knew what they were trying to make, *i.e.* scholars and gentlemen, there was no call for discussion between parents and masters. The fear of the undesirable parent is not a fear of "bad" parents. It is the bad parent whom every headmaster would like to see in the parent-teacher association, for it would give the school some opportunity of seeking the co-operation that it was not already getting. What headmasters fear is that the really good parents will stay away from meetings because they are busy at home with their children, which is where they can do most good, and the bad parents will stay away because they are bad; while the meetings will be packed with those parents who enjoy committees and who have private theories about education which they want to try out on the school. It is most unlikely that an experienced headmaster will have anything to learn from these which will make up for the amount of his time that they will waste.

which the movement has retained. Yet this is what Dewey has done in *Experience and Education* (1938); and if we want an idea of what the wisest and most experienced of the progressives mean by their faith nowadays we can scarcely do better than take Dewey's summary from that book. In contrasting the new education with the old, he says that the new "opposes to imposition from above, expression and cultivation of individuality; to external discipline, free activity; to learning from texts and teachers, learning through experience; to acquisition of isolated skills and techniques by drill, acquisition of them as means of attaining ends which make a direct vital appeal; to preparation for a more or less remote future, making the most of the opportunities of present life; to static aims and materials, acquaintance with a changing world". Dewey himself does not here claim, any more than he originally claimed, that it is the function of education to change society, but rather to acquaint pupils with a society which is in fact changing. The extreme view of education as a deciding factor in social progress continues to be common, however, among his followers; and in *Experience and Education* he does justify both democracy and the new education by reference to the same criterion, that they make possible a higher quality of experience.

It seems clear, then, that Dewey's work has been the main inspiration of the progressive movement, and that in many ways the movement is committed, whether it realises it or not, to his pragmatist [1] philosophy. This pragmatism in its simplest form is the belief that there are no eternal truths either moral or intellectual; that "good" and "bad" conduct mean simply socially convenient or inconvenient conduct; that truth means what works in practice, and that knowledge is only real to the extent that it affects our present conduct. Dewey is a consistent philosopher, and it is not surprising that he should find the aim of education to consist not in learning fixed truths or reaching a fixed moral ideal, but simply in increasing the capacity of the individual for experience. It is true that, like all those who reject

[1] Dewey maintains that his philosophy is not pragmatist but "experimentalist". This seems to save him from the philosophic attacks on James' position only at the cost of limiting his appreciation of a situation to internal analysis. "Experiment" will show whether a certain action produces the anticipated results. But there is nothing here from which we may derive a judgment of value, and he is left seeking experience (or experiment) for experience sake.

ultimate standards, he still talks of a "higher" form of experience (higher in reference to what standard, one might ask, if experience itself is the only aim?) and of "mis-educative" experience "distorting" future experiences (distorting them from what straight course, if there are no fixed landmarks?); but these are difficulties of language which the pragmatist always encounters. The fact remains that experience, more and more of it, more and more nicely distinguished, remains for him the true purpose of all human endeavour.

It was as inevitable that an educational theory based on such a philosophy should find acceptance in America as that it should be neglected in France. Margaret Mead has pointed out the extent to which all American thinking, and particularly moral thinking, is geared to the future. In a society where it is morally incumbent not merely to do as well as your father but to do better, the progressive view of education is almost the only one which it is possible to hold. In one other respect Dewey's views coincided with the trends of progressive thought in the first half of this century, for his pragmatist theory of knowledge (which is a vital part of his whole educational theory) is also the orthodox Marxist theory of knowledge.[1] In fact, progressive education was eagerly accepted by the U.S.S.R. in the 1920's and only abandoned as the Communist dictatorship solidified.

The "Neo-Thomist" reaction

By 1930 a reaction against the pragmatist and progressive theory of education had already set in in America. The belief that content as well as activity mattered and that there were certain established truths which were part of the western heritage and must not be neglected was exemplified in new courses at Chicago University and particularly, perhaps, in the 100 great books course of St John's College, Annapolis, introduced in 1937. The meaningless excesses of some schools, practised under the title of free activity, had awakened progressives themselves to the practical difficulties of operating a system that demanded

---

[1] "Marx insisted that we only perceive a thing as part of the process of acting upon it, just as a cat, when it sees a mouse, immediately pounces on it. The activist theory of knowledge—known to-day as instrumentalism—which insists that knowledge is indissolubly bound up with action, is the most distinctive feature of Marx's philosophy as opposed to his theories of history and economics."—R. N. Carew Hunt, *Theory and Practice of Communism*, 1950.

unusual abilities from the teacher, at a time when teachers were paid, treated and recruited on the assumption that they were semi-skilled labour. In the sphere of secondary education it was becoming clear that E. L. Thorndike had been right when he pointed out as long ago as 1932 that "one of the serious criticisms of the American system is that in the zeal to provide identical opportunities for all, the interests of the abler students have been sacrificed". In the enthusiasm for education for life it had been almost overlooked that a certain proportion of the pupils at least needed an intensive training in the arts and sciences; and it began to be questioned whether the methods which might be effective for the first would be of any value for the second. This intellectual reaction, combined with the psychological reaction produced by the failure in practice of much ostensibly progressive teaching, Dewey terms '"Neo-Thomism", because it involves a return to a fixed authority. It is in the clash between it and his own perpetually advancing experimental method in education that modern ideas of education for life are being formed; the side which any individual teacher takes in the dispute must depend on his deepest views about the nature of science, ethics and humanity.

CHAPTER SIX

SECONDARY EDUCATION

THREE great issues have dominated the history of secondary education in the last hundred years: the reform of the curriculum, the abolition of class distinction, and the provision of secondary education for all.

Throughout the nineteenth century it was assumed, as it had been assumed at all previous times, that only a minority of the population would receive secondary education. By this term was originally meant a general non-vocational education in the humanities, whether carried out at schools or colleges,[1] ending between the ages of seventeen and twenty. We have seen that up to the middle of the nineteenth century the content of this education in Europe was firmly based on the Greek and Latin languages, though ever since the French Revolution there had been a strong movement either for adding modern subjects on to this core or for using them to replace the core itself. This issue was debated at great length in the second half of the century, and the complete dominance of the classics had been brought to an end in the schools of most western countries by about 1900.

At the same time an attack had been begun on the rigid class distinction which reserved secondary education not merely to those families who could afford the considerable fees, but to those also who could afford to forgo for four or five years the youth's potential earnings. The distinction was so clear cut that in most European countries there were, even at the primary level, two completely separate systems of schools—the state system, which was used by the mass of the people, and a private system, preparatory to the secondary schools, which was used by the richer classes; it was most unusual for any pupil to move from one system to the other. The first attempt to reform this state of

[1] A European critic, in the middle of the century, even described the universities of Oxford and Cambridge at this time, not without justice, as "higher secondary schools".

affairs was concentrated at the primary level. It had always been accepted that a certain number of places in the secondary system ought to be made available at public expense to the abler sons of the poorer classes; but as long as there were two separate primary systems it was very difficult to effect this. For this and other reasons the reformers urged first the establishment of a single national system of primary education, alike for all.

In spite of its obvious democratic motive, this movement, which perhaps reached its height in Europe immediately after 1919, should not be confused with the third and latest development, the campaign for secondary education for all. Its advocates still believed that secondary education should be reserved for a minority; they were concerned only that that minority should be picked more on merit and less on income. It was from America, and particularly after the slump of 1930–31, that the radical innovation of providing secondary education for all spread to Europe.

This new development springs from economic as well as educational causes, and in this it is in the normal tradition of educational advance. Just as compulsory primary education was introduced in England mainly to save children from the factories, so universal secondary education is being introduced partly to save adolescents from the street corners; it is a direct result of a changing economic system, in which the adolescent has little or no earning power and is consequently excluded from the factory. He has therefore been found a home in the schools, in many cases before the teachers or educationists have formed any very clear idea what to do with him when he gets there. How far this movement will go, whether we are on the verge of a campaign for university education for all, it is difficult to see; but as the latest of the three great issues which have affected secondary education it must clearly be reserved for the end of the chapter.

Reform of the Curriculum

(a) *England 1850–1900.*—The movement to reform the curriculum of secondary education was not primarily an English one; indeed, Matthew Arnold pointed out to the uncompromising defenders of the classics that they were opposing a tide which had already gathered force all over Europe and to which they would inevitably have to give way in the end.[1] There are reasons for

[1] *Higher Schools and Universities in France*, 1868.

studying its development in England, however, quite apart from the local interest to English readers. The radical attack on the classics came earlier in England than in France, where science crept in as an "additional," rather than alternative, subject, and the legal ruling of Lord Eldon, which was effective up to 1840, meant that the attack was also concentrated here into a shorter time. In Germany the purely educational arguments for widening the curriculum were complicated at an earlier stage than elsewhere by the introduction of nationalist pressure for a German rather than international curriculum; while in America, where at the end of the century the greatest development took place, the question was never debated in its most acute form, because non-classical secondary education had been accepted almost from the first.

It is in England immediately after the Great Exhibition of 1851, therefore, that we see the defenders of the new and the old secondary curricula pleading their cases with the greatest concentration on the single educational issue. The dissatisfaction of the middle classes—and of a predominantly middle-class Government—with the existing system was stimulated by the discovery that, although the Great Exhibition had been a triumph of English organisation, it had exposed a little-known situation in the field of technical progress. The foreign exhibitors were rapidly overhauling and even passing England in the very techniques of manufacture which she had originally taught them, and to which she owed her commercial greatness. This fear of being out-distanced by other countries was widespread in Europe: the French sent Commissions to investigate English education just as we investigated French; but the English alarm at the state of secondary education was not ill-founded. The course of events which followed is, in the main, typical of the movement of English social history; the first decade, from 1850 to 1860, was devoted to agitation aimed at awakening the general public, the next from 1860 to 1870 to a series of Government enquiries in the form of Royal Commissions, and the next thirty years to an almost complete failure to act on the recommendations of these Commissions. In one respect only was the normal process interrupted. The Prince Consort needed no convincing that technical and scientific education in England was in need of encouragement. He was a man who could and would stimulate action without waiting on public opinion, and it was largely due to his influence that the Science and Art Department of the Board of Trade was founded in 1853, and in 1856 transferred to the Education Department. Such little government influence as was brought to bear on the curriculum came mainly from this body, which made grants to post-primary schools specifically for the teaching of science.

In general, however, the first decade after 1851 was one of public agitation and discussion. Discussion of the content of education has always tended to spring from one or other of two basic questions: (*a*) What studies are best suited to educate children? Or (*b*) what body of knowledge must every educated man possess? The demand for a "modern" curriculum took two main forms, in accordance with these two conceptions of education. Deriving from the latter were those who rejected the study of the classical languages on the grounds that the knowledge acquired was "useless"; Latin, they said, had been the staple of secondary education in the mediaeval and Renaissance periods because knowledge of it was a practical necessity as long as all learned work was published in Latin and all international correspondence carried on in Latin; its study had been preserved into the present day sheerly through the force of inertia and habit; what the modern man needed for the conduct of his practical life was a knowledge of the natural sciences, mathematics, geography, possibly foreign languages and history. Those who adopted this line of argument ranged themselves therefore with those who saw education mainly as the acquisition of a fixed body of knowledge and skills, to be later applied in adult life. This was, on the whole, the French rather than the English doctrine, and in England, where the conception of culture scarcely existed in the middle classes, it was difficult for those who held it to resist the middle-class pressure for even more "practical" studies, such as surveying and book-keeping. In America it proved impossible.

The chief exponent of this theory in England was Herbert Spencer, whose magazine articles, published between 1854 and 1859, had a great effect on public opinion and who was not without influence in France.[1] His work suffers as a whole from an attempt to find a rigidly rational and utilitarian criterion of value; as a result he laid it down that the importance of a subject in the curriculum depended solely on the necessity of that particular

[1] Compayré: *Histoire de Pédagogie.*

branch of knowledge to human life. As has been constantly pointed out ever since, it does not follow, even on the assumption that education consists in the acquisition of knowledge, that because health is a first essential for life, hygiene has an exactly equal importance in the curriculum.

The second line of attack on the purely classical curriculum was based on the other view, that education consisted not in acquiring knowledge but in training faculties of the mind. Its supporters held that what was important in the sciences was their method rather than their content, and that the dead languages were a bad subject of instruction just because, being dead, they could only be taught in a dogmatic manner. The spirit of enquiry and progress, with which the nineteenth century was permeated and which it so much admired, must be learnt, they maintained, through the medium of studies which were in themselves experimental. These views, combined with a less rigidly materialistic estimate of the value of scientific subject-matter, were put forward with great ability by T. H. Huxley, whose address on "The Educational Value of the Natural History Sciences", in 1854, was one of the landmarks of this period of public agitation.

By the 1860's the government had been sufficiently disturbed to set up an official enquiry, and the Public Schools Commission (Clarendon Commission) between 1861 and 1864 and the Schools Enquiry Commission (Taunton Commission) between 1864 and 1868 covered the whole ground of secondary education.

The Public Schools Commission dealt only with the nine great public schools, and its main criticism of the curriculum was that the liberalising process started by Butler of Shrewsbury had not gone far enough. They agreed that there must be a central core of studies and that this should continue to be the classical languages; but they pointed out that many boys, because of their inability to master Latin and Greek, were getting no sort of education at all, and they recommended the inclusion of additional subjects. All boys, they thought, should learn mathematics, at least one foreign language, two branches of natural science, history, geography, drawing and music.

No sooner had the work of this Commission been finished than the Schools Enquiry Commission began its survey of all remaining secondary schools. This was a much more important enquiry and revealed a much more serious state of affairs. Considered as specialist establishments for educating a small minority of the aristocracy in a traditional fashion, the great public schools were relatively efficient for their day. The second rank of public schools and the grammar schools presented a more diverse and at the same time more depressing picture. The best of both types had already made many of the reforms that the Commissioners proposed. At Cheltenham (founded 1841) there had always been a modern side, called the Military and Civil, in which all the subjects recommended above were studied, with the addition of Hindustani and engineering; at Leeds Grammar School there was "an excellent laboratory and a class well drilled in chemical manipulation and analysis". We have already seen, however, that throughout the country as a whole the provision of secondary schools was completely inadequate. Those which still attempted a secondary curriculum could be divided into two types, the classical and the non-classical. The "classical" retained the old-fashioned curriculum, similar to that of the public schools; but, except in the very rare cases where a considerable proportion of the pupils were preparing for the universities, this curriculum had become utterly meaningless, and consisted of learning the rudiments of a language which the boy never expected to master: in many such grammar schools the boy's acquaintance with Latin must have been very like Tom Tulliver's in *The Mill on the Floss*. The Commissioners found the non-classical schools, on the whole, worse. Most of them had introduced modern subjects, haphazard and with no scheme of instruction, either to impress parents or in order to charge fees for them as extras. In many grammar schools, for instance, a "writing master" was the first addition to the staff after the "Master" and "Usher", and only those who paid the extra writing fee were allowed to write. The recommendations of the Schools Enquiry Commissioners on curriculum were very similar to those of the Public Schools Commissioners. In the course of their enquiry Matthew Arnold had conducted a comprehensive survey of the secondary educational systems of Western Europe, and the Commissioners were clearly inclined to take the Prussian system, already described in Chapter One, as their model. Throughout the public and grammar school system they recommended the retention of a dead language core, becoming less important in the lower grades

I

of grammar school, with the addition of modern subjects, on the fringes but occupying rather more time than before.

In practice, no action whatever was taken on these recommendations: in theory they suffered from two serious defects. The first was that they were bound to involve an overloading of the curriculum if ever they should be adopted, since the classicists could point out that the essence of the scheme was to preserve the pre-eminence of the classics, and that therefore the new subjects must not encroach on their time.[1] Secondly, the importance of the new subjects was argued from the value of their subject-matter as knowledge, without nearly enough attention being paid to the methods of teaching them, or to their value as subjects of training. When the headmaster of Winchester told the Commissioners that he would like to include more history in the curriculum "but did not know how to teach it in set lessons", he was not being as stupid as people have sometimes thought; many of the new subjects were included, as a face-saving measure, before nearly enough was known about methods of teaching them; Herbert Spencer, for instance, wanted science taught "so that children should be led to make their own investigations", but nineteenth-century science lessons for the most part consisted of occasional lectures, in which the pupil's sole participation was either to listen or to go to sleep. It was clearly not enough, for those who abhorred learning by rote and dogmatic teaching, to substitute chemistry for Latin grammar, if the method of teaching chemistry was to be the memorisation of lists of formulae as meaningless as the Latin gender rhymes. No government action was taken to enforce any of the recommendations on curriculum, and the speed with which they were voluntarily applied may be judged from the fact that the author of this book contrived to pass through an education at one of the better public schools between 1922 and 1926 without any lessons in drawing or music, and without entering a science laboratory except to listen to a lecture on architecture.

The fact that no decision was imposed meant that the controversy could be extended indefinitely—as indeed it has been to the present day. The defenders of the old classical training found their strongest argument in the purely utilitarian nature of much of the attack. It is true that the Public Schools Com-

[1] This is what happened, for instance, in Prussia.

missioners claimed that the purpose of classical education was to enable the pupils to use English properly,[1] but the real classical defence was that the purpose of education was not the acquisition of any specific knowledge or skill, but the training of mental faculties, and that the classics were pre-eminently suited as a medium of such training.

"Something is required", said Thring, the great headmaster of Uppingham and perhaps the best, because the least prejudiced, of their advocates, "which shall be perfectly easy and at the same time perfectly hard; familiar to all and known to none; of universal use and universally strange to the users; so simple that babies learn it with ease, and so complicated that the ablest are ever learning it unsuccessfully; the most fixed of all things and the most shifting; plain, yet infinitely obscure; the common property of ignorance and wisdom; the joint inheritance of the ploughboy and the poet; holding nothing and yet full of all things; all these and many more paradoxes are reconciled in language." Having thus disposed of any possibility of a non-linguistic core, he goes on to show why the dead languages are so much better suited as a subject of instruction than the living ones—because, he says, once you are past sentence-structure the more difficulties in a language the better; because a dead language cannot be learnt parrot-fashion from a governess; because, being inflected, they train the mind in accuracy; because the difference in word order compels the pupil to attend to the sense. These are still the most valid arguments for a general study of dead languages. Thring was honest enough not to use the appeal to the value of classical literature, for he knew that the average pupil never reached the stage of appreciating it; nor did he refer to the aid given by a knowledge of Latin in English spelling, French roots or reading chemists' prescriptions. He took his stand firmly on the belief that language was the best medium for training the mind and that in choosing a language one must be guided entirely by its suitability for the purpose, and not at all by the subsequent advantages to be gained from a knowledge of it. Thring himself was no bigot, and in fact the arts and crafts owe their introduction into the public school curriculum more to him than to anyone else;

---

[1] This was also Thring's view: "The ultimate end of the study of the classics is to make the learner an artist in words, and a conscious master of his own tongue."

but he was convinced that there must be a solid core to the curriculum and that this core must be the classics. There was probably an unconscious motive also which influenced him, and many others, towards this conviction, and that was that they themselves knew how to teach the classics and were very doubtful how to teach anything else; at the same time they strongly suspected that the modernists knew nothing about actual teaching practice at all. This is well exemplified in Thring's comment on educational experts or "advisers": "It is a strange spectacle everywhere seen, though no one sees it; the spectacle of the nation putting their best hope, their children, under the charge of men whom they do not trust to do their work, and so put them in turn under the charge of others. And those others enjoy the singular advantage of not knowing the work . . . with the additional recommendation of very often having been in earlier years hopelessly left behind by the very men whom they now control."

Two factors, however, rendered the cause of the pure classicists hopeless in the long run. The first was the growing interest in science and scientific method which has characterised the last hundred years, combined with the actual need of trained scientists for industry. The second was the growth of educational theory. At first it was possible to oppose the demand for young men educated with a knowledge of the sciences by adopting the "training" rather than "content" view of education, and by constant reference to the mystique of the "grand old fortifying curriculum"; but as educationists, under the influence of Herbart, began to emphasise the importance of "interest" in the learning process, it became less and less easy to maintain that something as foreign to the natural interests of youth as the classical languages was the ideal subject of instruction. The final blow to this defence was struck by the demolition of the "faculty" and "transfer" theories about the turn of the century (cf. Chapter Four). If there were no separate faculties of the mind, and if training was not transferable, then it became impossible to argue that training in accurate Latin grammar was essential or even useful in acquiring the habit of accuracy in other subjects; and the Commissioners' contention that study of the classics was the best way of teaching children how to use their own language appeared to be scientifically untenable.

The result was that between 1900 and 1940 the classics steadily declined from their position as the core of the curriculum —in the great public schools by a slow shrinking in the numbers of those who specialised in classics, in the grammar schools by the actual abandonment of the study of dead languages by an increasing number of boys. The influx of new subjects in place of the classics was combined with an important change in school organisation; as long as language was the centre of instruction it had been possible for one teacher to take the class for most of the day; if "modernism" compelled him to add French to Latin he probably knew that language fairly well himself, and taught it in the same fashion that he taught Latin. The new subjects, however, were taught by specialists and, particularly in the more progressive schools, the "form-master" began to be replaced by experts in a variety of subjects each of whom visited the class for three or four periods a week. This was, at the time, considered a great advance, and educationists at the beginning of the twentieth century were inclined to measure progress by the extent to which specialists were employed. More recently some doubt has been thrown on this opinion, on the grounds that knowledge of the pupil is at least as important as knowledge of the subject.[1] For the old-fashioned form-master, though he may have been less expert in some of the subjects, knew the pupils a great deal better.[2] In the same way there has been a reaction against the disintegrated curriculum which at first resulted from the abandonment of the classical core, and a search for some other "core" subject which could take its place. In fact, most modern curriculum builders agree with the Public Schools Commissioners and with Thring that there should be some main body of study to which the rest is related, but are not prepared to find this core in language and certainly not in a dead language.[3] For developments in the curriculum since 1900 we shall do better to turn to America, after considering briefly the trend of events in Europe up to 1900.

(b) *Germany 1850-1890.*—We have seen that the Schools Enquiry Commissioners, influenced by Matthew Arnold, wished to introduce into England a system largely based on the Prussian,

---

[1] This is the belief behind the organisation of the "Classes Nouvelles" in France.

[2] I know one who, when asked by well-intentioned inspectors what he teaches, always replies: "Boys".

[3] There has been some revival in classics, however, since 1946.

and an almost equal admiration for Prussian methods existed among French educationists. But even at the time of Matthew Arnold's visit an attack on the purely classical tradition similar to that which shook England was in progress in Germany. There were two distinctive features in the Prussian situation, however: first, they, like the French, had a Ministry of Education which was prepared and accustomed to give directions in such matters; and secondly, there was a nationalist strain in the opposition to classical teaching even at this stage. Two quite separate motives can in fact be detected among the Prussian supporters of the new curriculum—a genuinely educational desire to fit the subject-matter more nearly to the real interests of the average pupil, and a nationalist desire that the schools should produce "virile" pan-Germans rather than scholarly bookworms always reading Latin and Greek. The teaching profession, with a few exceptions, were therefore concerned to repel what they saw as an attack on the intellectual standards of the *Gymnasium* conducted largely on political grounds. Moreover, Prussia differed from both England and France in that, since the recognition of the *Realschule* in 1859, a beginning at least had been made of an alternative form of secondary education to the purely classical curricula in use elsewhere; but it was only a beginning. It was not until 1870 that the graduates of *Realschule* were admitted to the universities, and then only those from the *Realgymnasien*, where Latin held almost as high a place as in the *Gymnasien* themselves. Moreover, under the materialistic influence of the German universities, the actual teaching of classics in Prussia became more philological and pedantic even than in England and France. What Europe admired in Prussia was not in fact a reform in the traditional secondary curriculum, but the creation of an effective alternative in the *Realschule*. It was doubted at the time whether this could be called secondary education at all, since most people accepted the French definition of secondary education as being that which led on to the university. Even this crown was added, however, for the pure *Realschule* student by the establishment of the *Technische Hochschule*, scientific institutions doing work which would be admitted elsewhere as of university standard, and to which the *Realschule* graduates were admitted in 1878.

The prestige value of the *Gymnasien* was not much impaired, however, and the very existence and success of the *Realschule* perhaps tended to confirm the *Gymnasien* in a more uncompromising classicism than ever. The German reformers were therefore faced with a slightly different problem from that which existed in England and France. It was not that no proper facilities for a "modern" education existed; it was that the curriculum of the nation's leading schools was hopelessly out of touch with the modern spirit.

(c) *France 1850–1890.*—Two features are noticeable in the French treatment of this controversy: first, the variety of solutions which were tried[1]; and second, the fact that no solution which seriously attacked the teaching of the classics was ever successful for long.

The first of these features is probably due to the highly centralised French system of control. Where the government directly controls the content of education there must be a great temptation to try new systems and new arrangements one after another. To this must be added the fact that the secondary curriculum became a subject of political dispute, the conservatives normally favouring the classics and the radicals "modern" subjects.

The continued resilience of the classical ideal is surely due to the French conception of secondary education's primary function, as the preservation of French culture. This naturally led to an unusual degree of conservatism. It is not only that the French, far more than the Americans or Germans and rather more than the English, have regarded education as the process of handing on from one generation to another a fixed content of skills and knowledge; over and above that, leaders of education in France have been conscious of the historical superiority of French culture over that of her neighbours. It is to preserve, rather than to achieve, French standards of culture that they are, consciously or unconsciously, struggling. This attitude of satisfaction with a standard already reached, and determination, as one's first duty, to preserve it, is utterly foreign to American ways of thinking, but it is constantly recurring in the official pronouncements of French policy and it runs through all French thought on education.

The first attack on the classics in France was part of the general

---

[1] Durkheim (*L'Evolution Pédagogique en France*, p. 172) notes no less than fifteen reorganisations of the curriculum in the nineteenth century.

radicalism of the Revolution, and the changes it made were reversed by Napoleon I; it was, however, generally accepted from that time on that the natural and physical sciences should play *some* part in secondary education, even if this part consisted only of one lesson a week until the last year, with the opportunity of some more detailed study at that stage. By a curious historical freak the Revolution and reaction of 1848 produced the reverse of the normal results on the curriculum. We have already seen that the schoolmasters were suspected, not without some reason, of having backed the revolutionary movement. It might have been expected therefore that the reaction would lead to a classical swing in education, but the new emperor, Louis Napoleon, was a curious mixture of autocrat and liberal. As an autocrat he considered that the *lycées* were producing too many journalists and literary men likely to oppose his régime; as a liberal he believed in "modern" educational ideas, and particularly that France needed scientists and technicians. Under his rule therefore a system of early specialisation in classical and scientific "sides", known as *bifurcation*, was introduced, but it involved specialisation as early as fourteen and was administered with such rigidity that it became very unpopular. Moreover, the French found the same difficulty that the English were to find later, that there was a great shortage of people qualified to teach the sciences or even of reasonable ideas on how they should be taught. In 1863, therefore, *bifurcation* was abolished and the old "arts" course became again universal, though it was possible to specialise at the end of the course. The Franco-Prussian War led to further modifications of this system. The victory of Germany, first over Austria and then over France, was widely attributed throughout Europe to the Prussian educational system, and increased the respect in which it was held both in England and in France. Imitation of it chiefly took the form of introducing courses that were clearly modelled on those of the *Realschule*; but the classics were also affected and it is no exaggeration to say that the battle of Sedan led to the abolition of Latin verses in the French *lycée*. In France, as in England, however, the main movement was towards a new form of post-primary education, in the establishment of "intermediary" or "higher primary" schools; but it was never very clearly established whether these were intended as an additional or an alternative form of education. Those who were

134

primarily interested in the reform of the curriculum were inclined to confuse the development of a new curriculum for these new schools with the reform of the curriculum in the existing schools. It is a confusion of thought which has been evident again in the last few years as a result of the creation of the "secondary modern" school in England.

(d) *The Reforms of 1890-1902.*—The end of the century saw the western countries turning to settle the curriculum of secondary education with a remarkable unanimity of timing. The Imperial Conference in Berlin was held in December 1890; the Ribot Commission in France and the Committee of Ten in the U.S.A. both date from 1892; and the Bryce Commission in England was appointed in 1894. Both in France and in England, systems of secondary education were established in 1902, mainly as a result of these commissions, which endured virtually unchanged until the second world war. There were great similarities in these two systems. In both countries the experimental intermediary courses or schools were taken up into the main secondary system and purged of the somewhat vocational and utilitarian character which they had gained, in France through separate existence as "*enseignement spéciale*" and in England through the special grants made by the Science and Arts Department to encourage the teaching of natural sciences.[1] In both countries the new system introduced in the public secondary schools a career divided into two halves, of which a considerable proportion of the pupils (in England a decreasing majority) completed only the first half. Latin was still retained as one of the subjects to be studied in this first half and, at first at least, all the abler students learnt it; but it was not obligatory. In the second half, to which students passed on at about the age of fifteen, four courses were laid down by the French reorganisation of 1902: (a) Classics, (b) Latin and Modern Languages, (c) Latin and Science, (d) Modern Languages and Science. It will be seen therefore that some language work was retained even for scientists at this stage. After two years of this the first part of the Examination for the Baccalauréat was taken, followed by specialisation either in philosophy or mathematics. The English courses approved by the newly created Board of Education in 1904 were very similar: (a) Classics,

---

[1] These had led to an over-specialisation on such subjects, and in 1904 all special grants for the teaching of individual subjects were abolished.

(*b*) Modern Languages and History, (*c*) Science and Mathematics, (*d*) Latin and History, (*e*) Geography with either a language or a science. The provision against undue scientific specialisation was not as clear as in the French courses, but was met by a regulation that at least one-third of a pupil's time must be spent on subjects outside his main course. Even this was later withdrawn and specialisation is now much more intense in the sixth forms of English schools than in either French or German.

In England the reforms of 1902–1904 really settled the curriculum controversy in state-aided secondary schools for the next fifty years. There was a slow drift away from the classics until about 1940, but the general principle of a wide common curriculum up till the age of sixteen with subsequent specialisation in one or other of a definite group of courses was never seriously challenged. The place of Latin in the first stage was safeguarded by the fact that it was retained as a compulsory subject for entry to the older universities and for arts students in most university faculties. In the independent secondary schools the same system was adopted, though it was still some time before science found a real place in the general curriculum of all pupils.

In France the objection to early specialisation in science and the strength of the classical tradition provoked what was probably the last attempt to reverse the decision of 1902, when Léon Bérard, the Minister of Public Instruction in 1921, passed through Parliament a reorganisation restoring compulsory Latin and Greek, and postponing the optional "modern" courses to the last two years before the baccalauréat. Though this return to compulsory classics was repealed by his successor in 1924, the new system introduced in 1925 avoided early specialisation in science by prolonging the general curriculum for all students until the end of the sixth year, with an option only between linguistic work in Latin or modern languages; complete specialisation was thus postponed until the last year of school. In Germany a system similar to that adopted in France and England had been pressed by the *Einheitsschule* movement; their plan, sometimes known as the Altona plan, also demanded a common curriculum for the first six years of the nine-year school course, followed by specialisation in the last three years.

In certain parts of Germany such experiments were tried, since until Nazi times education in Germany, as in America, was a State matter. In Prussia, however, which really led and controlled the education of most of the country, the conferences of the end of the century concentrated on freeing the *Gymnasium* from the appalling burden of memory work which it had shouldered in the attempt to adopt new subjects without lowering the standard of classics; and on regularising the position of the three types of secondary school. The upshot was a great reduction (at first fifteen periods a week) in the number of hours devoted to Latin in the *Gymnasium*, and the recognition of the *Realgymnasium* and *Oberrealschule* as enjoying "parity of esteem" with the *Gymnasium vis-à-vis* the universities. Those who have experienced the endless debates about "parity of esteem" in England will not be surprised to hear that the official pronouncement did little or nothing to alter the social supremacy of the *Gymnasium*; but at least the leaving certificates from the other schools could now be accepted by the universities.

The Breakdown of Social Barriers

We have seen that in much of the educational reform of the nineteenth century two problems were confused, how to bring the curriculum of the secondary school and the university up to date, and how to provide either a genuine secondary or an efficient post-primary education for those who were not going to the university. The former was mainly the interest of educationists, the latter of statesmen.

The statesmen were also concerned with a third related problem, how to enable the ablest members of the population to get a secondary or university education, irrespective of their parents' means. Just as the fierce competition of the nineteenth century drove England and France to reorganise their post-primary and technical education through fear of being outclassed in commerce or war by Germany, so the statesmen of each country began to see that a vast loss of national talent was involved by a system which deprived the great majority of the population of any chance of higher education because of the poverty of their parents.

The first obvious solution was the provision of a number of free places in secondary schools for the ablest pupils, and this provision had been made throughout Western Europe by the beginning of the nineteenth century. The establishment of universal free primary education produced an unexpected new problem. For centuries formal education of any kind had been confined to the richer classes, with the addition of a few boys selected from the poor for their ability or promise. There was no particular difficulty in making this selection, because it was made at the earliest stage, when all children started equal.

When a general system of primary education was introduced it was naturally assumed that this would provide for the first stage in the education of these poor but able boys, and that those who were to receive secondary education would now be selected at the end of the primary school life. As long as the selection continued to be carried out by charitable bodies and churches this method, though open to abuse, was not impracticable; but we have seen that very soon governments became interested in it, and this meant the expenditure of public money and selection by public authorities. Once this had become the rule, suspicious people demanded that the selection should be made by open and competitive examination.

A few years of open competitive examination were enough to show its serious disadvantages. That the whole future life of a child should depend on its performance in an examination taken at the age of eleven was, and has increasingly become, a most questionable system. The recognition of this has been one of the strongest arguments, first, in favour of secondary education for all, and then of comprehensive secondary schools on the American high school model. Apart from this it quickly became apparent that in many ways the examination was prevented from fulfilling its purpose. The *lycées*, *Gymnasien* and many of the grammar schools maintained preparatory departments of their own, so that there were, as we have seen, two separate systems of primary education— one for the rich and the other for the poor. When the "scholarship" examinations for entry to secondary schools were established, it was found that in some cases, mainly in France and Germany, candidates from the preparatory departments had an advantage over those from public elementary schools. The classes were smaller, the teaching often better, and the curriculum designed with the secondary school in mind. To some extent therefore the able children of the genuinely poor were still excluded.

In England the position was at the same time better than on the Continent and worse. The independent public schools were a complete class preserve, and there was no provision at all for free education at them; on the other hand, the grammar schools drew a larger proportion of their pupils from the public primary schools, and the free places were therefore more fairly competed for. Only in America was it the accepted custom for the children of all classes to start their education at the common primary school.

One of the guiding principles of liberal democracy was of course the "career open to the talents", and the anomaly of this situation was therefore attacked by liberal democrats in all Western European countries. As a result of this pressure, the new "democratic" system of education introduced in Germany in 1920, for instance, established a common primary school, known as the *Grundschule*, which children of all classes attended, while the preparatory departments were abolished. France, in 1925, took a similar, though less drastic, step. The private primary schools were allowed to go on, but their curriculum was compelled by law to conform to that of the state primary schools. Thus all children in France received an identical education at the primary stage even though they might receive it at independent schools.

In England, since the situation in the grammar schools was not so acute, preparatory departments were not abolished until 1944. The problem of opening the great public schools to a proportion of children from the state primary system was a much more difficult one, and though an attempt to tackle it was made by the Fleming Committee in 1942, which reported very favourably on the public schools as educational institutions, no real answer has yet been found to the problems of selection and finance. It costs approximately three times as much to maintain a boy at a public school as it does to send him to the boarding house of a grammer school, chiefly, of course, because at the public school tuition fees as well as board have to be paid. It is difficult to find any criterion by which a public education authority can select a small number of its children on whom this disproportionate amount of its funds would be fairly spent.

By the end of the first quarter of the twentieth century, therefore, the normal system in Europe was for the vast majority of the population to pass through a common primary education, and for a much smaller élite to receive a secondary education, ending with specialised study either of the arts or sciences. This élite consisted partly of those whose parents could afford to pay the fees at the secondary school, and partly of those who had won "free" places in open competition. The proportion of these free place-holders was approximately 30 per cent. in Germany and 35 per cent. in England.

At this stage a new development in France led almost accidentally to the amalgamation of intermediary with secondary schools; and since intermediary education was already free, the consequence of the amalgamation was the abolition of all fees for secondary education as a whole. Starting with the entry forms of 1930, therefore, secondary education throughout France became free; but it was still not universal, nor was it intended to be. In the first place, if the adolescent is capable of earning a useful wage, the abolition of fees alone does not open the secondary schools to the children of the poorest classes; it is necessary also to pay maintenance allowances which will compensate the family for the loss of the youth's potential earnings. And in France maintenance allowances at this period were not generous. Secondly, it had never been the intention of the French authorities that secondary education should cease to be the privilege of an élite, and since entry to, and continued attendance at, secondary schools now depended entirely on reaching the necessary academic standard, the intellectual quality of that élite was actually raised.

The democratic belief underlying this phase in European education, therefore, was that, in any society, roughly one-third of the adolescent youth, chosen on a basis of intellectual ability, could benefit from secondary education; and that it was the duty of the State to see that they received it. To appreciate its full force, it is worth stopping for a moment to consider the definition of secondary education on which it was based. This has probably been best expressed in French educational writing, but would have secured general acceptance throughout Western Europe in the 1920's. The theory then was that primary education supplied those children whose future was not likely to call for original thought with the essential skills and frameworks of knowledge which every man should have. Secondary education, on the other hand, was designed to train the élite in those habits of theoretical and original thought which future leaders of society would need to employ; and to give them the necessary ground-work of knowledge to enable them to study the arts and sciences at the university. The challenge to this conception of secondary education came from America, and it was a challenge, above all, to the assumption that secondary education should be reserved for an élite.

Secondary Education for All

We must now return and trace the developments in America which have led to the revolutionary conception of secondary education for all. It is of course impossible to generalise about American education with even the same degree of accuracy which can be achieved in respect of French or German. Particularly in the earlier periods one must allow for a wide variety of practice in different States and even in different districts within the same State. It is possible to discern general trends, however, and the nearer we get to modern times the greater the uniformity.

In general, American secondary education during the nineteenth century anticipated the practice of Europe in the twentieth in two ways. Americans were much quicker than Europeans to recognise the need for a type of secondary education suitable for those who were not going on to a university, and, as a result, much quicker to develop courses alternative or supplementary to the traditional classical curriculum. To a great extent the "academies" which flourished all over the States in the first half of the century were designed to impart that general culture which would act as a lower-grade substitute for a college education; the Boston English Classical School, founded in 1821, was clearly intended to provide a modern form of secondary education for those not going on to college; and the Committee of Ten in 1893 formally laid it down that: "The secondary schools of the United States, taken as a whole, do not exist for the purpose of preparing boys and girls for colleges. Only an insignificant percentage of the graduates of these schools go to colleges or scientific schools." It is worth comparing this with a European view expressed as recently as 1938: "By secondary education is understood uniquely that education which prepares for the university . . ." [1]

In the early years of the nineteenth century secondary education in America was almost entirely concentrated in these private "academies". Judged on pure statistics, the proportion of the population attending them was extraordinarily high, but it is

[1] Durkheim: *L'Evolution Pédagogique en France.*

difficult to be sure of the real meaning of these attendance figures, and the academies differed enormously in standards. It seems certain that a number of them would, by European standards, have been regarded as little more than primary schools; others were more comparable with the intermediary or "higher primary" schools of England or France; and some European purists would of course describe almost the whole of American secondary education in the nineteenth century as "higher primary" rather than secondary. The main thing which struck the European traveller, then as now, was the great diversity of the subjects taught and the immensely wide ground covered at a very superficial level. "The process of mental cultivation in America is somewhat analogous to their agricultural system", wrote Sir Charles Murray in 1834–36. "In both cases they look too exclusively to the quantity of produce immediately to be obtained, and pay too little attention to the culture and improvement of the soil. It has often been remarked that an American course of collegiate education extends over a field that would occupy a man of good abilities forty years to master." [1]   It is easy enough to find reasons for this characteristic in the mid-nineteenth century. The fact that America was still a "new" country meant that culture was still regarded as being something to be imported from Europe, and by many people as something to be "got" in pieces. As the academies competed with each other, there was an inevitable tendency to outbid one's rivals by offering to impart some new section of culture, often by some new method. At the same time the boundless energy and optimism of a new people led them to devise plans of study which assumed that a lively and hustling nation would be able to get through a vast amount of the learning of old-fashioned and decadent Europe in a very short time. Thus it came about that the curricula of the academies were inflated with astronomy, anatomy, meteorology, gauging, dialling (whatever that may be), Portuguese, elementary law, Biblical antiquities, mental philosophy, political philosophy, book-keeping, acoustics, phonography, phreno-mnemotechny and waxwork; and all this in addition to writing, spelling, Latin, Greek, etc.

Out of this welter of mixed sense and nonsense there developed in the first half of the nineteenth century a system of alternative

[1] Sir Charles Murray, *Travels in North America during the years 1834-6*. Quoted in S. G. Noble, *A History of American Education*.

Classical and English courses in most of the academies, which anticipated the alternative courses introduced in Europe at the end of the century. But in spite of this momentary crystallisation, it is worth noting that a wide and unco-ordinated superficiality has been the main weakness of American secondary education ever since, a weakness pointed out by none more vigorously than by American educationists. The academies adopted this form of curriculum largely because they were independent schools competing in the open market; there was no high court ruling tying them to the classics as in England, and no Ministers of Education jealous of their standards as in France or Germany; only in New York State did they receive aid from public funds. By the beginning of our period two things were already beginning to happen which changed the face of American education: the academy was beginning to give way to the public high school, and the college entrance requirements were beginning to impose some check on the secondary curriculum.

Although the academy was a perfect example of private enterprise, it was not really in the main tradition of American education, which has always regarded education as a public service to be controlled by the community and provided out of taxation. It seems probable from the Constitutions of those States incorporated soon after the Declaration of Independence that the system most commonly intended was that each State should have a state university, rather like the University of France, and that this should complete, and to some extent control, a public educational system including secondary schools. The beginnings of such a system had in fact been established by the University of Michigan, but were dropped in 1846. The demand for secondary education under public control and provided at public expense was such, however, that, although the state universities never played quite the part intended for them, most districts in the Eastern States had established public high schools by the outbreak of the Civil War. The wording of the Massachusetts Law of 1859 is significant: "Every town may, and every town containing 500 families or householders shall . . ." establish a secondary school. Thus by about 1860 the more highly developed areas of America were provided with an adequate system of free public secondary schools with a much wider—many felt, too much wider—curriculum than those of Europe.

K

Although free, these schools were still confined to an élite, partly by entrance standards, partly by the economic arguments which compelled poorer parents to send their children out to profitable employment as soon as possible. The opposition to secondary education provided out of public funds was continued, therefore, for some time, by those who argued that it was unjust that a man should be taxed for the education of "other people's children"; and that a service which was used only by the middle and upper classes should not be paid for out of general taxation. This opposition was finally defeated by the famous Kalamazoo decision (1874), a test case, brought up in respect of the township of Kalamazoo, which established the right of school districts to provide secondary schools out of taxation.

After the Civil War the academies gradually died out, although a few, such as Phillips Academy, have survived as predominantly boarding schools for the rich, very much after the fashion of the English public schools. At the same time the colleges or universities and the New York Board of Regents began to exercise some control over the curriculum and teaching methods of the new high schools through their entrance requirements. As in Europe, the older colleges in particular were slow to allow alternatives or additions to the old studies, and the struggle for recognition of "modern" courses in America was not so much a struggle for their inclusion in the high school, where they had long found their way from the academy, as for their "recognition for college entrance". The college authorities based their preference for the old studies on the theory of mental discipline, and to this the innovators replied, at first, not by challenging the theory, but by demonstrating that it was possible to teach the new subjects in as formal and disciplinary a way as the old ones. Physics could be taught direct from a text-book of rules, just as well as Latin syntax; English classics could be construed, parsed and learnt by heart just as well as Greek; French could be taught as if it were a dead language. Thus, although the growing importance of college entrance requirements played a useful part in persuading the high school to go in for rather more coherent and continuous courses, it was also leading, towards the end of the century, to a stultification of much that had been good in the old informal curricula. In America, as in Europe, the problems were brought to a head by the appointment in 1892 of a committee to investigate the work of the high schools.

This committee, known as the Committee of Ten, was appointed not by any official body, nor by an association of the schools themselves, but by the National Educational Association. The work of co-ordination and standardisation has progressed far in America since 1892, and has been mainly due to such independent professional bodies.

The Committee recommended a number of definite courses considerably more liberal than those accepted at the same time in Europe, viz.: languages, mathematics, general history, natural history, and physics and chemistry; but their main requirement was that any subject studied should be carried on for several years, at least three to five times a week. This was a criticism of the short ten-week courses in a wild variety of subjects which formed part of the curriculum of some high schools, and the Committee's chief concern was in fact to discourage the superficial smattering. They recognised that only a small proportion of high school students went on to college, but they recommended that the education of the rest should be the same as that of the college entrants, since what they were aiming at, for both types of pupil, was mental discipline.

This Committee was followed in 1895 by a Committee on College Entrance Requirements; and it was really this second Committee which established the American system of "Unit Counts", though the New York Board of Regents had already used it since 1891. This system has been generally adopted in America except among the eastern universities, where a Joint Entrance Board conducts examinations of the same type as is used in England. Its adoption was important because it provided an alternative to the European system of leaving or entrance examinations. To secure entrance to a college, a high school student was required to amass a certain number of "counts" during his school career; each count represented a definite period of work in a subject satisfactorily completed; and the Carnegie definition of a count, as a course of five periods a week continued for an academic year, soon gained national acceptance. The Committee approved the principle of "election"—that is, that pupils should themselves choose the subjects in which they were going to get counts, but recommended, though without insistence, that the course should be grouped round certain constants. The system has obvious advantages over the single crucial examination which faces the European secondary schoolboy at the end of his school career: but it has equally obvious difficulties and disadvantages.

From the point of view of the college, the main difficulties in such a form of selection seemed to be in ensuring that the courses from which counts were gained were genuinely educational, and that the standard demanded by the school authorities was adequate. They met the first by retaining in their own hands control of the subjects which would be accepted for counts, and the second by inspection, not of the individual candidates but of the schools. The normal arrangement was that fifteen counts in approved subjects, gained at an accredited school, qualified for entry.[1]

No sooner was this system of control by the colleges established than it began to disintegrate under the influence of two solvents, both strong in the first decade of the twentieth century. These were the growing demand for high school education, and the theoretical destruction of "mental discipline" as a principle of education.

The increased demand for high school education was a natural result of the phenomenal increase in wealth of the U.S.A., combined with the egalitarian feeling of a people who always suspected that it was wrong for some people to enjoy an "advantage" not enjoyed by all. More parents were able to do without the labour of their adolescent children, and at the same time there was more money available for the provision of public high schools. As a result of this situation there developed between 1900 and 1910 a great expansion in high school facilities combined with a growing concern that not enough of the adolescent population made use of them. This was not surprising so long as the curriculum remained essentially that which had originally been designed for an élite; secondary education may be an "advantage", but the kind of secondary education which is an advantage to an élite is neither attractive nor advantageous to the mass. The situation was well illustrated by a survey made in Chicago in 1900, which showed that the fees being paid to independent schools for

---

[1] The election system is discussed at greater length in Chapter Eight, "Universities"; and the accrediting system in Chapter Eleven, "Examinations".

vocational training in such subjects as book-keeping, typing and stenography exceeded the total annual expenditure for public secondary education.

A European Minister of Education, concerned only with the training of an élite, might have remained unmoved by such a discovery; but in a series of democratic school districts it could mean only one thing, that what the people wanted was further education in vocational subjects, and therefore that the public school system must give it to them.

There were still those who felt, however, that if such further training was given it should not be in the high school; and in many districts vocational and technical schools parallel to the high school system were at first set up. They failed because of the public demand, which constantly seems to cripple such institutions, that the subjects from the academic curriculum should also be included; and the final result of such enquiries as that made at Chicago was that the vocational subjects were included in the high school curriculum, and the special schools, where they had been established, were merged in the high school system.

It would have amazed the Committee of Ten that the high schools should be unable to resist this invasion of their preserve by subjects which had no "disciplinary" value; but the whole theoretical basis of their insistence on discipline had been attacked by Thorndike's analysis of the "transfer" problem. If disciplines acquired in one subject could not be transferred to general use, then there was no further justification for limiting the curriculum to subjects with a disciplinary value. American educationists at the beginning of the century accepted the conclusion that transfer is negligible to a considerably greater extent than it is now accepted, or than the evidence actually warranted. And the result was that the curriculum, which had been tightened by the Committee of Ten spread out again to accept almost any subject; from which it followed that the high school was enabled to cater not merely for an élite but for all those desiring secondary education.

The result of these changes has been a great increase in high school numbers and a great decline in the proportion of students "electing" academic subjects or studying them with any thoroughness. It has been stated, for instance, that of those taking history or foreign languages few study them for more than two years— and the value of two years' study of a foreign language at the high school level is very doubtful.   J. D. Russell and C. H. Judd (*The American Educational System*) give the following figures for six representative high schools between 1890 and 1930:

Percentage of pupils taking—

	1890	1930
Foreign Languages	38·7	17·6
Mathematics	16·0	13·5
Science	17·7	10·1
Non-academic Subjects	3·6	21·2
Social Studies	10·9	16·3
English	13·1	21·3

With this should be compared the system which prevailed throughout Europe over the same period, according to which *all* high school students studied foreign languages, science, mathematics and their native tongue, and none vocational subjects.

With this change in the curriculum the high schools had lost their last connection with the education of an élite, and secondary education for all became a possibility.   This was the end to which economic causes had been leading since the beginning of the century.   With increased urbanisation, and even in the farm districts increased mechanisation, the labour of adolescents found a smaller and smaller market;   in the really modern and well-designed factory they were a nuisance.   When the great slump of 1930 hit America it was therefore the adolescents who were stood off first.   Society was quick to realise that once barred from productive work they would be better off in school than at the street corner, and the new high schools, inspired largely by the doctrines of "education for life", were well suited to absorb a whole generation.

Such was the birth of a conception of secondary education which is influencing the whole western world to-day.   Its disadvantages, in the retardation of the able pupil, are admitted—it is, for instance, American educationists who point out that academically the American college entrant is two years behind his European counterpart and that "pupils who have studied any given subject in the secondary school do not succeed any better in college than those who have not studied it".   It is also very difficult to apply in small units, with the result that city high schools are, by European standards, impossibly big, while the large number of rural high schools with enrolments of under a hundred and fifty cannot possibly provide the intended curriculum. These difficulties loom very large in the eyes of American educationists to-day, but in the main the defence of the American high school is social or political rather than educational, and is well expressed by Russell and Judd (*op. cit.*):

> "Some attempts have been made to promote the idea that segregation of young people destined to enter employment on the completion of their school work from those who will go on to college is desirable from an educational standpoint. Many educators are of the opinion, however, that segregation results in an undemocratic form of organisation and savours too strongly of the European ideal of a dual system of schools for a two-class society. It may be confidently stated that the cosmopolitan secondary school, serving all the children of all the people, is one of the great triumphs of educational democracy."

Although secondary education for all is in origin an American ideal, the great diversity of living conditions, the existence of a large negro minority, and the number of scattered farming communities mean that universal school attendance at any age is not so nearly achieved in fact in America as in Europe. Both England and France accepted at the end of the second world war the conception of secondary education for all, at least up to the age of fifteen or sixteen, at which the "break" in the secondary course had come since the beginning of the century. In England the new Act of 1944 left room for a wide variety of experiments, including the provision of comprehensive secondary schools on the American model; but the overwhelming trend of practice in both countries was first to set up alternative secondary schools designed to cater for differing types of pupil. The English system, for instance, envisaged the provision of grammar schools for those who were capable of profiting from an advanced academic type of education; technical schools for those who were capable of profiting from an advanced technical education; and modern schools for those who were not intellectually above the average, and who would not in the past have gone beyond the primary stage, but who were now chiefly being "educated for life".

In terms of social origin it is a questionable point whether this is more or less "democratic" than the American system. It is easy, as American experience has shown, for the boundaries of the "catchment area" of Comprehensive High School to be so drawn that its pupils are limited to a socially homogeneous "neighbourhood". And some gerrymandering on these lines has gone on. A selective school on the other hand must have a much wider catchment area. To take an English example, it might be possible to fill a comprehensive school almost entirely with the "upper class" children of Belgravia; but a grammar school of equal size would have to extend its catchment area as far as Pimlico.

The social objection which both England and France have found to the selective secondary school is that it is "undemocratic", not in the sense of perpetuating class distinctions but in that of creating them. There is a justifiable fear that selection at eleven virtually stratifies men and women from this age onwards into a managerial and an operative class; and that if these are educated separately from the start the recent trend towards a more equal society will be reversed and we shall find ourselves returning to Disraeli's "Two Nations". These social arguments have combined with a growing realisation that we cannot make the selection at eleven with the degree of accuracy which would give us the level of social justice we expect. There are too many hard cases for the law to be accepted as a good one. Both countries are therefore experimenting with methods of mitigating or postponing selection, just as America is beginning to move slightly in the selective direction. It seems likely that the next ten years will see Europe and America arriving at a compromise somewhere between their two original positions.

CHAPTER SEVEN

THE EDUCATION OF WOMEN

THE systematic higher education of women has developed almost entirely within the last hundred years. In primary schools there has normally been no difference made between boys and girls, either in Western Europe or in America, and it is therefore unnecessary to treat of primary education separately in this chapter. Efficient secondary schools for girls, on the other hand, scarcely existed in 1850, and entrance to the universities was barred to them altogether. This does not mean, of course, that girls never received a good secondary education or never went to a secondary school. Individual daughters of enlightened parents received at all periods what was possibly the best education of all, within their own homes [1]; and anyone who has read the conversation of Helena and Hermia in *A Midsummer Night's Dream* can see that Elizabethan girls in England knew what it was to be school friends. Unfortunately, the girls who went to school got very little real education.

The development of higher education for women was, of course, a by-product of the general movement for feminine emancipation. As long as it was accepted that women were weaker vessels, always dependent on men as wives, daughters or "female dependents", there was little inducement to educate them for any other station than that to which it had apparently pleased God to call them. There were two types of institution which undertook this work, the convent and the young ladies' academy; the main difference between them was that the convent aimed at producing good wives or good nuns, while the academy aimed at training girls to catch husbands. The education of the convent was therefore moral and practical, that of the academy meretricious. Neither were concerned with the intellect.

---

[1] C. M. Yonge in *Womankind* ranked the types of education available in this order of merit: (*a*) Home education by the father, (*b*) home education by the mother, (*c*) a good governess, (*d*) a good school.

As the movement for feminine emancipation was essentially part of the liberal-democratic movement, we shall find that the higher education of women has flourished only in this type of society. The Roman Catholic Church has never taken kindly to it, and in those countries where an authoritarian political regime replaced liberal democracy it was immediately curtailed; in the Nazi view the proper interests of women were *Kinder, Kuche, Kirche* (Children, Kitchen, Church), and to such a conception the convent or academy type of secondary education was clearly fitted. It is for this reason that higher education for women has been developed chiefly in the free, Protestant communities of Western Europe, and in America.

From the start there were obviously two different ways of providing girls with the same educational opportunities as boys: the existing boys' schools and universities could admit girls on an equal footing; or separate and parallel institutions could be established for girls only. Both methods have been tried in most countries, but, roughly speaking, it is true to say that America and Scandinavia have pursued the first and the rest of Europe the second. It is also roughly true that in admission to the universities there was usually a progress in three stages, from separate women's colleges, through a period of admission to the male universities with unequal status, to full equality. Since co-education involves considerably fewer external administrative problems than separate schools and was therefore established much more rapidly, it will be convenient to turn first to America, where co-education quickly prevailed.

The Higher Education of Women in America

The situation in America during the first half of the nineteenth century was very much the same as that in Europe, except that the American spirit of innovation and the degree of local freedom in educational matters allowed for sporadic experiments like the Georgia Female College, founded in 1839, which pointed the way to later developments. Although, in general, there were no girls' secondary schools other than the ladies' academies, and no opportunity for girls to get a college education, it is probably true that the reformed seminaries of such pioneers as Mary Lyon and Almira Phelps were providing a more solid education than their counterparts in England. Certainly it seems clear that, by the middle of the century, the "educated American female" was a figure of ribald fun, fairly well known to English humourists, whose predominantly male audience found feminine education very laughable.

As usually happened, there were two separate problems for the feminists to solve—how to get university education, and how to get secondary education. To many, particularly in the Eastern States, the first seemed the more important of the two—as it did to such English reformers as Elizabeth Garrett and Emily Davies. As long as secondary education was confined to an élite in any case, it was possible for the small proportion of women who wanted it to get it in one way or another, either at home, through special courses, or at the reformed seminaries. What was impossible was to get university education. Moreover, the rise in the standard of the teaching profession and any progress whatever in girls' secondary education demanded a certain number at least of university-trained women.

The fact that America was in the van of this movement probably accounts for the adoption, in the Eastern States, of a device which was not tried elsewhere and which seems to have been an early solution, quickly abandoned in favour of complete co-education. In the mid-nineteenth century it was commonly assumed that if women were to attend universities these would have to be all-female institutions; they were discussed all over Europe but only in the Eastern States of America were they actually established.[1] The foundation of Vassar (1865) came only eighteen years after the publication of Tennyson's *Princess*, and three years after the University of London had turned down, though only by one vote, a proposal that women should be permitted to graduate. London, with its vast number of external students whose only connection with the university was an examination, must have seemed the one male university where there could be no reasonable objection to the admission of women, at least to the examination hall. Vassar was followed in 1875 by Wellesley and Smith Colleges, and in 1880 by Bryn Mawr. This separation persisted, so that college education is still largely divided between the sexes in these Eastern States, the existence

---

[1] The English women's colleges, such as Bedford College in London and Newnham at Cambridge, attained their full "college" status only when incorporated in the male universities of London and Cambridge.

of the women's colleges having undoubtedly enabled the older universities of Harvard and Yale to remain, in this respect, more conservative than Oxford and Cambridge.

Further west, a different line of development was followed. It is generally held that the practical necessities of the frontier led to a higher valuation being set on women's capacities, and certainly in such a society it was not possible to bar them from college on those grounds of mid-Victorian propriety which were constantly adduced in England. Whatever the reason, we find co-educational colleges in the West even before 1850, and several of the Middle Western and Western State universities were co-educational from their foundation.[1] Even where the university was not entirely co-educational, the establishment of co-educational high schools made it inevitable that the Education Department or normal school should be co-educational; and from this beginning, as often happened in Europe, the women students gradually gained admission to all other departments. The decisive moment was probably in 1870 when the University of Michigan, then the most important and progressive State University in the Middle West, threw open all its faculties to women students.

America was only anticipating British practice in admitting women on equal terms to the universities. Where she has broken away from it entirely has been in the establishment of a co-educational secondary system, and in the country as a whole this preceded the provision of equal opportunities for women at college. This movement also spread from the West (New York is still one of the very few cities where the public high schools are not co-educational), and was one of the changes which took place when the public high school replaced the academy. On the whole, while the boys' and girls' academies had been separate, the high schools were co-educational. The reasons for this are not easy to determine. It was probably due to a number of causes: the social attitude of the pioneering States to which I have already alluded; American feminism, whose leaders pleaded continually for co-education in the ladies' journals from 1850 onwards; the administrative convenience of providing one secondary school rather than two from public funds, especially

[1] *E.g.* Iowa (1865), in the Middle West, which was exactly contemporaneous with Vassar in the East.

since many of the new school districts would have been too small to support two; finally, the fact that secondary education in the new territories grew up as a prolongation of public primary education, which was already co-educational, and not as an extension of an existing system hitherto preserved for an élite.

The decision in favour of co-education commended itself very quickly to the American people. By the end of the century the girls in the secondary schools outnumbered the boys (the women teachers were soon to swamp the men), and with a very few exceptions—notably the independent boarding schools and a few of the older cities—the secondary education of America is now entirely co-educational. In the wide variety of courses always provided by the American secondary curriculum there was never any difficulty in fitting in a few more specially suited to girls, and the problem of the differentiated curriculum which loomed large in Europe scarcely arose. Apart from domestic science, hairdressing, beauty culture and such vocational courses, the curriculum of the American high school girl has not differed much from that of the boy.

Higher Education of Women in England

In England, as in most European countries, the higher education of women began with the necessity for better teachers. It is true, of course, that there were occasional girls' schools, particularly in the North and among Nonconformists, which could really claim to be giving a secondary education even in the eighteenth century. In this, England was in advance of the rest of Europe. The great majority of girls in the richer classes who received any education beyond the primary stage, however, did so either at home from governesses, or at young ladies' academies, or, among the small Roman Catholic community, in convents. The girls of the poorer classes did not receive any such education at all.

English convent education, though later used to quite a considerable extent by Protestant parents, was at the beginning of our period confined to a small minority, and deeply influenced by French convents. It combined piety with practical domestic training in an atmosphere of strict supervision, much more French than English, and its effect on the general education of girls was very slight.

The young ladies' academies differed rather more from the boys' schools than they did in America; as the boy's curriculum at the better schools in England was more solid and concentrated, so the girls' was more frivolous and meretricious. The gap resulting from this differentiation at both ends, was such as to make the development of joint co-educational high schools much less probable in England, even from the point of view of curriculum, had there not been, as there were, other almost insuperable objections. It also meant that there was little chance of a general and gradual development from the young ladies' academy to the girls' secondary school.

It was rather from the first attempts to improve the training and capacity of the governess that girls' secondary education developed. The movement has been so recent, and so much influenced by a few great personalities, that although there lies behind it the whole feminist movement, it is possible to trace its development quite clearly through the lives and interactions upon each other of a few people. And this is even true of the influence of American progress on British. The whole fashion in which this interaction worked is exemplified in one story: Elizabeth Blackwell, the first American woman to be graduated from a medical college (Geneva, New York, 1849) was allowed to study at St Bartholomew's, London; in England she met Elizabeth Garrett who, fired by her example, began to study medicine herself in 1859, but was refused permission to take the matriculation examination by the University of London; and this led Emily Davies to found the Committee for securing the admission of women to university examinations, from which the whole agitation that ultimately opened the universities to women derived.

The first step in the progress, then, was the foundation, in 1843, of the Governesses Benevolent Institution. The purpose of this body, which still exists, was to raise the status of the governess by giving her the opportunity of training for her work in a more serious way than was possible at ladies' academies. In other words, it was designed to take, in a governess-educated society, the place of the continental normal, or training, school. It was soon found that the Institution needed a centre for its work, and classes were started, with the help of liberal-minded professors from London University, at Queen's College, Harley Street. This was more like a series of "extension courses" than a college by modern standards, but it was the first institution for the higher education of women in England to attempt work at a university level. The usual rivalry between Anglicans and Dissenters meant that it was followed in 1859 by a similar institution which, in 1869, became Bedford College. Among the first pupils at Queen's College were Miss Buss and Miss Beale, who became headmistresses, in 1850 and 1855 respectively, of the two secondary schools on which the subsequent education of girls in England has been based—the North London Collegiate School and Cheltenham Ladies' College.

At this stage the two problems which we noticed in America become distinct: there is the development of girls' secondary education on the one hand, and the struggle to secure admission to the university on the other; and while the same pioneers were hotly engaged in both, and the same feminist, as opposed to educational, influences affected both, it will be convenient to concentrate first on the earlier movement for the secondary education of girls. From the North London Collegiate School, founded by Miss Buss in 1850, are really descended practically all the girls' schools in England; for Miss Buss not only provided the model after which the independent high schools were fashioned but it was largely the evidence which she gave, and the pressure which she and Emily Davies exerted on Matthew Arnold, that led to the recommendations on girls' education of the Taunton Commission of 1865. In the opposite direction she provides a link with the past, for her school started as an old-fashioned private academy in which the teaching was largely carried on by the Buss family—her father's chemistry lessons being particularly popular.

In two respects the school was notable from the start, in its insistence on the education of the whole personality and in its absence of class distinction: it is the latter quality above all that justifies its claim to be the ancestor of the present-day high schools. But Miss Buss might have had no more effect than previous successful headmistresses of individual schools, if the Taunton Commission had not been persuaded to take girls' education seriously. They recommended the establishment of a girls' secondary school on the new model in every main town in the country, and the provision of at least some of the necessary finance by diverting the existing endowments of boys' schools, where the money could not be effectively used, to provide girls' schools. It was this action which really gave a start to a general system of girls' high schools and led to the foundation, for instance, of Girls' Secondary Schools at Bedford, Birmingham, and Rochester.[1] By 1900 eighty such girls' schools had been provided in this way.

The finance provided from the diversion of endowments was not enough, particularly in the new centres of population, and in 1872 the Girls' Public Day School Trust was founded to supply the deficiency. This was a commercial venture, in that it derived its income from fees, but its object was to provide schools which would pay for themselves rather than to make a profit. Its sponsors were the Workers' Education Union, and its supporters included many of the leaders in educational thought. Its first school, in London, was opened in 1873, and by 1891 it had thirty-six. Although the numbers have slightly declined since the establishment of a State secondary system for girls, the G.P.D.S.T. played, and is still playing, a part in girls' secondary education roughly similar to that of the great endowed day schools for boys such as St Paul's or Merchant Taylors.

From these two sources sprang the girls' equivalent of the nineteenth-century grammar school; but one further line of development in this century remains to be traced. In 1858 Miss Beale, who had been a mathematics tutor at Queen's College, Harley Street, was appointed headmistress of Cheltenham Ladies' College, and proceeded to establish a girls' equivalent of the English public school. Cheltenham was almost immediately successful,[2] and was followed by a number of others, chiefly boarding schools. Since they were all independent foundations, they did not imitate Cheltenham as closely as the standardised Girls' Public Day Schools followed the North London Collegiate; but the influence of Cheltenham and the Scottish girls' schools was very strong, and where new foundations departed from it, it was usually to follow more closely the boys' public schools, as in the emphasis originally placed on team games at Roedean.

"It is to be wished", said Miss Beale in 1865, "that croquet could be abolished. It gives no proper exercise." But it was

[1] Barnard: *Short History of English Education*.
[2] It had five hundred girls and ten boarding-houses by 1883.

the newer public schools which actually abolished it in favour of hockey and the American importations, netball and lacrosse.

The curriculum and organisation of these schools, whether "high schools" or "public schools", undoubtedly suffered from their connection with the feminist movement. It was inevitable, of course, that in broad outline they should be modelled on boys' schools; there was no other precedent to follow; but many of the feminist leaders felt a passionate determination to show that girls were "just as good as boys". This was a natural result, no doubt, of years of male condescension and superiority, but it meant in practice that too often girls were loaded with the same type of curriculum, the same team games and the same prefectorial system as their brothers. Even the first theoretical advocates of co-education (which, like feminism, was a "progressive" movement) were apt to support it by the claim that if only boys and girls were educated together in "frank cameraderie", there would —horrible thought—be virtually no difference between them. The determination to prove that girls could do just as well as boys also led to too much concentration on success in competitive examinations; and although each step in the admission of girls to the public examinations conducted for boys was heralded as a triumph, in fact it meant a further extraneous check on the natural development of the girls' secondary curriculum.

This subservience to the existing curriculum for boys was probably most marked in the Girls' Public Day School Trust, with its uniform system of marks and prizes, and its loyalty to the original feminist principles of Miss Buss. It was of them that it was reported as late as 1911 that "a few girls who are backward in intellectual work learn cookery".

In 1902 the first comprehensive Education Act, covering the whole country, placed on the local education authorities the duty of providing secondary education in accordance with the needs of their area, and this included the secondary education of girls. The Girls' County High School was soon as familiar a sight as the County Grammar School, and by the time of the second world war the numbers of girls and boys at secondary schools were approximately equal. A small but appreciable number of these L.E.A. schools were co-educational, but this arrangement was usually adopted only on financial grounds, where the numbers of secondary pupils were insufficient to justify two separate

L

schools. For the same reason co-educational high schools had long been popular in Scotland.

Co-education as a principle rather than an expedient has always been connected with the "progressive" or experimental school in England. Where in fact it was practised as an expedient in the establishment of mixed secondary day schools, it has approximated to what is called on the Continent co-instruction rather than co-education—that is to say, the classes are mixed, for practical reasons; but no positive attempt to mix the sexes out of school was made at first, and often there was a considerable attempt at segregation. A small number of positively co-educational boarding schools, of which the best known is probably Bedales (1893), grew up, partly, like Bedales, inspired by co-educational boarding schools in Scandinavia, partly in an attempt to meet the accusation that single-sex boarding schools foster the homo-sexual instinct. The original arguments in their favour, that they were more "natural" than segregated schools and that homosexuality was a product of the public school, have been largely exploded by the more recent discoveries of anthropology and psychology—and incidentally, as far as the second is concerned, by everyday observation. On the other hand, the original arguments used against them have been proved equally false; and it seems probable that both the advocates and the opponents of co-education considerably overstate their case. The general trend in England has been towards the maintenance of the single-sex secondary school, with very much increased contact between senior boys and girls at the sixth form level. If there is any arrangement which is "natural", in the sense of responding to the instinctive behaviour of the adolescent, this is probably it. The curiously sexless nature of the American "dating" system among very young adolescents, and the common prolongation of this "high school" attitude towards sex into mature life may not be effects of the American educational system, but if they are, they do not seem to be very strong arguments in favour of positive co-education at all stages.

The establishment of the county high schools meant that the secondary education of girls became more directly a concern of the government, and in 1920 the Board of Education instituted an enquiry into the differentiation of boys' and girls' curricula. This report drew attention to the way in which the girls' curriculum was still dominated by university entrance examinations originally designed for boys, and recommended that more allowance should be made for their greater conscientiousness and susceptibility to nervous strain: it also endorsed Miss Buss' principle of rather shorter hours and the retention of specifically feminine interests such as domestic science. One of the difficulties in developing a girls' curriculum in England was clearly that the extension on any wide scale of secondary education to girls was really one move, perhaps the first, in the development of secondary education for all; and therefore it demanded that widening of the curriculum and inclusion of practical subjects which inevitably resulted from giving up the conception of secondary education as the pre-university stage in the training of an élite. It was forced through, however, by the feminists before this stage had been reached in the organisation of the boys' curriculum; and therefore the girls' curriculum was designed from the first for what was, in most cases, the wrong purpose. Even so, the girls' schools were free of a great deal of the traditional reverence which bound the boys to an outdated curriculum; and in English literature, artistic subjects and gymnastics they quickly outdistanced them.

From the point of view of a "blue-stocking" élite such as this curriculum suited, admission to the universities was, as we noticed in America, almost more important than the provision of secondary education; and the struggle for this privilege went on at the same time as that for secondary schools, considerably to the disadvantage of the latter.

There were in England also two different conceptions of the part which women should play at the university. The idea of a purely feminine college such as Vassar was never fully developed, but Miss Clough, the founder of Newnham (Cambridge), which was opened in 1875 and incorporated as a sort of "external" college in 1880, believed that women should be allowed to study at the university in their own way, rather than that they should be admitted to the men's examinations. Emily Davies, on the other hand, the founder of Girton (opened as a private house in 1869), had been spurred on, largely by the refusal of the university authorities to allow Elizabeth Garrett to sit the qualifying examination in medicine. She believed that the rights of women would never be recognised until they could qualify for the professions, nor their claim to equal intellectual status until they could compete in the examinations. It should be remembered also that the middle of the nineteenth century was the heyday of the public external examination, when the improvements it had produced in educational standards led to a considerable overestimation of its value. Emily Davies, therefore, concentrated on securing the right of girls and young women to sit for the public examinations. This involved them in following the same curriculum as the men, and it was her influence rather than Miss Clough's which triumphed. It seems clear that she was right as far as genuine university studies were concerned, but it must be remembered that the type of work for which Newnham was originally designed was certainly that of the "*haut lycée*" rather than the university; and in securing from the Cambridge Syndicate's permission for schoolgirls to compete in the "Cambridge Locals", Emily Davies probably did the schools a bad turn.

It was at Cambridge that these two founders of women's university education established the hostels which have ultimately become women's colleges; but it was London, in 1878, which first admitted women to full degrees. This meant that Bedford College was the first women's college to become a genuinely constituent part of an English university. Cambridge formally admitted women students to the examinations in 1881 and published their names in the Pass List,[1] but did not admit them to full degrees until 1948. At Oxford, colleges on the model of those started in Cambridge were founded from 1879 onwards, and women were admitted to degrees in 1920. The Scottish and Welsh universities had admitted them by 1893, and the modern universities from their foundation.

The penetration of the older universities by women was, therefore, a slow business; and even when Oxford admitted them to full degrees, they were at first hedged round with social conventions reminiscent of the French *lycée*, forbidden to entertain male undergraduates in their own colleges or to visit the men's colleges unless accompanied by a chaperone.

The Higher Education of Women in Europe

Surprisingly enough, the country which shared with England the lead in women's education was Russia. Just as the Marxist

---

[1] There were great rejoicings among the feminists in 1890, when, in spite of the general prejudice that girls could not do mathematics, Philippa Fawcett was placed above the Senior Wrangler.

now claims that the tiny but highly developed industries of Russia, though quite isolated from the life of the country, were the most advanced example of the capitalist system, so the social historian finds in the records of the rootless and limited Russian aristocracy some of the most modern educational practices. Only a very minute fraction of the Russian people received education of any kind, and a still smaller proportion secondary education, but in this privileged class secondary education for girls as well as boys was provided by the State from the time of Catharine II; and women were admitted to university courses at St Petersburg in the same year that Emily Davies went to Cambridge—1869. Readers of the great Russian novelists must have been struck by the emancipation and culture of the Russian women of rank, compared with their contemporaries in France, Germany or Italy.

In the remaining European countries the example of America and England was followed at varying intervals and to varying extents. The chief deciding factors were the progress of the general movement for feminine emancipation and the influence of the Roman Catholic Church. That the Roman Church has never been a believer in secondary education for all is clearly demonstrated, not only by the very much lower proportion of children receiving secondary education in purely Roman Catholic countries, but most clearly in countries of divided faith such as Holland or Canada. N. Hans (*Comparative Education*, 1949) records that "whereas under the Protestant system in Canada, for instance, 25 per cent. of boys and girls of appropriate ages attend secondary schools, under the Catholic system only 17 per cent. of boys and 6 per cent. of girls have that opportunity". But quite apart from its conviction that among boys secondary education should be reserved for an élite, the Roman Church has always regarded it as even less suitable for the average girl. And, except in Portugal, where presumably financial considerations played a very large part, co-educational secondary schools are very rare in Catholic communities. In Holland, for instance, 95 per cent. of Protestant schools are mixed, as opposed to 18 per cent. of Catholic secondary schools.

It was not to be expected, therefore, that the higher education of women would make much progress in France until the régime of Napoleon III was brought to an end. France had her share of feminist writers, notably Mme Necker de Saussure, but the State was determined not to antagonise the Church. It is also true that Napoleon I set a precedent by establishing a school for daughters of officers of the Legion of Honour, but this was not intended to grow into a national system, nor did it do so; and by the time of Napoleon III girls in France were educated much as they were in England, with a much higher proportion attending convents. It was not until 1867 that girls even began to attend special courses, conducted for them out of normal school hours by *professeurs* from the boys' *lycées*—and therefore consisting purely of a dilution of the boys' curriculum. Girls' secondary schools were not introduced as part of the State system—and it should be remembered that the State system was everything in France—until the law of 1880 led to the foundation of the first girls' *lycée* at Montpellier in 1881.

From the first, the girls' *lycées*, as in England, seem to have been freer to experiment than the boys', and freer also to relax some of the excessive pressure and discipline from which French boys' *lycées* of the nineteenth century notoriously suffered. Contemporary observers seem to have been struck by the happier and less strained atmosphere of the girls' schools, and this although all except those in Paris developed boarding departments. It was clear that if the State was to foster the secondary education of girls it must also make provision for women secondary teachers; and in the same year as the first *lycée* the women's normal school at Sèvres was opened. The early descriptions of this also have a great charm, and bear out the favourable impression created by the early *lycées*. Camille Sée, the inaugurator of the law of 1880, quotes the following description from Mlle Lejeune of the first entrance examination to Sèvres:

"The examiners tried to find out not what we knew—alas, we knew so little—but what we were worth. The chief effort of these men seemed to be to find questions which we could answer. When our answers were good, they were positively enchanted."

It is an idyllic picture, and pleasant to think that Mlle Lejeune passed her examination. Later the examinations became much more stereotyped and harder, as the girls' schools began to compete with the boys' in preparing for the baccalauréat, as they did with increasing frequency from 1905 onwards.

The law of 1880 and the re-organisation of secondary education after the Ribot Commission in 1892 provided for girls' secondary schools; but the normal procedure in any town was to start with "courses" at the boys' *lycées*, such as had been going on since 1867, and to establish a college if the attendance at these courses demonstrated a sufficient demand. The large Catholic community still preferred the convent, and by 1908 there were still nearly four times as many boys as girls in secondary schools in France, although by this time numbers in England were nearly equal, and in America girls outnumbered boys.[1] By 1930 there were 59,399 girls to 138,301 boys, and to-day the boys still greatly outnumber the girls.

In Germany the development of higher education for women came later than in France, but once accepted it expanded more quickly. The preservation of "the ideal position of the German woman in the family", as one Minister of Education in Prussia called it, was always an effective battle-cry, and as Hitler showed later, it could be used to reverse even the degree of sex equality which had been achieved. Up to the end of the nineteenth century women were not admitted to the universities, and for the greater part of this time the only post-primary education open to girls was provided by the Municipal "Higher Daughters Schools", which were really intermediary rather than secondary schools, and which, as their name implies, concentrated largely on the domestic skills and virtues. The fact that the government, in such a state-ridden country as Prussia, took no interest in these schools is a measure of their importance.

A department dealing with girls was not created in the Prussian Ministry of Education until 1899, though girls privately educated had been allowed to sit for the boys' final examinations three years earlier. It was not until 1908, moreover, that the secondary education of girls was really integrated into the Prussian system. Under this reorganisation the *Lyzeum* provided girls with a ten-year course from six to sixteen, which could be followed either by two years further education with a domestic bias at a *Frauenschule*, or by further academic education at a *Studienanstalt*, which led to a leaving certificate equivalent to the boys' abitur, and entitling the holder to enter the university.[2] Not much change

---

[1] Though the boys only outnumbered the girls by four to one, they received seven times as much in the way of state funds (Farrington, *op. cit.*).

[2] Admission to the university had come earlier than this, Baden being the first to admit them in 1901; but up till 1908 few German girls were qualified to take advantage of it.

was made in this system after the 1914-1918 war, though the increased political importance of women was recognised in slightly improved opportunities for girls to reach the university. By 1911 there were approximately half as many girls receiving secondary education as there were boys, and this proportion remained roughly constant up to 1936, by which time the Nazi "reforms" had already begun to reduce the total secondary school population. Under the Nazis, of course, the higher education of women was strongly discouraged and every effort made to force women back into purely domestic life.

CHAPTER EIGHT

UNIVERSITIES

IT seems reasonable to open this chapter with a definition.
Before discussing the development of university education
we should surely know at least what is and what is not a
university. But this would lead us in fact into a critical and not
a historical enquiry. Historically, universities have varied so
much at different times and places that no definition is possible,
and we must fall back on common consent. In the first half of
the nineteenth century, for instance, no one would have hesitated,
in common parlance, to call Oxford, Cambridge and Harvard
universities; yet the remark of a French critic that the first two
were doing the work of higher secondary schools was probably
justified, and Harvard was academically no better. Again, the
criterion of distinction between a university and a "university
college" in England to-day is the power to grant degrees: yet
London University is nothing if it is not a degree-granting body,
and of it Abraham Flexner, writing in 1930, says that he is
"unable to understand in what sense it is a university at all".
Moreover, the British Courts have just ruled that St Davids
Lampeter, which is empowered by charter to confer degrees, is
not a university.

It would be possible, of course, to give an opinion about what
a university ought to be, and many people from Newman onwards
have done so; but to stick to any definition in a historical sketch
could only lead to confusion. The one point which is perhaps
worth repeating is that the mediaeval terms *universitas* and
studium generale are best left alone. The historical meaning
of *universitas* has no connection at all with universal knowledge,
as the German idealists apparently thought, nor with admitting all
and sundry as students. It meant simply a corporate body, and
it cannot therefore be used to suggest that, unless institutions
are prepared to teach everything or admit everybody, they are
not truly "universities". Similarly, *studium generale* has

nothing to do with "general education"—a context in which it is now becoming fashionable to use it. It meant, according to Sir Charles Grant Robertson,[1] simply "a centre of general resort", a place to which people came from considerable distances for higher education.

Let us abandon, therefore, any attempt at definition and admit as the subject of this chapter those institutions which have generally been recognised as universities in their own countries. It is possible then to trace three separate European traditions, the German, French and English; and to find in America the continuation of all these three with the addition of something new. There is one wide generalisation about this diversity, however, which, however inaccurate at any one time, may save a great deal of confusion later on. Roughly speaking, if we take the bachelor's degree as being of a certain average standard of academic attainment, it is true to say that this was and is reached in Germany and France (where it is then awarded) at the beginning of the university career; in England at the end of the second year (though it is not awarded until the end of the third or fourth); and in America at the end of the fourth (when again it is awarded). Those who are familiar with an English or American university will always find it difficult to understand a nineteenth-century German one, for instance, until they realise that on our standards it did not cater for undergraduates at all, and that all the students were studying either for final professional examinations or for a doctor's degree.

The three European traditions had this in common, that in all three countries university life had reached its lowest point of decline in the eighteenth century. Vicesimus Knox, speaking of some of the Oxford colleges, describes them as "seats of ignorance, infidelity, corruption and debauchery"; and the best that Gibbon could find to say for Cambridge was that it had not sunk quite so low as Oxford. Similar complaints of "boorishness, ignorance and futility" were brought by the Prussian reformers against the universities of Germany, and probably deserved by all of them, though perhaps least by Göttingen and Halle. Of the French universities a National Commission reporting in 1932 says: "Their history under the Ancien Régime was one of progressive decadence. It can be shown that by the eve of the

[1] *The British Universities.*

168

Revolution the progress of learning was being maintained outside them or even actually in opposition to them."

The common cause of this decay seems to have been dependence on an authoritarian Church and the inherent conservatism of corporate bodies, responsible to no outside authority and governed always by their oldest members. The chief complaint of the reformers was, in fact, that the universities had preserved a "mediaeval" form which was completely out of touch with the needs of the new centuries. Even the purely professional studies of law and medicine, which had flourished in the universities of the Middle Ages and the Renaissance, were now better pursued outside the universities than in them. Thus doctors were trained by the Royal College of Surgeons in England and the Royal Collegium Medico-Chirurgicum in Prussia, while lawyers attended the Inns of Court or the chambers of private advocates as apprentices. The only profession for which university training was of any value was the Church, and the Church was intellectually at a very low ebb. At the same time the universities clung to the mediaeval conception of their function which was that of training institutions in the four traditional faculties of Law, Theology, Medicine and Arts. The idea that a university should be either an institute of research for the furtherance of learning, or for teaching the arts and sciences in their purest form had not yet been born. The consequence was that since they were useless, either to real scholars or to serious entrants to the professions, they attracted only a proportion of the clergy and a crowd of idle and dissolute young aristocrats, who found them a pleasant place for working off the exuberance of a protracted adolescence.

The complete inadequacy of these universities for any useful purpose was so apparent that the outcry against them was equally strong in England, France and Germany. In the end it led to reforms in all three countries which produced the three streams of tradition mentioned above; but it is worth noting that the dissatisfaction with the "mediaeval" universities was so complete, both in France and Germany, that men seriously advocated their complete abolition, on the grounds that they were beyond reform. In Prussia the first reaction of the authoritarian state during the greater part of the eighteenth century had been simply to ignore and by-pass them—in the hope presumably that they would die a natural death; but Revolutionary France actually proceeded with the murder.

The German Tradition

The first great change came in Germany and was part of the humanist reforms of education brought about by Wilhelm von Humboldt after the defeat of Prussia by Napoleon. Since von Humboldt was also responsible for the creation of the German secondary school system, which has profoundly affected all secondary education elsewhere, there is good reason for counting him among the greatest practical contributors to higher education in the western world.

Von Humboldt became Secretary of Education in the Prussian Government in 1809 and enjoyed less than one year of office. Even the educational movement which he represented, the liberal humanism of Goethe, held sway for less than ten years. Nevertheless, von Humboldt succeeded during his one year of office in founding the University of Berlin and leaving to Germany a tradition of university freedom, which, however much the German universities sinned against it, remained powerful, both inside and outside Germany as an ideal. There were other reformers in Prussia at the time who wanted to abolish the universities, as the French had done, and erect in their place a single central Institute of Learning. Von Humboldt preferred to found a new university which should enjoy that academic freedom without which the humanist education was impossible; for since the humanists held that true education consisted in the activity and self-discovery of the human mind, it was clear that the mediaeval universities could not supply it, tied as they were by the rigid fetters of Church, State and an outworn system of knowledge. While Berlin was therefore the first university of this new type, designed for the serious study of man and nature, von Humboldt was enough of a conservative to retain in it the old professional faculties, and in fact it absorbed the old Royal Collegium Medico-Chirurgicum which had long been the seat of medical knowledge in Prussia. His conception of the university soon spread to the other universities of Germany of which at least twelve survived the upheaval of the Napoleonic Wars.

The great legacy of this brief period of liberal humanism was therefore that of academic freedom, and for the remainder of the nineteenth century this remained one of the proudest boasts of the German universities. Their other distinctions derived from a different source.

Humanism in Germany could not survive the political re-. pression of the 1820's, and its place as a national philosophy was soon taken by the nationalist and doctrinaire idealism of Fichte and Hegel. This change had profound consequences for the future of university studies throughout the West. It was one of the principles of this extreme idealist philosophy that since Reason and Nature were ultimately one, it must be possible to deduce the true nature of the physical world from the speculations of pure reason, and merely base or "mechanical" to investigate it by painstaking research, after the despised method of Sir Isaac Newton. The vague and misty generalisations which were produced by such confidence were suspected by the world at large; and in England parodies and lampoons of "German metaphysics", "The Higher Transcendentalism" and "high priori" thinking were soon a common-place. In Germany itself the reaction was more serious and more dangerous. The onset of the higher transcendentalism coincided almost exactly with the beginnings of serious study of the natural and physical sciences in the universities; the first official chemistry laboratory to be opened in any university was, for instance, that of von Liebig at Giessen in 1826. Since, for political reasons, the intensely conservative governments of the German States favoured, for the most part, the higher transcendentalists, it was natural enough that the experimental scientists should become more and more exacerbated by the nonsense which they talked when they attempted to describe the physical world. How fantastic that nonsense was, it is difficult to conceive, but Lilge (*The Abuse of Learning*) quotes an example from one of Schelling's lectures on medicine which gives some idea of what the scientists had to put up with:

"In the general formation of the animal kingdom the union of the soft and the hard presents the greatest problem in Nature. The gradual receding of the bone structure toward the inner part of the body is the gradual uniting of the hearing and the feeling animal. The organ of feeling is represented by all the soft parts of the body, and the organ of hearing by all the hard parts of the body."

As a result of this sort of nonsense there grew up among German scientists an antagonism towards philosophy as such, and a concentration on detailed research, which spread from the natural sciences to history, literature and every other subject of enquiry. The vague theorising and generalisations of the idealists bred a generation which distrusted theorising and generalisation of any sort, and therefore found the meaning of education no longer in the activity of the mind but in endless accurate research, for the acquisition of minutely detailed knowledge. Thus, in opposition to a misty adoration of the Absolute, the new God of Research was set up.

By the middle of the century, then, the two elements of which the German universities were most proud were their academic freedom and their devotion to research. It was these elements which were imitated to a greater or less degree by the universities of England and America, and which justify the claim that the German was the most influential of the three strains of university tradition in the nineteenth century.

We have seen that the principle of academic freedom spread from Berlin to the other universities of Germany, at least in theory, fairly early in the nineteenth century. It had three facets: academic self-government, freedom of instruction and freedom of learning.

Academic self-government was intended to put an end to that censorship by the State which even Kant had found irksome. It was organised on an oligarchic basis; each faculty managed its own affairs under an elected Dean, but within the faculty only full professors had any say. These full professors in the nineteenth century numbered rather more than half the teaching faculty. They were appointed by the State, to whom the faculty sent in three names for choice, and they drew a fixed income in addition to the fees paid by those who attended their lectures. Such intervention by the State had been deliberately accepted by von Humboldt who feared the extreme conservatism and "inbreeding" which might result from an unfettered choice by the faculty. In fact, it gravely limited the reality of academic self-government, since the State could and occasionally did reject all three candidates suggested, and substitute one of its own nomination. Two appointments which did much to steer the University of Berlin away from von Humboldt's principles—

those of Hegel and Ranke—were in fact made by the State in this way.

In order to become a full professor, and a member of this self-governing faculty, it was necessary to start as a lecturer. There were no "appointments" and no salaries for lecturers, and they required the licence of the faculty to teach, though they had no say in the faculty affairs. Their only remuneration was the fees they could collect from those who attended their lectures.

Academic self-government was carried above the level of the faculties, since the affairs of the university as a whole were managed by the Senate, which was largely made up of representatives elected from them.

This great principle, so essential to the health of a university was limited in practice by two factors—finance and human weakness. It is probably true that the universities in the nineteenth century were more genuinely free of governmental control than most German institutions; but in States which, during the first half of the century, were still governed as absolute monarchies this did not amount to much. As the century progressed and absolute power was modified by constitutions, finance began to play a bigger part. Berlin, after all, was founded as a State university, whatever its humanist constitution said, and by the middle of the century the State provided virtually the whole of its income. He who pays the piper almost inevitably calls the tune, however unwilling he may be to do so, and the Prussian State was not such as to prove unwilling. Moreover, the greater the development of scientific research, the greater became the dependence of the university on finance. Even apart from finance, however, the State was able in the last instance to control the universities directly; in 1898, for instance, academic freedom was modified to the extent of a law laying it down that "the deliberate promotion of social-democratic purposes is incompatible with a teaching post in a Royal university"—a point of view much criticised by liberals at the time, but which is logical and closely parallel to that often maintained, that the deliberate promotion of Communist views is incompatible with a teaching post in a democratic university.

The effect of human weakness on academic freedom is harder to trace. The position of a full professor in a German university in the middle of the nineteenth century was probably higher both financially and in social esteem than that of any other teacher in Europe or America.[1] At the same time the necessity of reaching it through a probationary period as an unpaid lecturer meant that it became more and more reserved to a monied professional class. This class contained some notable heroes of the liberal democratic movement in Germany, but inevitably it developed the vices of a privileged class, and these were accentuated by the extent to which nineteenth-century Germany was class- and privilege-ridden as a whole. Like most privileged classes it tended to support the reigning authority, and as a result the German State, whether Imperial or Nazi, was able to control the universities to a very great extent without any technical infringement of academic freedom.

The second facet of this freedom—freedom to teach—meant that the professor or even lecturer, once appointed, could teach what he pleased and how he pleased. To the universities of the early nineteenth century, still largely censored by the Church, this was a great step forward. The strong man enjoyed a real freedom and made magnificent use of it; but to many professors and lecturers the freedom was meaningless and, when combined with the later passion for research, dangerous. The system by which lecturers were paid wholly, and professors partly, from enrolment fees at their lectures may have been a stimulus to good teaching; but it was also a temptation to teach only the popular subjects and a positive barrier to new subjects and to young enthusiasts. Unless a lecturer had exceptionally ample private means he could not afford to embark on an unfamiliar subject. Added to this was the same strong social pressure from the government, the faculty, society, and very often the "Old Alumni Societies", which kept the potentially eccentric or revolutionary professors within safe bounds. Lecturers, of course, were not likely to receive their licence to teach unless their work won the approval of the professors. It is not surprising that men like Nietzsche and Burckhardt should have preferred the genuine freedom of a Swiss university.

The third facet of academic freedom—freedom of learning—was peculiarly German, and was really only operative in its

---

[1] Except that possibly a housemaster at an English public school was better off financially. Many of these made small fortunes, but in their capacity as boarding-house keepers not teachers.

entirety in the early part of the nineteenth century. Freedom of learning meant that a student was free, at the university, to attend what lectures or courses he pleased, and to organise his studies in whatever way he chose. He was even free to migrate from one university to another, the only check on his work being the final examination or "proving" for which he could present himself whenever he chose at whatever university he pleased. By the middle of the century some slight check had been imposed, since the universities, in their examinations for their own doctorates, demanded certificates of attendance at a number of lectures as well as an adequate performance in the examination. This check was more apparent than real, however, since most students concentrated on the state "proving" examination, which opened the door to the professions, and only a small proportion ever sat for the university doctorate. Moreover, the certificates themselves were often a formality, imposed as much for financial reasons as any other. The professor made no attempt to count or identify his audience, and provided that a student was enrolled and paid his fees the certificate would be granted without question. The extreme of student freedom, the migration from one university to another, declined steadily throughout the century, under the pressure of organised courses in scientific subjects, research seminars, and university "loyalty". Even to the present day, however, the German university student remains much freer in the organisation of his studies than either the British or the American, and the habit of migration has left its mark in the much greater freedom with which lecturers and professors have moved from one university to another in Germany.

We have seen that the second crucial development in the German university was the growing importance attached to research. To the German universities certainly belongs the credit of reminding Europe that one of the functions of the university is to enlarge knowledge as well as to pass it on. It was unfortunate that this enthusiasm coincided with the materialist reaction against idealism described above, for this meant that the research which was glorified was research into fact rather than meaning. As human knowledge increased, the intensity of specialisation required to discover new fact was accentuated, and learning was broken down into innumerable compartments, whose workers almost took a pride in their ignorance of the field

M

of knowledge as a whole. An illustration of the attitude of mind involved in this type of research is perhaps best taken from one of its critics. Burckhardt, writing in the middle of the century of the type of historian who now ruled the German academic world, says: "God, too, wants some fun at times, and then he creates those philologists and historians who think themselves superior to all the world when they have scientifically ascertained that the Emperor Conrad II went to the privy at Goslar on May 7th in the year 1030—and things of like world-wide significance." [1]

This preoccupation with detailed factual discovery, and the specialised factual knowledge which was necessary for it, was accompanied by an almost romantic cult of objectivity. This, too, seems to be derived from a reaction against the preachers and political prophets of the idealist period, and it attracted the nobler minds in the universities in proportion as those enthusiasts were replaced by the demagogues of popular nationalism. In a world where society and the State were following after false gods, objectivity provided an illusory avenue of escape. Thus there was developed the conception of the true scholar as a man devoted to detailed research in one ever-narrowing field, conscientiously shutting himself off from any attempt to interpret life as a whole, the ascetic, or, as Nietzsche called him, the slave of factual knowledge. Browning's *Grammarian's Funeral* is a romanticising of this type, which represents faithfully a very prevalent German attitude throughout the latter half of the nineteenth century. This subdivision of knowledge may also have been responsible for a further development of German university organisation which has had considerable influence outside Germany, the establishment of the institutes of technology. [2]

In the early nineteenth century many German towns developed trade schools which gradually grew into polytechnic institutes following perhaps the example of the École Polytechnique at Paris. From these to a university faculty of engineering was a very short step, but the idealist character of the universities in the first half of the century made it most improbable that the universities would accept such an additional faculty. It is not surprising, therefore, that the technological institutes went their

---

[1] Quoted in Lilge, *op. cit.*
[2] I prefer this translation to "technical high school", since "high school" to the ordinary English or American reader denotes a secondary school.

own way, and in 1865 the first of them, that of Karlsruhe, acquired university status, with the title of *Technische Hochschule*. This separation involved a certain amount of duplication, since chairs of mathematics and pure science were, of course, established at the technological institutes. As soon, therefore, as it was clear that the universities had thrown over idealism and adopted a materialist and scientific approach to all subjects, there was a movement to unite the technological institutes with them as faculties of engineering. The leader in this movement was Meyer, who saw not only the danger of duplication, but the much greater danger that the students of the technological institutes would be deprived of any sort of general education.

The objection to merging the technological institutes with the universities, apart from such natural prejudice and jealousy as may have affected individual leaders, was the great increase in the size of the universities which it would have involved; and the validity of this argument has steadily grown with the increase in demand for technicians and the complexity of technological equipment. By 1880 the demand for fusion had died down, and the two forms of university, for that is really what they were, were established as separate entities. The problem was not solved, and from the end of the nineteenth century onwards repeated efforts were made to solve it by fitting some sort of cultural courses into the framework of the technological institute; chairs of philosophy and even of philology were established at them, but inevitably the students tended to treat such subjects as "extras", for which the increasing pressure of their research work in their own branch of technology left them no time. The latest solution proposed (1949) is the addition of a faculty of "the humanities and social sciences".

The German universities of the nineteenth century were therefore established as genuine corporations, enjoying considerable theoretical independence, whose members, students and faculties alike, were engaged in the specialised study of some branch of pure learning. They were, in fact, centres of teaching and research, and this combination remained the ideal to which western universities were committed well into the 1930's.

Freedom of learning was a mark of the extent to which the German universities had outstripped the English or American in reaching it. It was based on the view that the student was a genuine seeker after knowledge, capable of choosing his own way and directing his own studies, without the aid of a dean or tutor. While the English undergraduate was writing Latin verses for his tutor, and the American was drearily "reciting" his lessons to the "overseer", the German was working in the seminar, or small research group, that gathered around each professor or lecturer engaged on some piece of original scholarship. The contrast between the schoolboy and the student atmosphere was so glaring that the German universities became a model for "progressive" university teachers throughout the West, whose shame at their own neglect of research perhaps blinded them to the extent to which Germany was beginning to neglect teaching. For the combination of freedom of teaching with the almost exclusive value set on the results of research led many professors and lecturers to concentrate their lectures and seminar work entirely in the limited field of their own contemporary research; and this meant that the students were deprived of any wider teaching and found their interests narrowed to a focus which might be intelligible to a man who was already master of his subject, but which was a barren and meaningless specialisation to many of them.

The French Tradition

From the point of view of administration the French university system was almost the reverse of the German. The reason for this was the historical centralising tendency in France. We have already seen that the decline of the universities in the eighteenth century led, in France, to their complete abolition during the Revolutionary period. Instead of restoring the universities, Napoleon I adopted the "modern" solution, which had been proposed in Prussia also, of creating a new central institution of Higher Learning. This he christened the Imperial University, and on it, centred at Paris but operating through its provincial "academies", he conferred a complete monopoly of education. Its charter included the provision that "No one may open a school or teach publicly without being a member of the Imperial University and without having been graduated from one of its faculties". He compared it to the Jesuit Order, and openly stated that his purpose in founding it was to "be able to direct political and moral opinion". This centralisation of educational control was not foreign to French tradition, as exemplified by the domination of the University of Paris in the later Middle Ages, or of the great teaching orders in the seventeenth and eighteenth centuries. It was not abandoned, therefore, at the Restoration, though its complete monopoly of school education was taken from it in order to restore freedom of instruction to the Church. The Imperial University merely changed its name to the University of France and continued to supervise State education, changing its name again later to the Ministry of Public Instruction. In the mid-nineteenth century, therefore, there were still no independent universities in France, and their place was taken by professors of each faculty teaching in the various academy districts; it did not follow, however, that all the faculties would be represented in each district and the great majority of serious university students were attracted to Paris. Problems of academic freedom did not arise because the University and the Ministry of Public Instruction were one and the same body. In spite of this apparent totalitarianism, it did not, of course, follow in practice that political or other pressure was exerted on university teachers any more than in Germany, where lip-service was paid to free enquiry but the social climate was more authoritarian. In one institution particularly, the Collège de France, the most complete freedom both of teaching and research was zealously cherished.

In France, as in Germany, the higher technological institutes were separated from the traditional faculties of the university; but this, typically enough, arose from the fact that they were established and controlled by the Ministries who needed technicians. Thus the Minister of Works controlled the School of Mines, the Minister of War the Military Academy, the Minister for the Colonies the Colonial School, the Minister of Agriculture the Institut Agronomique, etc. These "grandes écoles", like the German technological institutes, but to a much smaller degree, attracted students from America, including C. S. Storrow, who inspired the foundation of the Lawrence Scientific School at Harvard, the first beginnings of a faculty of science in an American university.

Between 1875 and 1880 the rigidity of the central control was broken to the extent that independent bodies were permitted to establish schools or courses of university level, but not to adopt the name of university nor to grant degrees. Their students were, however, free to present themselves for the public examinations of the "faculties", and so to secure a degree from the Minister of Public Instruction. In 1896, under the influence of Louis Liard and the regionalists, the separate universities of France were revived by the simple expedient of turning each "academy district" into a university. Sixteen were thus created in 1896, and a seventeenth, Strasburg, added in 1919. The intention of the reform had been well expressed some years before by Victor Cousin:

> "The intention of the Government is to create a certain number of centres of University instruction scattered throughout France, which will be able to provide a source of enlightenment for the provinces in which they are situated. Separate faculties may have their value; but it is from the combination of these that the new institutions will derive their greatest advantage. A faculty of Law can scarcely do without a faculty of Letters, and a faculty of Science is both the basis and the culmination of a faculty of Medicine. All the branches of human knowledge are interlinked in this way, and thus those who study them acquire an education which is both wide and deep— that is to say, true enlightenment. Moreover, there are certain political and social advantages in keeping in the provinces many young people whose talents, ripened in the national system of higher education, can turn advantageously to building up and strengthening that provincial life, once so flourishing and now so decayed, whose revival in a strong and unified France would be an unmixed blessing."

Two things are remarkable about this passage. The first is that it could still have required saying in the latter half of the nineteenth century; the other is the extreme nervousness of decentralisation which it still shows. In fact, though the provincial universities were restored, they continued to form an integral part of the centralised system, and the degree of formal academic freedom which they enjoyed was considerably less than existed in Germany, England or America.

By many of the standards which had been adopted by this time in other countries they would hardly have qualified as independent universities at all: thus many of them had only three or even two faculties, like that of Besançon which had only those of science and letters. Their independence was seriously modified by the fact that the Rector of the university remained also the Rector of the Academy District, and was appointed, not by the university, but by the Minister. The old centralised system was also retained parallel with the new universities, and there were always more state professorships than university professorships and more candidates for the state examinations, which alone opened a road to the professions, than for the university degrees.

The two outstanding features of the French nineteenth-century tradition were, therefore, extreme centralisation and the close connection between the university and the secondary schools of its area. This close connection was not merely fostered by the fact that both were elements in a central and organised national system of education; it was apparent also in the dual function of the Rector of the university, who, in his capacity as Rector of the Academy District, was "charged with the direction, in the Academy District where he resides, of higher secondary, higher elementary and technical education". This conception of a local university controlling and encouraging secondary schools through-out its area seems to have been in the minds of those who planned the system of state universities in America; something very like it was in fact tried in Michigan in the 1840's. It seems likely to prove the most fruitful French contribution to the general western theory of university organisation.

The English Tradition

England throughout the nineteenth century was remarkably short of universities. Until 1832 she had no more than two against Germany's twelve, and in these two the vices of the eighteenth century persisted much longer than on the Continent. The German universities had, no doubt, their students' clubs and their duelling, their whole atmosphere of "Old Heidelberg", and their perpetual students, intending vaguely to take a degree in something, somewhere, some day; but these were faults on the surface; by 1850 they had become, above all, places of serious—even too serious—study.

At Oxford or Cambridge, on the other hand, it was the serious student who was the exception. The average undergraduate, well born, well supplied with money, and bringing little education with him from school, lived in the atmosphere of horses, dogs, duns, tobacco and drinking which is caricatured in *The Adventures of Mr Verdant Green*, and more faithfully portrayed in *Pendennis*. Where there was a group of "thinking men", like the "Noetics" or the more famous "Apostles" at Cambridge, it was from their own meetings and conversation that they profited, more than from any teaching provided by the university.

The general causes of this situation throughout Europe have already been described. In England they were aggravated by the schism within the Protestant Church and the appalling state of English secondary education. The universities were the closed preserve of the Church of England, of which many of the college fellows were ordained members; and the Church of England was then at its lowest ebb, such educational interest and activity as existed being almost confined to the Nonconformists. The shocking state of secondary education meant that the universities, even if they had wished otherwise, were compelled to spend much of their time imparting that secondary education which the undergraduates had been unable to get elsewhere. An Oxford tutor in the first half of the nineteenth century was, in fact, doing the work of a sixth or even fifth form schoolmaster; and the fact that Shrewsbury schoolboys actually won university prizes only meant that sixth form teaching at Shrewsbury was better than at Oxford.

The prolongation of this situation was probably due in part to the victory of England in the Napoleonic wars: there had been no overwhelming social cataclysm in England, as there had been in France and Prussia, to sweep away the remnants of the Middle Ages and give the radical reformers their chance. There was, however, a secondary cause in that feature of the English universities which distinguished them from all others in Europe, and which has been their greatest contribution to the common stock—the fact that they were residential and collegiate. Whereas in the universities of Europe the student attended the university to study, and lived in lodgings or as he pleased, the English undergraduate came to Oxford or Cambridge primarily to live there as a member of a college. As a result, the loyalty to the college was much stronger than that to the university as a whole, and it was to the individual colleges, not to the university, that the benefactions were made. Oxford and Cambridge were remarkable in being rich enough, right up to 1922, to do without aid from the State, but it was the colleges not the university that held the purse strings.

This was reflected in the seventeenth-century constitution

of the universities, under which all power lay ultimately with the heads of the colleges. There was no question of "academic freedom" in the continental sense, for it would have been quite contrary to English thought for the government to interfere with a private and self-supporting corporation; but, equally, the university had little or no control over the colleges. The faculties, which counted for so much in a continental university, simply did not exist.

Reform of such institutions was more difficult, and a slower business, than reform elsewhere, because instead of winning over or coercing a central governing body, it was necessary to win over the heads, usually elderly and clerical, of a number of independent and deeply conservative colleges. It is not surprising, therefore, that university life in England was slow to follow the recovery which had been started in Germany, nor that the movement for reform took two forms—the reawakening of Oxford and Cambridge and the foundation of rival universities.

The first step in reform of the existing universities was to introduce some element of genuine study, and this was effected by the introduction, towards the end of the eighteenth century, of written examinations instead of formal interviews for degrees. These degrees remained, however, at the bachelor level, the level at which continental students began their university studies, and teaching for them continued to be carried on by college tutors, using the methods of the higher secondary school. This was not as severe a strain on the colleges as it appeared, since up till 1850 neither university taught anything much except classics and mathematics. The two were separated at Oxford in 1807, but it was not possible to take a degree in any subject but mathematics at Cambridge until 1832; and even then the concession was only extended to those who had already taken the Mathematical Tripos. New honours schools were introduced in the 1840's but were very little patronised. Barnard (*Short History of English Education*) quotes the figures taking the newer schools at Oxford in 1850 as: Modern History 8, Botany 6, Arabic, Anglo-Saxon, Sanskrit and Medicine o—and this out of a student body of fifteen to sixteen hundred. When one remembers that modern history and law were at this time a combined school, it can be seen how far Oxford was from the continental conception of a university with its four great faculties of law, medicine, theology and arts. Another feature in which the English universities had broken away from tradition was that the student body consisted entirely of under-graduates studying for their bachelor's degree. Post-graduate study, which elsewhere was considered the real function of the university, simply did not exist, and the master's degree remained, as it remains to-day, a formality which any bachelor can attain "by staying alive five years and keeping out of gaol". Research, therefore, is more easily dealt with than teaching, for, as a function of the university, it simply did not exist. That the two older universities were ever reformed is due primarily, as might have been expected, to the reawakening of the Church of England.

Two new universities were founded in England during the first half of the nineteenth century, Durham and London. Durham is of no particular significance since it was only an attempt to give the young men of Northern England an institution on the same lines as Oxford or Cambridge but at rather less expense. London, however, was and remains one of the strangest universities in the world. Its foundation was due to three factors, dissatisfaction with the old universities, the demand for some university that should be open to Nonconformists, and the desire which England shared with other countries, to emulate the University of Berlin. It started with the foundation of two colleges, one Nonconformist and the other Anglican, each of which might have developed into a university; but the religious schism was so violent that neither would give way to the other, and the compromise reached in 1836 was to set up a "University of London" which did neither teaching nor research, and had no powers but the conduct of examinations and the granting of degrees. These degrees were open to members of the two colleges or to members of any other institution which might become affiliated to the "university". It is constantly pointed out that this was no university, and certainly not what the pro-moters had intended, a university in the world's greatest capital city which might rival that of Berlin. London University, as an examining board, however, did provide the nearest equivalent in England to those state final examinations which were so important elsewhere, and in the absence of any official body, like the University of France, it performed a valuable and necessary function. At least it gave, for many years, some sort of university status to many who would otherwise have been totally excluded from it.

The second half of the century saw the reform of the existing universities and at the same time the foundation of new ones. Reform at London took the form of recognising the university's strange function and throwing its degrees open to all who were successful in the examination, whether they had attended any institute of higher education or not. As a result the external candidates for degrees far exceeded the members of affiliated colleges or internal candidates, and London became, for the rest of the century, mainly an examining body for those who had not attended universities.

At Oxford and Cambridge reform was crystallised by the reports of two Royal Commissions, welcomed by the small reform party at both universities, but positively demanded by outside opinion. On these reports were based the Oxford University Act of 1854 and the Cambridge University Act of 1856. These Acts repealed the seventeenth-century constitutions of the universities and broke the absolute power of the college heads; they abolished the Anglican monopoly (though religious tests for degrees were not finally eliminated till 1871); they increased the number and powers of professors, as opposed to college tutors; but they did not radically alter the college system, either of life or teaching.

The reforms in fact indicate that although impressed by the way in which continental universities had outstripped English in learning, the Commissioners felt that the English system had something of great value in the college and tutorial system. It is significant also that they criticised the extreme expense of university life, and suggested some remedies for it. This concern with the life of the student at the university as well as with his learning and research is in fact the great English contribution to the western tradition. The actual reforms suggested by the Commissioners in this respect were not very effectual, but a new type of young man was beginning to come up to the universities from the reformed public schools, and the exuberance of youth was soon worked off in rowing and football, which every one could enjoy, rather than horses, dogs and card parties. The problem was one shared by American universities and the first annual boat race between Oxford and Cambridge dates from 1856 —four years *after* the first Harvard–Yale race.

The great advantage of the college system was that fellows and students lived together instead of merely meeting at the seminar, and that in a small corporation of this kind minds of different types and calibres fertilised each other and a tradition of values could be developed and passed on. When the colleges were corrupt, Oxford and Cambridge were probably the worst universities in the world; but as the colleges began to become centres of good living, as well as of advanced thought, they had a growing claim to be considered the best.

The advantage of the tutorial system lay in the close contact between the tutor and each individual pupil, closer even than the contact of the seminar. Where the standard of scholarship was little above school-level and the tutor himself was doing no research work of his own in his subject, little no doubt was gained; and at first this was probably the usual situation in England. At all times a bad tutor may be a positive barrier between a student and the faculty professor. But the tutorial system was gradually improved throughout the nineteenth century, the greatest single reform being the establishment of inter-college lectures. As a result of this, the old system by which a student's teaching was limited to the few professorial "university" lectures, supplemented by the help of his tutor and what lectures were given in his own college, was done away with. Instead, lectures given in one college were thrown open to members of all other colleges, so that a man might attend what he pleased, and the majority of tutors were also lecturing in some subject. More recently still, the habit has grown up of students being sent for purely intellectual guidance to a tutor in some other college, if their own provides no expert in the special branch of the subject which they are studying.

That the English conception of the function of the university was consciously recognised as early as the middle of the century is clear from the emphasis which Newman lays upon it in *The Idea of a University*. He is emphatic that a university must concern itself not merely with teaching and research, but must "administer a code of conduct and furnish principles of thought and action". The devotion to this ideal throughout the second half of the century consisted rather of a reluctance to abandon traditional advantages than of a conscious intention to exploit them. "Progressive thought" was more concerned with raising the standards of teaching and research to the German level, and with bringing in to the university the modern scientific subjects.

The serious introduction of science at the older universities dates from between 1865 and 1880, as anyone who observes the architecture of the earliest science buildings can tell. But there was a very general feeling, among the new, prosperous, Nonconformist, radical, provincial middle class, that this reform was not going fast enough; and that, in any case, Oxford and Cambridge were haunts of Toryism, snobbery, luxury and sin, whispering the last enchantments of the Middle Ages to practical business men, who wanted a modern, scientific education. To this combination of feelings, and to the immense generosity of the new rich, England owes her provincial universities. Again, their foundation dates exactly from the half-century, with Owens College, Manchester, in 1851; and soon, in the great manufacturing towns of the North, colleges like it were founded, usually with a strong scientific, sometimes almost vocational bias, and nearly always including or absorbing a medical school. None of them were specifically founded as universities, and at first Manchester, Liverpool and Leeds were combined in a single "federal" Victoria University; but by the end of the century the example of Birmingham in combining what had once been a theological school, with a medical school and a higher technical school into a university had obviously pointed the way. Manchester and Liverpool, which had received their first charters in 1880 and 1881, became independent universities in 1903, Leeds in 1904, Sheffield in 1905 and Bristol in 1909. All were founded as independent corporations, as the result of immense benefactions by private citizens; although the State now contributes a very large sum to the maintenance of the British universities, it has never financed the founding of one.

As was natural for progressive institutions, the new universities differed considerably from the old; they sought their model more in Scotland—whose universities had been much influenced by the German—than in Oxford or Cambridge. Apart from the late foundation of Reading none was residential, and none tried to reproduce the tutorial system. Their method of government, through the Senate and Faculties, was continental rather than traditionally English. It must be remembered, however, that apart from the prevalent admiration for German methods, a residential, tutorial university is a much more expensive place both to provide and to attend than a "continental" one; and one of the reasons for founding the new universities was to provide higher education for those who could not afford Oxford or Cambridge. It is unfortunate that in their anxiety to be strictly utilitarian, materialistic and scientific, the founders should too often have chosen sites and buildings as different as possible from the despised colleges with their lawns and quadrangles.

The American Synthesis

The United States inherited from colonial days a number of residential universities, which were in effect liberal arts colleges, on the Oxford and Cambridge model. Their standard of education during the first half of the nineteenth century was no higher, and in their treatment of the students they were even more like overgrown secondary schools. At Harvard, for instance, at least until 1857, a student's progress towards his degree was judged mainly by his marks in "recitations", which were daily construe lessons prepared the night before and recited to the tutor in class. The professors themselves complained of this system, which left them no time to teach, since they were too busy hearing and marking recitations. The corporate life of these colleges was also expensive, riotous [1] and unintellectual, though there were a number of later foundations which were more serious and austere than Harvard.

Apart from these foundations, it was clearly intended, as early as 1787, that each state should have a state university, and in the newer states land was set aside for their endowment. The earliest of these were modelled very much on the existing colleges —Georgia (1800), for instance, being particularly connected with Yale; but in the University of Virginia (1825) Jefferson sketched out a new and much wider basis of studies, including ancient and modern languages, pure and applied mathematics, natural sciences, medicine, law, political economy, history, rhetoric, *belles lettres* and fine arts.

It was clear from the first that the issue between privately endowed colleges on the English model and state universities on the continental would have to be settled. At first the state legislatures tried to take over the control of the independent

---

[1] S. E. Morison, *Three Centuries of Harvard*, lists no less than six "rebellions" between 1766 and 1834. Rebellions were common at English public schools but not at universities.

colleges, but the legality of this was tested in the courts, and the Dartmouth decision of 1812 established that it was beyond the state's powers. The two systems therefore continued parallel to each other, and the U.S.A. reached the middle of the century with its old independent colleges now developing into real universities on the eastern seaboard, and a growing number of state universities in the newer states. This pattern has been preserved to this day, and the only states which have not got state universities are those in which the original independent colleges were founded.

The dominant influence in the reform or creation of true universities was the German. During the first half of the century it became common for graduates to spend a year or two in Europe and these on their return reproduced what they had learnt. There is only one specific instance of French influence, apart from any part it may have played earlier in forming the whole conception of a state university; that, as we have seen, was at Michigan in the 1840's, and it was soon brought to an end by the appointment of a President who was an enthusiast for German methods, and who introduced, for instance, the B.Sc. degree before it existed at any English university. At Harvard also it was the appointment of professors with German Ph.D. degrees that really began the reform of teaching methods, although Yale had preceded Harvard both in the organisation of a graduate school and in the serious teaching of science. From England the older universities had already derived all that England had worth offering—their independence and the residential system; and there seemed nothing for the state universities to admire.

The chief lessons which the American universities learnt from Germany were the importance of research, and the incorporation of the professional faculties in the university. In the first half of the century their student body, like the English, consisted of young men, acquiring for a bachelor's degree that secondary education which they had not been able to get at school; loosely attached to the "college" were a number of prospective lawyers or doctors, nominally perhaps members of the university school of law or medicine but actually apprentices in the surgeries or offices of local practitioners. President Eliot's reform of the Harvard Medical School is a good example of how these were raised to genuine university faculties and by the end of the century the university schools of law and medicine had taken their rightful place. At the same time, post-graduate work was gradually becoming, for serious students, the real purpose of the university.

This second change took place at all the greater universities but it is most dramatically illustrated in the foundation of Johns Hopkins University, Baltimore, in 1876. Johns Hopkins was founded with the deliberate intention of superimposing the German university course leading to a Ph.D. on the traditional four-year course of the American college. The graduate school was the whole *raison d'être* of the university, and in fact it really rather grudged having any undergraduates at all. It was founded with strong support from President Eliot, and its methods were almost immediately adopted by the other eastern universities. One further reform of the very greatest historical importance may be attributed partly to German influence. This is the elective system introduced at Harvard in the 1870's. It was not, of course, an entirely new idea: in its worst aspect the practice of the early nineteenth-century academies foreshadowed it, and there was never any shortage of "practical" men who urged that schools and universities should adopt the sacred principles of private business and teach their "customers" whatever they wished to learn, the salaries of the professors depending, like those of lecturers in Germany, on the number of pupils they could attract. This belief that the customer is always right has in fact been the bane of the American state university and high school for many years, and has led to the accusation that the most widely expanded of them are no more than vast educational "bargain basements". No such idea was in President Eliot's mind when he introduced the system at Harvard, but such ideas undoubtedly account to no small extent for the rapidity with which it spread all over the United States.

The elective system, in its pure form, meant that the student alone chose what courses he would take for his first degree. Its connection with the German principle of freedom of learning is of course obvious. It was limited at Harvard by the fact that the university did not offer trivial or vocational courses, but it was, nevertheless, a revolutionary change. Jefferson's plan for the University of Virginia had allowed a choice only between groups of courses, but even that was far more liberal than the normal American college system, in which not only the majority of the courses, but the order in which they were taken, were prescribed. As these prescribed courses consisted very often of the "recitation" of specific chapters of a prescribed book, the intellectual progress of each individual student was cramped and confined even more severely than in the worst days of the English public school. It probably needed something as explosive and revolutionary as Eliot's championship of completely free election to break these bonds. By the end of the nineteenth century it had been adopted by almost every university in the country. Yale alone held out till 1904.

The Twentieth Century

The outstanding feature of the twentieth century has been the recession of German influence and the spread of English and American ideas. The reaction of the leaders of German thought to the two great aggressive wars into which their government plunged them, bred, even in Germany itself, a suspicion that all was not right with the universities; while in America it was becoming clear that the imitation of German models was combining so ill with the natural developments of American life as to produce very serious problems in the rapidly expanding universities and high schools. The fundamental criticism of German claims and ideals was associated with the movement for "education for life" described in Chapter Four, and it took the form of a return to something more like the English conception of the function of the university. This movement of thought was general throughout the West. As late as 1932 it could still be officially stated that the purpose of the universities in France was confined to teaching and research, but in this, as in many other respects, France was clinging to a traditional definition. In point of fact the re-creation of the provincial universities in France in 1896 was one of the first moves in the new direction. The view that the university was concerned not merely with the intellectual studies of its members but with their whole lives, and the life of the community as a whole, had never died out in England and America, though in both countries the newer universities were much less inclined or able to undertake the first responsibility. The German tradition of pure research was seen now as a doctrine of intellectual surrender and despair, which gave up the moral leadership of the

N   191

country to the uneducated; and the scholars who had bartered their responsibility for a quiet life, found that the quiet life also was taken away from them. The attempt by the university to keep aloof from the maelstrom of public life had left it a slave to political mass movements. The danger was pointed out in two books published around 1930, which had a considerable effect all over Europe, Julien Benda's *Trahison des Clercs* and Ortega Y Gasset's *Mission of the University*.

By the middle of the twentieth century a new conception of the function of the university had gained general acceptance. Teaching and research were no longer to be worshipped in isolation. The best definition of the new attitude, as well as the most significant considering its origin, is to be found in the Report of a German Commission on University Reform, published in 1949:

> "At the beginning of the report we defined the function of a University as being to serve man through teaching the truth which is reached by scientific study of the real world. The three most important words in this definition are man, research and teaching. In these words are found the oft-quoted trinity of tasks of a University—research, teaching, education; but we wish to interpret this trinity in a certain way.
>
> "We dissociate ourselves from those conceptions which put, not man, but research in the foremost place. We believe that University activity is justified only in so far as it renders service to man. This service is not restricted to the student who is to be taught, but extends directly or indirectly to the whole people."

In England the increased provision of halls of residence at the new non-residential universities and the great expansion of university "extension" courses were part of the new movement; so was the attempt to make a genuine university rather than an examining board out of London University; but in England, which had never fallen so deeply beneath the German spell, the ill-effects and the reaction are not so marked. It is in America that both may most easily be observed in their extreme form.

In the first quarter of the twentieth century, then, two German institutions, the graduate school with its doctorate thesis, and "freedom of learning" under the name of the Elective System, were firmly established in America. Both began immediately

to develop inherent faults, much exaggerated by transplantation to
a new soil. The American universities had always included in the
first two years of college work much intellectual experience which,
in Europe, was passed through at the secondary school; this was
inevitable, partly because of the low academic standard of the
secondary schools and partly because so many students attended
college in America who would neither have wished nor qualified
for a university education in Europe. To them a college education
was often just one more of those "advantages" which their fathers
had lacked, and which they accepted with all the eagerness of a
democratic and progressive tradition. Often such students were
—like the "hearty" ex-public school undergraduate in England—
basically uninterested in university studies, and they treated the
principle of free election simply as a means of avoiding failure
with the minimum · of inconvenience. The most ill-assorted
courses were fitted together purely on the grounds that they were
easy, or conducted at convenient times of the day, and the example
of such dilettantes debased the value of the bachelor's degree,
and discouraged any serious study. The fact that the degree
was granted on the completion of the requisite number of independent courses, and did not depend on any final examination,
meant that a subject could be "swotted up" at an elementary level
one term and immediately forgotten the next. It was even
possible to take a degree solely by pursuing a series of elementary
courses in the widest possible variety of subjects without ever
pursuing any of them beyond the freshman standard. The
absurdities of the whole system are well exemplified by an
imaginary conversation reported by Professor Leacock:

"Well, young man," says the Professor to the undergraduate,
"what subjects are you taking this year?"

"Music, Turkish and theology, Professor."

"Ah. You intend to become choirmaster at the Anglican
Church in Istanbul, no doubt?"

"No, sir. They are the classes at nine, ten and eleven in
Room X, and that is the room nearest my lodgings."

President Eliot's defence against such attacks was that these
things were the abuse of the Elective System, and that in giving the
good student the opportunity to educate himself, the university
inevitably permitted the bad student to waste his time. There
is clearly much force in this argument, but even if it could have

been maintained at the university level, it was clearly disastrous when free election, supported by the "anti-transfer" school of educationists, spread to the high schools. Undergraduates of sufficient maturity might just possibly benefit from completely free election. For high school children it could mean nothing but an education in unco-ordinated snippets. The first reactions against the pure Elective System were already appearing before 1914, and took the form of insisting that the courses chosen should be grouped around a "major" field of study; and along with this went the introduction of final examinations in the major subject. Thus the American system was brought nearer to the English honours school type of organisation. This reform satisfied the critics for some time, and the freely elected curriculum made up of a "major" and a number of related or unrelated "minors" was the normal arrangement of the 1920's. Free election in the high schools, however, had had its effect, and the universities became more and more concerned with the complete lack of any background of general education among their students. The specialisation imposed in the graduate school at the other end of the process meant that it was possible for a man to leave the university with a Ph.D. in advertising, but a completely fragmentary education.

The lead in countering this tendency was taken by the University of Chicago, which had a tradition of general education. In 1931 President Hutchins introduced a radical reorganisation, by which the first two years of college were devoted to a compulsory course in general education, including the natural sciences, social sciences, humanities and English. Success in the course was judged on final examinations, not termly credits, and led to a diploma. In 1942 this diploma was changed to the Bachelor of Arts degree. Thus Chicago recognised two facts, that the average undergraduate was not ready for true university work until he had completed what would in Europe have been his secondary education, and that, since a great number of undergraduates would not stay at the university beyond the second year, the course for the first two years should be designed as a self-contained whole. The Chicago baccalaureate thus came to represent the same stage in education as the French. The University of Chicago plan was only one of a number of such reorganisations which took place from 1930 onwards. Perhaps the most revolutionary was the Great Books plan at St John's, Annapolis, which built up a four-year course round the study, mainly in translation, of about a hundred of the world's greatest books. Some idea of the breadth and variety of this course can be gained from the fact that the books included Homer, Herodotus, Hippocrates, Aristarchus *On the Sizes and Distances of the Sun and Moon*, Plotinus, Marx' *Capital*, and Flaubert's *Bouvard et Pécuchet*. The importance laid on going back to such works in their entirety was a protest against the "potting" and "cramming" which had been among the worst features of the ten-week "credit" courses in unrelated subjects.

By the end of the Second World War it was widely accepted that the universities must demand a period of general education from all students. In France (Langevin Report) and in Germany (British Zone Report on University Reform) it was proposed that the years between eighteen and nineteen should no longer be organised as the last year of school, but as the first of the university, and devoted to general education. This is a system very similar to that which was developed at Chicago in 1932, when the last two years at high school were integrated with the university general education course. It is a principle which has found wide acceptance in the founding of "junior colleges" in many American districts. In England it is most clearly seen in the compulsory general education course in the University college of North Staffordshire, the youngest university foundation in the country.

The German concentration on research has proved equally difficult to acclimatise in America. The largely secondary nature of the undergraduate work soon led to an increasing conviction that anyone who was to get the best out of a university training must go on to post-graduate work. This was particularly true of those who intended to teach in any college or in the better high schools; a Ph.D. became almost an essential qualification for such posts, and the various "accrediting agencies" began to judge the worth of the institution by the number of Ph.D.s on its staff. Such a degree is in fact far commoner in the better American high schools than it is in English secondary schools, although in academic standard the pupils in the former are a full two years behind those in the latter.

This meant a rapid increase in the number of Ph.D.s—1000

per cent. between 1900 and 1947. In spite of this increase, however, and in spite of the fact that the majority of those taking the Ph.D. never intended to do any further research, they continued to be trained purely as research workers, and the graduate schools continued to demand, as qualification for the degree, a thesis containing original research. Hence came the passion for expressing in scientific or mathematical terms the most banal conclusions, and the fevered search for some nook or cranny which had not yet been counted or measured and so could provide a field for a Ph.D. thesis. Abraham Flexner (*Universities*, 1930) records that at Teachers' College, the graduate school of education of Columbia University, Ph.D.s have been awarded for theses on "An Analysis of Janitor Service in Elementary Schools" and "Our Girls and what they tell us"; and M.A.s at Chicago University for theses on "Photographic Studies of Boiled Icing" and "A Time and Motion Study of Four Methods of Dish-washing". The degree of specialisation involved in this insistence on original research was such that it would presumably have been in order to submit another thesis to Teachers' College on "An Analysis of Janitor Service in Secondary Schools".[1]

This sort of thing was clearly research run mad and brought nothing but discredit on the American higher degrees. It is not surprising, therefore, that the 1947 presidential report on higher education recommends most strongly that the graduate schools should be reformed, and the training in research and insistence on a thesis reserved for those who are really being trained as research workers.

The two German importations failed because the American universities were not what the German universities had been—corporations of highly trained students, drawn from a single class, with a single background of intellectual training and a single aim in view. They were independent corporations, consisting, again to quote Abraham Flexner, partly of "secondary schools and colleges for boys and girls"; partly of "graduate and professional schools for advanced students"; partly of "service stations for the general public."

[1] Flexner's tirade does not seem to have been entirely effective. A recent article records the following among the courses which count towards a degree at Columbia: "Cookery 103: *Meal Management*. This course stresses entertaining in the home" and "Dance 193C: *Social Dance*. Basic steps in foxtrot, waltz, rumba, tango and samba".

These were characteristics which they shared with the English universities. Their independence meant that finance has depended primarily, as it once did in England, on the generosity of benefactors. The extent of such generosity in America has almost passed the bounds of belief, but it has not proved an ideal way of financing a university. Apart from the obvious flaws, such as the tendency of rich alumni to pay more attention to football than to scholarship, too many bequests have been made for specific purposes, when the university either needed something else, or had not the permanent income available to make use of the buildings donated. The English system of a block grant from the national Treasury, which the university itself administers as it thinks best, is clearly a better system, provided that it does not entail detailed state control of the university. Their combination of an undergraduate college with a graduate school also meant that American universities were inevitably places of corporate living as well as corporate study, and training schools of men as well as of scholars. In developing the small units of corporate life the American colleges, however, followed the example of the German *Korps* or *Bruderschaft* rather than of the English college. The advantage of the College over the Fraternity is that it contains university members of all grades from professor to freshman, and that membership of it is automatic. The German students' *Korps* and the American Fraternity lacked the steadying influence of the senior members, and the social implications of election or rejection were, at the height of their influence, far too important. The student who failed to belong in either country got very little out of the corporate life of the university. Nevertheless, American universities were much nearer to English than to German in their concern for the whole welfare of the student as opposed merely to his scholarship. This is a concern for which Flexner berates them, but it is being increasingly recognised that it is one which the university must display unless it is to be purely a graduate school of mature scholars.

Finally, the American universities developed a wide new field of activity in adult education: they became "service stations" for the whole area. In this they followed the English example and possibly the French theory. The discussion of this work must be left to the next chapter. All that need be said now is that both in Europe and America it has been officially recognised as an important and legitimate function of the university. Flexner's attack on it was not a criticism of the work done so much as of the confusion of standards which arose from treating it, not as the university's contribution to adult education, but as an integral part of the university itself.

CHAPTER NINE

ADULT EDUCATION

ADULT education is a phrase to which a variety of meanings may be attached. The one of which this chapter will treat is the further formal education of those who are adults in the sense that they have left the primary school and already taken up full or part-time employment. It will be seen that this definition rules out literacy campaigns or devices for supplying a primary education to adults who missed it at the primary stage. This was the chief concern of adult schools in the eighteenth century, but for the last hundred years it has generally ceased to be necessary in the West. It also rules out the innumerable cultural activities of adult life; drama leagues, sports clubs, rifle clubs, Women's Institutes, etc. No one could deny that these are educational, but the whole process of life is educational in some sense, and for convenience sake a line must be drawn somewhere.

Adult education, so defined, has been of two clearly marked types, (a) education in the liberal arts and sciences for those who have been unable to attend secondary school or university, and (b) part-time technical training for those engaged in agriculture and industry.

Throughout the nineteenth century it was almost, by definition, intended for the underprivileged, and therefore rarely succeeded altogether in avoiding a politically partisan flavour. Only the original Danish Folk High Schools seem definitely to have set their faces against this danger. As they, more than any other institution, have influenced adult education in the liberal arts, it is with them that we will start our enquiry.

Nineteenth-Century Developments

(a) *The Danish Folk High Schools.*—The Danish Folk High School was the creation of the great educator and churchman Nikolai Grundtvig. Like many of the important figures in the history of education, he was a man of markedly individual genius, and a great many features of the folk high school movement derive from his personality. Born in 1783, he was a romantic nationalist, a convinced Christian, and a great opponent of book-learning. His almost mystical belief in the spoken word, as opposed to the written, led to doctrinal disputes in the ecclesiastical sphere, and to an unusual emphasis in teaching on folk-lore, oral tradition and the lecture. It must be remembered, however, that the oral teaching which Grundtvig really favoured was much more like an informal and inspiring monologue, given by the teacher at the dining table, then a formal university lecture. Finally and most important, he was convinced that adolescence was the wrong period of life for secondary education. He believed that the boy or girl should spend the years between fourteen and eighteen apprenticed to a trade or learning the duties of the housewife; then, when they were approaching maturity, when they knew something at least of the world, and began to feel the desire and the need for education, was the time for them to go to school. This was a strange and original theory, but there can be few who have taught adolescents who do not feel that it embodies some part at least of a profound psychological truth. For Grundtvig it meant that the right form of secondary school was what we should now call the residential adult college. The first of these he set up at Rödding in South Sleswig in 1844.

Grundtvig's original intentions are clearly set out in the programme for this school: "Our aim", he said, "is to found an institution where townspeople and peasants can acquire such knowledge and ability as may be of use and pleasure, not so much with regard to their special trade and occupation as with regard to their position as sons of their country and citizens of the state."

Two things are noteworthy in this statement: the clear denial of vocational training and the nationalist intention. The choice of South Sleswig is also significant in the latter sense, for Grundtvig's intention was clearly to make good Danes out of the largely German population. The curriculum of Rödding was not very different from that of an ordinary secondary school, but particular emphasis was placed on history, Danish language and literature, and on singing. These were always features of the early folk high schools. The importance of history was partly nationalistic, but also partly due to Grundtvig's belief in the spoken voice, and the teacher as an inspired storyteller. Later in the century, when educationists elsewhere were pressing the experimental and heuristic methods of science teaching, the Danish folk high schools stuck to their courses in historical physics and historical mathematics. For adult education at least, there is good reason to think that Grundtvig was here many years before his time; and although the folk high schools to-day have adopted a more factual and less romantic attitude towards history, they still make use of the popular lecture more widely and more successfully than any other kind of school.

As well as the academic curriculum, he believed that as much practical work as possible should be done—again to get away from book-learning—and that therefore farms and workshops should be attached to the high schools wherever possible. When the government began to treat them as vocational agricultural schools, however, and to demand that the students should take the entrance examination for the Royal Agricultural College at Copenhagen, he used all his influence in a long and successful fight to preserve the liberal nature of the schools and to keep them free from all examinations. The latter freedom he regarded as of vital importance, for his whole theory was based on the belief that the young people would come to him at that age for the sheer love of learning, and that any form of examinations or certificates would destroy the atmosphere which he wished to build up.

That atmosphere was most nearly akin to the spirit of a family, living together in cheerful simplicity and devoting their time to learning, singing, gymnastics, telling stories and practical tasks. Grundtvig wanted to admit women from the first, but this was not actually done until 1862 when his great disciple Kristen Kold ran a summer course for them at Dalum.

Rödding was perhaps too academic and expensive for a real folk high school, but it was undoubtedly the germ from which the whole movement started. The work which Grundtvig had begun was continued by Kristen Kold, who started as a disciple but really went further than his master. He started his first school on Grundtvig's lines in 1851, living with his pupils, sleeping in the same dormitory with them and sharing a much greater simplicity of life than prevailed at Rödding.[1] His greatest

[1] The consumption of sugar for a school of 26 pupils and the headmaster during one entire winter was 2 lb. (*Education for Life*, Noelle Davis).

achievement, perhaps, was to see from the first the danger to the movement which might arise either from nationalism or political bias. "My school is the best", he says. "At Rödding they work for Danish culture as against German culture, and when the former is triumphant the task of the school will have passed; at Hindholm they work for the rights of the peasants, and when the peasants have gained the upper hand (and they have already done so) there will be no further use for Hindholm High School. But in my school we work for Life against Death, and that work must continue as long as the world exists."

That seems one of the finest school mottoes ever coined, but Kold was actually wrong in his prediction. It was not Danish culture, but German force, which triumphed at Rödding, and after the "Schleswig-Holstein incident" the school found itself annexed by Prussia and had to be transferred across the frontier to Askov.

Meanwhile, however, the movement had spread throughout Scandinavia. The first folk high schools were established in Norway in 1864 and in Sweden in 1868, though in neither of these two countries were they able to keep entirely clear of political associations; and in Sweden they took a more vocational form than in Denmark. Finland started with one—for women—in 1889, and by 1910 there were 19 in Norway, 42 in Sweden, and 41 of a rather smaller type, in Finland. In Denmark itself a Folk High School Association was established in 1878 with its headquarters at Askov, and by that time the number of folk high school students had passed three thousand. By this time the folk high school courses were more or less stabilised at a five month's course for men in the winter and a three months' course for women in the summer. Apart from these courses, they enjoyed wide support as "community centres" for their areas. The golden age of the Danish folk high school was, in fact from 1870 to 1890. When we consider that every one of them was started by the enthusiasm of private individuals, that the pupils were all adults coming voluntarily, in search of a liberal education and initially at least under very austere conditions, we must admit that the folk high school was one of the most successful of all nineteenth-century experiments in adult education.

(b) *The English Mechanics and Literary Institutes.*—While Denmark was concerned primarily with peasants, it was almost inevitable that England, with her great lead in the Industrial Revolution, should take the lead also in developing adult education for industrial workers. Before the end of the eighteenth century Dr Birkbeck had established in Glasgow his first technical courses for mechanics or artisans, designed primarily to give them some knowledge of the scientific theory on which their daily work was based. Historically the most interesting features of Birkbeck's classes were the great response which they aroused and the fact that they were, in some degree at least, connected with a university. The enthusiasm which they excited awoke in him a lasting interest in adult education, so that he, more than anyone else, was responsible for the foundation of the London Mechanics Institute in 1823; and the connection with the "Andersonian" University of Glasgow foreshadowed the link between universities and adult education which was later to become of such vital importance.

Following the example set in London, Mechanics Institutes were founded in most of the great industrial towns of Northern England in the 1820's, and regular publication began of what must have been one of the first of all educational journals, *The Mechanics Magazine*. The purpose of these institutes remained that of the Glasgow classes, "to supply at a cheap rate, to the different classes of the community, the advantages of instruction in the various branches of science which are of practical application to the various trades or occupations".[1]

There was, however, another motive besides this purely practical one behind the demand for adult education. The retrospective literature of the second half of the century shows again and again the unsatisfied longing for a liberal education which existed among the poor at this time, and which showed itself in the lengths to which exceptional individuals would go to get for themselves in later life what no school had given them. In answer to this genuine demand, and because the educated patrons of adult education fostered them, there grew up alongside or within the purely vocational Mechanics Institutes, Literary Institutes whose aim was more widely cultural.

The size of these Mechanics and Literary Institutes was never

[1] Purpose of Leeds Mechanics Institute, quoted by S. J. Curtis, *op. cit.* It is worth comparing this with the purpose of the Folk High School quoted above.

very great; up to four or five hundred had attended the classes at Glasgow, but shortage of accommodation alone meant that an active membership of over a hundred was large for a Mechanics Institute. The period of their greatest prosperity was around 1840, and by 1850, when Hudson (*History of Adult Education in England*, 1851) estimated their total membership at 102,050, they were already in a decline, which was accentuated in the next ten years. This decline was probably due to a variety of causes. It may be attributed partly to the lack of elementary education, which meant that very few mechanics or artisans were sufficiently literate to profit from them; but this, though undoubtedly a great handicap to adult education in England, was a diminishing, not an increasing, difficulty. Other probable causes were the general economic depression of the 'forties which put even the "cheap rate" beyond the means of the artisan, the "invasion" of the Mechanics Institutes by clerks and the lower middle classes generally, the increase in other facilities for secondary education after 1850, and what one might almost call the Law of Diminishing Enthusiasm which seems to operate particularly in adult education. Since all these causes exemplify factors which are more or less constant in the history of adult education it is worth considering them here in rather more detail.

The first two go together. Institutes of adult education have usually been founded in the first place with the intention of serving the manual labourer—or, in nineteenth-century phraseology, the "working classes". But, in the nineteenth century, manual labourers as a whole had neither the desire for further education, the educational equipment to profit from it, nor the money to pay for it, to anything like the same extent as the clerical workers of the lower middle class. It was believed, at the time, that the clerical workers "invaded" the Mechanics Institutes, "as the interest of the working class members flagged"; but the process was probably more reciprocal than that, and the influx of clerks increased the discouragement of the workers. Those who were rigidly working-class in their interests left the Mechanics Institutes and joined People's Colleges, set up in connection with the Chartist movement, which died out with the death of that movement in 1848. The political problems involved in adult education are treated in a later section, but even apart from them the question of class or occupation has remained a difficulty.

Even where the subsidies provided by an association or out of public funds are great enough to put such education easily within the reach of the manual labourer, organisers have found themselves faced with the inescapable fact that the greater part of the demand comes, not from uneducated manual labourers, but from the educated or half-educated "black-coat" worker, who wishes to continue his education—or in some cases even feels obliged to "support adult education". It is a significant fact that even in the courses organised in England in the twentieth century by the Workers' Educational Association there has never been a majority of manual labourers or working-class students; and the occupations from which the largest number of full-time students have come have been "teachers", or "commercial clerks, typists, agents and travellers". Except where a political "working class" qualification is introduced, this tendency seems a permanent feature of adult education. It is the manual labourer whom the educational idealist wishes to attract, but it is not the manual labourer who comes.

The relationship between the demand for adult education of a certain type and the existence of other educational facilities is obvious. In so far as adult education is supplying the underprivileged, the demand for it must inevitably decline as the walls of privilege are broken down. There may always be a certain number of people to whom the desire for serious study comes late in life, there should always be many who wish to keep their own knowledge up to date; but the easier it becomes for everyone to attend a secondary school or university, the less will be the demand for substitutes in the form of "people's colleges" and evening classes. It seems probable that each development of adult education, like the Mechanics Institutes, has begun by attracting an élite of enthusiastic students who used it as a substitute for the secondary or university education from which they had been debarred. As soon as secondary or university education was opened to them, this élite fell away and the standard of genuine scholarship and enthusiasm declined.

Finally, the Law of Diminishing Enthusiasm is a phenomenon, arising perhaps largely from a combination of the other factors, which seems almost universal throughout the field of adult education. It is seen only too frequently in the history of individual classes and institutes—as many village and district organisers can confirm. It is found, too, on a larger scale, in the history, not only of the Mechanics Institutes, but of far more successful experiments such as the W.E.A. and the folk high schools. A. L. Smith said of the first ten years of the W.E.A. that a quarter of the work sent in to him was up to the standard of work done by students who gained first class honours in the final school of modern history at Oxford; no one would dream of making such a claim to-day. Why is it then that the first flush of enthusiasm so rarely lasts, and the first standards are so rarely maintained? Partly, of course, because of the factors mentioned above, but partly, I think, because of a quality inherent in adult education. Because it is by its nature voluntary, a work of supererogation, it flourishes when its students are attracted either by some great personality or by some new educational ideal. In this respect it is like the "experimental" school; and, like the experimental school, schemes of adult education tend to decline as soon as the inspiration of the great personality is lost, or as soon as the new educational ideal has proved, as it so often does, not to be that short cut to human perfection which its most enthusiastic supporters first imagined it. But this law—if it is a law—is not necessarily a weakness. Adult education more than any other type of education needs constant change, constant re-inspiration, and there is no reason to lament that one form of institution should decline or one great teacher's work be swept away, provided that its place is taken by new forms and new enthusiasts. The greater danger seems to lie in that natural loyalty which tries to maintain the old forms after the life has really gone out of them.

As the Mechanics Institutes in England declined, their place was taken, in the purely vocational sphere by the work of the Science and Art Department, and in the more cultural sphere by the great movements for university extension. The institutes themselves, with a typically English capacity for adaptation, were merged sometimes in the evening institutes and classes later established by public authorities (see section (d) below) and sometimes in the newly arising provincial universities (see Chapter Eight); their "literary" branches are still to be found here and there surviving as social clubs.

(c) *University Extension.*—The idea of university extension was again English in origin. When it was first discussed, about the

middle of the nineteenth century, its supporters had in mind something like the establishment of the provincial universities in the great
manufacturing towns, which took place at the end of the century.
By "extension" they meant the foundation of new colleges which
should be open to the working classes, in the same way that the
Mechanics Institutes were, but which should give them something
much more like a university education. Experiments of this type
were tried, first at Sheffield and then at London, where F. D.
Maurice founded the Working Men's College in 1854. Maurice's
plan was quite simply to extend to the working classes the benefits
of university education, and the university he had in mind was,
not unnaturally, his own, Oxford. The curriculum of the College
was liberal and humane, and great emphasis was placed on the
development of the true communal spirit, which we have already
seen was the one great achievement of the English universities.
The College attracted the support of many of those earnest
Christian reformers who did so much for mid-Victorian social life;
Ruskin, Charles Kingsley and Hughes (the author of *Tom Brown's
Schooldays*) all served it. Individually it was remarkably successful, but it depended too much upon the patronage of individual
men of exceptional character to be copied elsewhere and the
colleges founded in imitation of it had short and disappointing
lives.

What was needed was a method of linking the spirit of social
service which welled up continually, but uncontrolled, among
the educated classes with some existing and continuous body
which could regulate and distribute it. This was found in 1871,
when James Stuart, a Fellow of Trinity College, Cambridge, who
had been giving lectures on astronomical subjects to women's
classes and Mechanics Institutes in the North of England,
persuaded a number of them to petition the University of Cambridge to undertake the provision of such lectures as a regular
activity. Stuart had long been interested in the general idea of
university extension, and had originally conceived the idea of "a
sort of peripatetic university, the professors of which would
circulate among the big towns". He had, moreover, been led
to a most important new development in the technique of this
kind of work by an experience when lecturing to a Co-operative
Society Institute in Rochdale. Having left his diagrams in the
lecture hall at the end of one lecture, he discovered, on returning

O

for the next, that they had excited so much interest and discussion among members that he was persuaded to explain and discuss them with a small class before the lecture began. In this preliminary discussion with the tutor, which Stuart made a regular feature of his lectures from then on, lay the germ of the "tutorial classes" introduced into the University Extension movement at the beginning of the next century.

It says much for the rapid progress of reform which had been going on in the English universities since the middle of the century that Cambridge immediately agreed to the request made to it by Stuart's classes. Cambridge was followed by London in 1876 and Oxford in 1878.. By the end of the century the movement had spread beyond England (Vienna, 1895; Jena, Munich and Leipzig, 1896), so that when the new provincial universities were founded it was already part of the normal activity of a university. Indeed three of the new universities, Sheffield, Reading and Nottingham, began as University Extension centres.

Although the establishment of adult extension classes as part of the university's functions secured them against too great a dependence on individual—and mortal—promoters, it did not solve the other problems of adult education. The universities had neither the wish nor the funds to subsidise them heavily, so that the cost had to be covered by fees. If, as usually happened, the working classes were admitted at cheap rates, that only meant that a proportionately larger income had to be found from the fees of middle-class students; the type of education given therefore had to be such as would attract a sufficiently large middle-class audience. This normally took the form of "interesting" and "stimulating" lectures rather than serious social study or technical training. And to such lectures the working class were not particularly anxious to come. The inspiration of Stuart had served a great purpose in bringing the universities directly into the field of adult education, but there remained two demands unsatisfied by the extension movement, the demand for vocational and technical training of artisans, and the demand for the political education of the working class. The first of these was beginning to be satisfied by the State and the second by the Socialist movement.

(d) *Vocational Education and State Aid*.—Throughout the nineteenth century it was more usual for the State to encourage, support and inspect the voluntary bodies providing adult education than actually to provide facilities itself. This was the position, for instance, with the Danish folk high schools and, to a great extent, with adult education (mainly agricultural) in France.

Where the State was most deeply concerned was in the provision of technical and vocational education, and here it exerted its influence most strongly. The Department of Science and Art, set up in England in 1853, was in many ways typical of the nineteenth-century government attitude. In the first place, since England was primarily a manufacturing country, it began as a department of the Board of Trade, just as agricultural education in France remained throughout the century the concern of the Ministry of Agriculture. When it was transferred to the Board of Education in 1856 it confined its activities to the "encouragement" of scientific and technical teaching by the payment of grants to anyone who, having passed its qualifying examination, taught such subjects, either to children in a full-time school or to adults in evening classes. It was not surprising, therefore, that although the number of classes being taught science doubled in the first ten years of the Department's existence, the type of teaching remained theoretical and of little practical use for vocational training. At the Paris exhibition of 1867 the British public got a shock even more severe than they had received at their own great exhibition of 1851. Whereas they were surprised to find in 1851 that British manufactures did not win every prize, at Paris they found them winning prizes in only ten out of ninety divisions. Something was clearly wrong with the technical training of British craftsmen. This time it was private enterprise which tried to set things right. The ancient City Guilds and Livery Companies of the City of London had a traditional responsibility for the standards of craftsmanship, and they set up, in 1880, the City and Guilds Institute to exercise this responsibility in the new setting. The weakness of the Science and Art Department was clearly that it encouraged, but never provided, vocational training, and that it made no provision for the adequate training of the teachers who held its certificates. The City and Guilds Institute adopted the much more practical expedient of founding, at Finsbury in 1883, a "model" technical college designed for both full-time and adult evening students, and closely connected with the chief local craft of cabinet-making. In the following year they opened their Central Technical College for the training of technical teachers.

During the last quarter of the century the government was slowly coming round to the view, stimulated by constant German competition and a series of Commissions of Enquiry, that the promotion of technical and vocational training was a public responsibility; but it preferred at first to carry on the Science and Art Department's "encouragements", and to devote to the aid of such institutions as the new Polytechnics and Technical Schools any financial windfalls which were not earmarked for anything else. In particular, they benefited from the redundant charities of the City of London and from an unexpected budgetary surplus known colloquially as "whisky money". It was not till the reorganisation of the whole educational system in 1902 that the support of the growing network of evening classes became a regular and acknowledged part of the public educational services.

The development of this type of adult education in France runs closely parallel to that in England. In a predominantly agricultural country it is not surprising that the first widespread or serious efforts were devoted to agricultural education. As in England they were made by private corporations, and the Société des Agriculteurs de France began in exactly the same way as the Department of Science and Art, by paying a gratuity to any teacher who was prepared to conduct classes in agriculture after school hours. About the middle of the century it extended its activities to the support of agricultural departments in existing institutions and finally to the support of agricultural colleges, of which the Institut Agricole de Beauvais was the first. Since the agricultural districts were mainly Catholic, the Church authorities showed a particular interest in this type of education.

It was not until 1879 that the State undertook the organisation of an agricultural education service, including an organiser for each district in charge of adult classes, farm institutes, etc., as well as of the teaching of agricultural subjects in schools. A number of travelling lecturers were included on the staff of the organiser, whose function was to tour the district giving talks and demonstrations. Technical education in the towns was organised more slowly. The first national law laying down a system of technical education was passed in 1880, and placed the technical schools under the joint control of the Minister of Public Instruction and the Minister of Commerce. This was reversed in 1892 and full control given to the Minister of Commerce. Alongside these technical schools were organised vocational courses on a municipal basis, which became eligible for grants from the state and were under the general control of the Department of Technical Education. By the end of the century, therefore, France was slightly ahead of England, in the organisation both of full-time technical schools and of publicly aided vocational education for those who had left school. There was, on the other hand, no parallel to the development of adult education on the social and cultural side which had taken place in England. To some extent this was probably due to the superiority at this time of French secondary education, just as the earlier establishment of *Realschule*, *Burgerschule* and technical colleges in Germany had done much to meet the demand there for vocational training.

(e) *Political Influences in Adult Education.*—We have already noticed that throughout the nineteenth century and well into the twentieth one of the main functions of adult education was to provide, for the underprivileged, those opportunities which they had been denied in their youth. Many social reformers felt the injustice of this exclusion, and both the People's Colleges and the University Extension movement had been started largely for the benefit of the working classes. But there was another motive also behind the demand for working class education. As early as 1848 the leaders of the Radical and Socialist movements had seen clearly that if the working class was to capture political power it would need an educated élite drawn from among its own members. It was to provide such an educated élite that the adult education movement within the working class, not *for* the working class, arose. The objects of this movement were frankly political, and the subjects taught—such as were likely to prove useful to political leaders—predominantly Marxist economics. The protagonists of the movement were usually sceptical of the good faith, and also of what they termed the patronising air, of those from the richer classes who were trying to organise adult education *for* the workers. There arose, therefore, in most countries a conflict between those working-class leaders who were prepared to put education first and accept it from whatever hands it came, and those who regarded education as a means in the political and economic struggle and were therefore determined to control it themselves.

The purely political motive behind adult education was most clearly seen, perhaps, in Prussia. In England the Chartist People's Colleges died with the Chartist movement, and in the second half of the century the increased prosperity of the nation as a whole and the genuine efforts made by social reformers for working class education momentarily obscured the conflict, though it may be seen again in the split between the W.E.A. and the "Plebs League" in 1908.

The political education of the working class in Prussia, under the influence of Lassalle and the early Marxists, had the advantage that it could build on a more effective system of primary education than elsewhere, and therefore one of the main causes of failure in England was not operative. Moreover, its frankly political bias led to the formation in 1871 of an anti-socialist Society for Adult Education, so that the genuine "workers" were not squeezed out by any influx of respectable petty bourgeoisie who naturally preferred the rival society. However unfortunate it may be that men should seek and organise education, not for itself, but as a means to a political end, there seems little doubt that, in adult education at least, such a motive is a great stimulus; people will flock to the party schools in order to educate themselves for the class struggle, whom the appeal of culture and self-development would leave apathetic. The frankly political movements of Prussia were in fact remarkably successful in attracting students whenever they were not actually banned by the government; but by the end of the century it was clear that they suffered from educational defects quite as grave as those which affected adult education in England. The ambition to equip the largest possible number of party members with the doctrines and knowledge required for the political struggle led to the superficial presentation of undigested information to large classes in Prussia, just as much as the necessity of attracting large numbers of fee-payers did in England. In both countries therefore the chief problem at the beginning of the twentieth century was how to make adult education more serious and more intensive, more genuinely an educational effort of the whole man and less the attendance at a series of lectures. Leaders of the working-class educational movement tried to solve this problem in two ways,

by the organisation of "tutorial classes", and by the establishment of residential colleges, such as Ruskin College at Oxford
(1899).

Twentieth-Century Developments

There have been three main lines of development in the sphere
of formal adult education in the first half of this century—the
attempt to deepen the content of adult education, partly by
the extension of the residential college, or folk high school; the
expansion of publicly sponsored vocational classes; and the
spread of university extension. These were paralleled by a great
increase in informal adult education through such organisations
as Women's Institutes, Theatre and Music Clubs, which it
would be impossible to treat adequately in this compass.

The example of the Danish folk high schools, which, as we have
seen, was taken up enthusiastically in Scandinavia in the nineteenth
century, spread also, at a rather later date, to Germany, England
and America. In America they were, of course, originally the
contribution of the Danish communities, who started their first
at Elkhorn, Iowa, in 1878. They became fairly popular in areas
with large Scandinavian populations, but on the whole they were
not widely accepted and their influence on education has been
indirect. It can be clearly seen, for instance, in the great success
of that typically American social and educational vacation centre,
the "summer school".

Nor have they spread very much more widely in England, and
where residential colleges have been established in this country it
is hard to tell how much is due to the native tradition—from
which in fact Grundtvig himself drew much of his inspiration—
and how much to Danish influence. We have already seen that
the Socialist movement, seeking to deepen the nature of its adult
education, turned to the residential principle at Ruskin College;
and even earlier than this, Toynbee Hall, in London (1884), had
followed the same lines. The model for these, however, was the
residential college of the English university, and the first college
to be founded in England on the true lines of the folk high school
was Fircroft in 1908. As in Germany, the colleges have often
been founded for a particular group, Fircroft for industrial workers,
Hillcroft for women, Avoncroft for agricultural workers, etc.
The Danish influence is apparent, too, in such nationalist founda-

tions as the Welsh Coleg Harlech (1927). These residential colleges usually give a year's or even two years' course, and although vocational subjects are included they are never allowed to play too large a part in the curriculum. Another feature of the Danish experience which attracted a large following among English educationists was the way in which the folk high school acted as a centre for the cultural life of a whole agricultural neighbourhood; and an attempt has been made to establish such centres in the Cambridgeshire Village Colleges (1928) where they are linked with primary or secondary schools. On the whole, however, England did not develop residential adult colleges in the pre-War years to anything like the extent that might have been expected, and in 1938 there were only seven, with one each in Wales and Scotland. After the War there was a considerable increase in the number of residential colleges offering short courses of a week or week-end, and many educationists have pleaded that the new County Colleges, which are to be set up for the benefit of those who leave school at fifteen, should be as far as possible residential; but the true folk high school has not been accepted any more widely in Britain than in America.

The country which, in the twentieth century, developed most widely the Scandinavian system was Germany. Germany, as a result of the war of 1864, had actually acquired the site of the first folk high school at Rödding, and not unnaturally the first of her own folk high schools were started in Sleswig. The nationalist elements in Grundtvig's thought found fruitful soil in Prussia, but after the defeat of 1918 there was a real attempt to free the folk high schools from any chauvinistic tendencies. The "youth movement" in Germany at this time, and the genuinely liberal and idealistic views which were enjoying a new freedom of expression, favoured the folk high school movement, and in 1927 there was founded an all-German Society of Folk High Schools on the Danish model. Unfortunately, this society was far from comprehensive; in the interests of academic freedom, it embraced only those schools which were free of partisan affiliations, and in Germany, as in Norway, many of the folk high schools had been founded as centres of a particular faith—Evangelical, Catholic, Socialist or even "proto-Nazi". By the end of the Weimar period, however, there were, counting these "partisan" schools, approximately eighty true folk high schools in Germany and over two hundred non-residential institutes acknowledging the folk high schools as their model. As in Denmark, the State aided them but did not control them. All this the Nazis, when they came into power, quickly abolished.

The most significant move towards deepening the content of adult education, outside the residential system, was probably the establishment of "tutorial classes" by the W.E.A. in England. The W.E.A. (Workers' Educational Association) was founded in 1903, though it did not take that name until 1905. It was formed by a union of a number of bodies interested in the higher education of working men, and from the first enjoyed the support of the universities. So far was it from being the revolutionary body which it sounds that its first president was William Temple, later Archbishop of Canterbury.

The W.E.A., after some years of experiment, worked out, in conjunction with the University of Oxford and later the other English universities, the "tutorial class" method. This was a class of thirty adult students who undertook a three-year course under the direction of a tutor from the university. The course usually involved a weekly two-hour session of lecture and discussion during the university term, together with the writing of "essays" by the students, exactly like those produced weekly for their tutors by undergraduates at the universities. The standard of the work was well up to that of undergraduates in residence, and the whole system therefore approached, more nearly than anything else had done, to the idea of the "peripatetic university" which had been in Stuart's mind when University Extension was founded. The subjects studied were usually the arts and social sciences, with a strong emphasis on economics, and as far as possible the type of subject which public authorities were beginning to offer in evening institutes was avoided.

For the first ten years, from 1908 to 1918, these classes formed the greater part of the W.E.A.'s work, but since then three tendencies have shown themselves, of the kind we have noticed in adult education as a whole: the proportion of serious students in tutorial classes has fallen, with a corresponding increase in "popular lectures" and fall in the academic standard of work; the proportion of manual workers in the classes has fallen, with a corresponding increase in teachers, civil servants, etc.; and there has been a transfer of interest from academic subjects such as economics to the more vague and topical such as "international relations".

In the field of state-aided vocational education the twentieth century saw, with the expansion of secondary education for all, the absorption of the English junior technical schools and French *écoles pratiques* or *écoles des metiers* in the general secondary system. Neither had achieved enrolments much exceeding 30,000, and it was clear that the lead in this sphere of education was still held by Germany. It also saw, in England at least, a great increase in the number and improvement in the organisation of evening classes, now under the control of the local education authorities.

In America the fact that vocational subjects already played so large a part in the curriculum of the high schools and that there was no equivalent to the European Ministry of Education which could take charge of adult education produced a rather different development. The demand for adult education was very great, but the only public body capable of organising it on any scale was the universities. With no clear differentiation at the secondary level between vocational and non-vocational education, it was not unnatural that the universities should have moved to meet this demand in all its variety. Not only did they organise extension classes in the academic subjects, after the manner of European universities, but they catered for the whole range of technical training from corset-making to confectionery. In this the State universities in particular were influenced perhaps by their duty towards the whole educational needs of the community and the similarity of their position to that of the universities in France, where the establishment of vocational classes of this kind depended on the agreement of the Prefect and the Academy Rector. This expansion of their interests brought on them a bitter attack in Abraham Flexner's celebrated book on universities. Flexner in this attack concentrated largely on the Extension Departments of Columbia and Chicago, in which he saw two great weaknesses. The first was that these departments were not conducted in response to a demand for a genuinely liberal education, as the original Cambridge extension courses had been; on the contrary, they were more vocational than liberal, and promoted themselves by every device of advertising that the university could think of. It was not that the hungry sheep looked up and were not fed;

everything, whether digestible or not, was forced down then throats; and the public were continually bombarded with invitations to secure a college education, "of university grade", either by attending extension courses or by post.

The second weakness arose from the first. Once the university had imposed on itself the duty of creating rather than meeting a demand for adult education, the customers' wishes began to become the final criterion of what was taught. Not only were courses offered in subjects which were not capable of treatment at university level, such as fire insurance, juvenile story writing or elementary typewriting, but, in order to attract a gullible public, degrees were solemnly awarded on such work. It was in this that the real gravamen of Flexner's attack lies. What is open to objection is not that this type of adult education should be carried out, nor even that the universities should assist in it, but that they should advertise it to their customers as genuinely academic study on a level with that of the established faculties. In doing this some American universities seem to have been led astray by their enthusiasm for "graduate school" methods, which have been already criticised in Chapter Eight. One or two of Flexner's collection of Ph.D. theses have already been quoted, but there are plenty more to illustrate the results of treating all adult education as if it were on a level with university studies—an M.A. degree at Chicago granted for "A Study of Controlled Conditions in Cooking Hams" is as good an example as any. By such practices, Flexner maintained, the university was not only led by its extension department and allied "institutes" into a degrading form of catchpenny publicity, but the whole significance of its more serious degrees was debased. The final criticism was that this descent of the university into domestic and vocational training was a fraud even at its own level. Flexner quotes two universities which had tried in vain a series of domestic science Ph.D.s to manage their own catering, and finally fell back, with complete success, one on an experienced but untrained boarding-house keeper, and the other on an intelligent young instructor in French. Such a result is not surprising. There may be good justification for technical research in food preparation but there is no reason whatever to suppose that the composition of a degree thesis on "Some Sugar-Saving Sweets for Everyday" (Ph.D., Columbia) will be any guarantee of competence in a practical caterer. And it is certainly no part of a liberal education. The whole phantasmagoria of research, theses and degrees was part of the twentieth-century malady of the American graduate school, and its connection with adult education brought nothing with it but an odour of pretentious hypocrisy. Such degrees were sought for their commercial value only. It is significant that whereas the extension departments of the English universities could not carry on without considerable grants from the Treasury, that of Columbia cleared in 1929 a net profit of $300,000. It is hard to believe that a great part of this was not derived from the fees for courses which consisted of no more than translating into pompous pseudo-scientific language the practice of various trades or household activities, which the students could have learnt equally well as apprentices in industry or children in the home. Flexner's attack had considerable success, not fortunately in discouraging the universities from an interest in extension courses and adult education generally, but in modifying their views about the award of degrees in all sorts of subjects to the authors of largely artificial research theses. The concern of the American universities for adult education in fact increased, and it was natural that it should have done so. The State universities, as we have seen, had never entirely got away from the French element in their foundation, the design that they should control or supply the whole needs of the State in higher education. The need for adult education was one of these, and the taxpayers of the State felt that they had a right to secure this service from their own university. This point of view is emphatically stated in the Report of the Presidential Commission on Higher Education (December 1947): "The Colleges and Universities should elevate adult education to a position of equal importance with any other of their functions. . . . It should be the duty of the English Faculty or of the Physics Faculty, for instance, to teach English or physics not just to those who come to the campus, but to everyone in the community or the State who wants to learn, or can be persuaded to want to learn, English or physics."

Granted the American faith in education, it is difficult to see how this conclusion could have been avoided. No other body exists in America which could undertake this duty if the colleges and universities did not. Two factors make the duty appear one of supreme importance, the belief that only an educated community can make democracy work, and the conviction that there is a widespread need and demand for adult education if the American community is to become fully educated. The first of these involves philosophical questions so profound and beliefs so deeply held that it is impossible to debate it here; it is worth putting in the caution, however, that it is self-evident only for certain definitions both of democracy and education. The second conviction is based on two social facts: first, that in 1947 only just over half the electors in the United States had attended school after the age of fourteen; and, second, that a Gallup Poll also held in 1947 showed that 41 per cent. of the voters "wished to engage in some form of adult education". Thus both the need and the desire for vastly increased adult education seems established. The figures of partially educated voters could be paralleled in any European country, but the number of people demanding adult education is really staggering—even allowing for the fact that in all probability far more people record on the poll that they want to enter classes than would actually enter them. (In fact it must take a certain amount of moral courage to say that one does not. want to continue one's education.)

That this demand is not an optimistic myth is confirmed, however, by the very rapidly rising adult enrolments in existing institutions. In 1947 the State of California alone had nearly a million adults enrolled in evening high schools or in special junior colleges of an adult type (*cf.* the 103,757 enrolled in W.E.A. classes in England).[1]

It seems likely, therefore, from the social and economic trends in America as a whole that a vast and rapid expansion of adult education will take place in the next few years, parallel to and supplementing the expansion of college education. To the outside observer this expansion seems endangered by the superficiality which afflicted Europe at the opening of the twentieth century. The possibilities are very great, but whether they will be realised must depend on three as yet undecided questions, of crucial importance to all democratic countries:

(*a*) Is the increased wisdom and responsibility which such democratic communities seek from their voting members really going to result from increased adult education of a formal type?

(*b*) Is the demand for adult education which exists, a demand for the type of social education which could produce such increased

[1] S. G. Raybould, *W.E.A. The Next Phase.*

wisdom? Or is it a demand for light amusement and vocational tricks of the trade? [1]

(c) Granted that such education as we desire demands the very highest type of teacher, where are these teachers coming from?

One solution to the problems raised by the shortage of teachers is of course the use of educational television, through which one first class teacher can lecture or demonstrate to an almost indefinitely large audience. For voluntary adult education such methods have obvious advantages and less disadvantages than television in the schools. Certainly the immense popularity of serious educational television programmes in America and the vastly increased sales of "non-fiction" paper-back books are encouraging signs.

The issue which is raised here of a greatly increased demand for higher education on an academic level below that which the University requires for a degree, and with a content more "general", cultural or vocational than that of established University courses, is one which might well be receiving more attention in England. Are we sure, for instance, that what we need most is more Universities producing more graduates with specialised honours degrees in History, Modern Languages or Economics? Or do we need some sort of new institution more like the American Liberal Arts College? And if we resist the pressure to establish University degree courses in Creative Writing or Home Economics, as I, for one, think we should, what provision should we be making for the perfectly legitimate demand that courses of this kind leading to some qualification should be widely available in some full time Institution of higher education? Already the parents of the present generation of American children expect that two-thirds of them will "go to College". What American parents expect for their children and what an affluent society can afford is likely to be the pattern of the future. England is already a singularly backward nation in the proportion of its population receiving higher education. If the next twenty-five years are going to see a "College education" accepted as the birth-right of every citizen who chooses to avail himself of it (and we should remember how visionary "secondary education for all" appeared twenty-five years ago), then some hard thinking needs to be done to-day and some rapid expansion tomorrow.

CHAPTER TEN

THE SUPPLY AND TRAINING OF TEACHERS

THE most important problem in education throughout the last hundred years has been the provision of enough good teachers. No educational research, no building regulations, no system of grants or compulsory attendance, no supervision of curricula can hope to be effective unless there are enough good teachers in the schools.

The expansion first of primary and then of secondary education has faced society with a continuing problem of supply which is as acute to-day as it was a hundred years ago. In 1850 the *Pittsburgh Saturday Visitor* was writing: "If the Legislature does not take some steps to supply the Common Schools with teachers. it had better abolish the system altogether." Between 1950 and 1960 the U.S. Bureau of Labour Statistics estimated that it was necessary to recruit and train nearly a million new teachers. And in Great Britain also it has been the shortage of teachers and of training capacity that has governed the rate of progress.

It is not merely the problem of securing *enough* teachers that has presented the difficulty. Unless the quality of teachers is at least adequate to the work required of them, the schools will do as much harm as good. Every step forward in the expansion of primary, secondary and finally of higher education has demanded an increased proportion of teachers of high intellectual capacity, as well as teaching ability, so that with the new developments in education a new problem in the supply of teachers has constantly arisen.

This problem has always had two sides. It has been necessary, on the one hand, to provide adequate training for those who wished to teach, and, on the other hand, to attract enough suitable men and women into the profession. The importance of training has been recognised by almost all educationists. Professor Kandel, for instance, writes in his *History of Secondary Education*:

221

"Fundamentally, however, the success of secondary education as of any other education, does not depend either on definitions of aims, statements of objectives, or discussions of subject values, but on the academic and professional preparation of the teachers."

The importance of supply is a consideration rather for statesmen. It is useless for the educational system to maintain the most admirable training institutions, if the general social and economic structure is such that few, if any, suitable candidates present themselves for training. Supply is therefore the first consideration and training the second.

Supply of Primary Teachers in the Nineteenth Century

(a) *Monitors and Pupil Teachers.*—The greatest educational revolution of the nineteenth century was the spread of free and universal primary education, and the teaching problem lay, therefore, in the supply of an adequate number of qualified teachers for primary schools. We have seen in Chaper One how hopelessly incompetent to teach was the typical dame who kept a Dame School, and the founders either of voluntary or State primary systems had therefore to find a new supply of teachers, and, at the same time, to improve the quality.

The first temporary expedient to meet the actual shortage was "mutual instruction" on the system of Bell and Lancaster, and this had a brief vogue in the first half of the century in England, France [1] and America.

By the middle of the century mutual instruction had been almost entirely abandoned [2] in favour either of licensing teachers, sometimes after training them in State "normal schools", or of the employment of pupil-teachers. Of these two methods, licensing had been adopted by the centralised states, France and Prussia, and pupil-teachers by England and Holland. The pupil-teacher system has ultimately been superseded by training and licensing throughout the western world, and it will be convenient, therefore, to describe it first before going on to the general history of the more widespread system.

Pupil teachers were a Dutch invention. Instead of using the older boys in any school as monitors, to eke out the shortage of

---

[1] See Chapter Four. It is even claimed by Compayré as a French, not an English, invention.
[2] A few monitorial schools still existed in England in 1858.

teachers, the Dutch allowed a number of the most promising pupils in the primary schools to stay on, acting under the headmaster exactly like an apprentice in a trade. In this way they not only helped the master in the conduct of the school, but learnt the art of teaching themselves. The first normal school for training teachers had already been opened in Holland by 1816 and it was not intended that service as a pupil teacher should be the only way into the profession. Moreover, Holland, had developed the first really adequate corps of inspectors, who saw that the pupil teacher was really trained.

The same idea had apparently occurred to Kay Shuttleworth in England from his own observation in charity schools, though it was probably strengthened by a visit to the Dutch schools, which had a very high European reputation in the early part of the century. In 1846 he secured the approval of the Committee of Council for a general scheme of training and using pupil teachers, which remained in force with some modification until the end of the century, and which was once described by Matthew Arnold as "the sinews of English Public Instruction".[1]

At first, boys and girls entered this apprenticeship at the age of thirteen and served five years. For five and a half hours each day they were engaged in helping the master to run the school, and for one and a half hours each day the master was expected to teach them. At the age of eighteen they competed for "Queen's Scholarships" at a teachers' training college—the first of which Kay Shuttleworth had set up at Battersea in 1840. It must be emphasised that although teachers who had taken this form of training received special proficiency grants from the government, there was absolutely nothing to compel teachers to take any sort of training at all. This extreme freedom persisted a long time in England and America, and is still technically true in independent schools, though in fact completely unqualified teachers are very rare. It shocked the more rational Europeans. "It is only in England and America that individual liberty has been pushed to the point of charlatanism," said Langlois at the beginning of the twentieth century, "so that anybody at all is free to teach anything at all."

The pupil-teacher system had one great advantage, which it shares with all forms of apprenticeship, that the intending teacher

---

[1] *Report on the State of Education in France.*

was able to find out by practice whether the profession suited him. It was also surely of great value that the entrants to the training colleges had already a considerable experience of teaching and of school life. The objections to the system were that the pupils had no experience of any but elementary schools, that they entered it too young, and that too much depended on the skill and conscientiousness of the headmaster to whom they were bound apprentice. Moreover, any defects in the established system tended to be reproduced in the training of the pupil-teachers. Nevertheless in spite of a considerable setback in 1862, when the Revised Code narrowed their syllabus and rigidly restricted their grants, pupil-teachers supplied the most important source of trained teachers in England during the latter half of the century-- and also a considerable help to the overworked masters during the period of their apprenticeship. When the School Boards were set up in 1870 some of them tried to improve the standard of teaching received by the pupil-teachers by setting up pupil-teacher "centres" at which a number of pupil-teachers from different schools could receive their further education in classes.[1] In 1884 the Cross Commission tackled both problems by recommending that the starting age of pupil-teachers should be raised to fifteen and then sixteen, and that the pupil-teacher centres should "approximate to secondary schools". That was of course the real point. The further education which the pupil-teacher received either from his master or in a centre ought to have been normal secondary education, and as soon as it became possible for the intending primary teacher to attend a secondary school before going to the training college, the pupil-teacher system withered away. It still existed in rural areas into the 1920's, but by then the vast majority of intending teachers were going to the secondary school and the training college.

(b) *Training and Certification.*—Those countries which pursued the other course of training and certification were met from the first by an almost insoluble problem. The low esteem in which teachers were held was not confined to the dames of British and French Dame Schools. It was not a recent development. And it had a perfectly clear economic cause.

A sixteenth-century writer in England, for instance, says: "For if they hire a Schoolmaster to teach in their houses they

---

[1] Something of this kind had long been the practice in Holland.

chiefly enquire with how small salary he will be contented, and never do inserche how much good lernyng he hath." [1] This opinion of the value of schoolmasters spread to the New World, and a seventeenth-century Rector of Annapolis recorded that, on the arrival of every ship containing either bondservants or convicts, schoolmasters were regularly offered for sale, along with weavers, tailors and other tradesmen. He noted little difference except "that the schoolmasters do not usually fetch so good a price as the others". Society gets out of the labour market roughly what it wants and what it pays for, and by the beginning of the nineteenth century the opinion was almost universal, in Europe and America, that schoolmasters were the dregs of the population. "Many elementary schoolmasters in Prussia", said a witness before the English Commission of 1834, "come from the ranks of non-commissioned officers, organists and half-drunken people." "The teacher was often regarded in the community on the same footing as a mendicant", writes M. Lorain [2] "and between the herdsman and himself the preference was for the herdsman." In America the teacher often actually was a mendicant of a special type, and would accept, instead of fees, a few days' board and lodging from each of his pupils' parents. The following is an extract from the diary of one such peripatetic: "Weighed and found I had lost six pounds in the last week; grew alarmed; had a talk with Mr. B—— and concluded I had boarded out his share." [3]

Along with the recognition of this situation went a conviction on the part of the educational reformers that it was totally irrational. It was preposterous, they said, to put the care of our children into the hands of men we would not trust with a threepenny piece, it was ridiculous that teaching should be the one activity in which no skill and no qualifications should be demanded, etc.

The cure, as the reformers in the authoritarian States of France and Prussia saw it, was that no one should be permitted to teach unless he could prove that he was morally and intellectually a fit person. Here they were met by a difficulty which has plagued education ever since. To raise the status of a whole profession, by increasing the qualifications for entry and the length of training,

---

[1] Elyot: *The Governour.*
[2] *Primary Instruction in France*, 1837.
[3] Quoted in J. D. Russell and C. H. Judd: *The American Educational System.*

leads, in the normal course of economics, to higher rates of pay for the trained and qualified practitioners. The general public, however, particularly among the poorer classes, for whom extended primary education was now being planned, and the middle class, who would be expected to pay for it out of rates or taxes, did not regard the teacher's function as being nearly so skilled or important as did the educationists. As long as the free market persisted, they had paid primary teachers, and regarded primary teachers, as being on a level with domestic servants. They did this because, at heart, they considered their main function to be that of keeping the children out of the way during the day, and teaching them no more than their parents would have done if they had not been occupied on more important business. It was a job like housework, which anyone could do who was fit for nothing else. Crabbe, in *The Borough*, describes the Dame School children as:

> "Infants of humble, busy wives, who pay
> Some trifling price for freedom through the day."

That was indeed all they paid for, and all they were prepared to pay for.

Guizot, one of the most shrewd and practical of educational reformers, knew this well. His circular of 1833, one of the crucial documents for French primary education, makes this clear. "However, as I well know," he writes, "the foresight of the law and the resources at the disposal of public authority will never succeed in rendering the humble profession of village teacher as attractive as it is useful. Society could not reward him who devotes himself to this service for all that he does for it. . . . It is necessary that a profound sense of the moral importance of his work sustain and animate him."

This attitude towards the payment of teachers was common throughout the nineteenth century. It has some degree of general justification, for there are a number of people to whom teaching, like any art, is a pleasant job, and it is reasonable that between equally skilled trades the pleasant should be less highly paid than the unpleasant; it had also a degree of truth, high at first but gradually declining, in a partly illiterate age, for to become a teacher was for a long time one of the few ways in which a poor man could aspire to educate himself; but it was recognised by the McNair Report (1944) that it is not, and never could be, a sufficient incentive to recruit the vast army of teachers required for universal primary and secondary education.

The nineteenth-century governments were committed, however, to raising the standard and qualifications of teachers without appreciably raising their pay. They were able to do so only at the cost of creating a discontented, radical and almost revolutionary class; and only because virtually no other form of independent livelihood was open to women. It must be remembered that at this time primary and secondary education were quite separate, and that it is of primary education only that we are speaking.

The most complete and logical system in Europe was the French, introduced by Guizot in 1834. Under this, the teacher had to produce a certificate of his ability to teach, and of his moral character; in order to train teachers for the first of these, normal schools were set up, and there were already seventy lay normal schools by 1856, to say nothing of those operated by the religious communities. These normal schools, of course, accepted only pupils from primary schools and trained them only to teach in primary schools. Once appointed, the teacher got a house and a minimum salary of £8 a year, which he was free to augment by fees, or as he often did, by taking on such clerical jobs as town clerk. In Holland, where we have already noticed the pupil-teacher system as well as normal schools, a certification similar to the French was introduced. In Prussia certification was demanded, and controlled by the Church, but special training facilities were less.

Even in a frugal country like France it was soon clear that the pay of the teacher was much too low, and a proposal was put forward in 1847 to introduce three grades, paid £24-£36-£48, with a special Paris allowance bringing it up to £60 a year in the capital. This proposal was overtaken by the revolution of 1848, when the school teachers were strongly suspected of revolutionary tendencies—perhaps because the revolutionaries had proposed doubling the government's contribution to their pay. In Prussia, also, after 1848 the school teachers were reproached for an equal ingratitude to the government which had called them into existence. These are the words of Frederick William IV, addressing teachers from the training colleges in Berlin, early in 1849: "All the misery which in the past year has overwhelmed

Prussia is your fault and only yours, the fault of the specious culture and irreligious mass-learning which you disseminate as wisdom, and with which you have destroyed faith and loyalty in the minds of my subjects and turned their hearts from me."

The years following 1848 saw little improvement in the teacher's lot. In France, instead of the rise in pay, a regulation was introduced that where the combined proceeds of the teacher's £8 a year and the fees did not come to a total of £24 a year, the government would make it up to that sum. Even this put such a strain on the public finances that a system grew up by which every teacher had to serve for three years as an "adjoint", or assistant, before he finally qualified as a teacher—and adjoints were paid at a lower rate.[1]

In England and America, rates, if not quite so low as in Europe, were still well below what a qualified or enterprising man could earn in most other trades, and the whole system could never have been maintained if it had not been for pupil-teachers in England and the economic subservience of women. Moseley, H.M.I., estimated in 1844 that the average annual salary of male teachers in England was £51, 12s. 4d. and of females £26, 5s. 1d. Mrs Hale, one of the pioneers of women's education in America, puts the position very clearly, though her intention is rather to commend the economy of employing women teachers than to deplore their low pay: "To find 20,000 young men who would enter the office of pedagogue would be utterly impossible, while the great West, the mines of California, and the open ocean laving China and the East are inviting them to adventure and activity" (1852). The manpower problem in America was, of course, worse than anywhere else, and the proportion of male teachers in American schools dropped heavily as soon as any form of secondary education or teacher training for women had been introduced. The total proportion of women teachers in America, which was 57·2 per cent. in 1880, had risen to 70·1 per cent. in 1900 and reached its peak of 85·9 per cent. of all teachers employed in primary and secondary schools in 1920. The social implications of this must have been considerable and have been discussed by many American sociologists.

---

[1] Of course these are minimum rates and the best schools paid a good deal better. Other minima at this time were £25 a year in Switzerland, and £34 in Holland and Belgium.

Women teachers were cheap compared to men, and the short-age of other outlets for their talents certainly meant that society secured, well into the twentieth century, a considerable number of primary teachers whose devotion and qualifications were far higher than those of the men—and higher than society was paying for. Moreover, in primary schools women are often more suitable than men, even as teachers of small boys. They have, however, one great drawback—they tend to get married and, on marriage, abandon teaching. In the nineteenth century this was even more true than it is now. It was almost unheard of, and in many areas forbidden, for a married woman to continue as a schoolmistress.[1] This meant, of course, a very serious wastage of talent and experience in the teaching profession. It has been said, and it is probably not far from the truth, that a young teacher is a liability to his employers for the first two years of his teaching life, at his best for the next ten, competent for twenty after that, and then a liability again. The trouble with young women teachers, particularly in America, was that they tended to abandon the profession for marriage within the first three years of their teaching life. As late as 1914 the average length of service of all American teachers was four years, and by 1941 it was only nine years. Quite apart from the waste of time in training teachers for so short a period of usefulness, it inevitably meant that in the least popular schools, i.e. the rural schools where pay rates were lowest, the replacement rate was far too high. Even to-day in some American rural schools it is as high as 50 per cent. —and no children can hope to get the best out of their school life if half the teachers are new every year.

It was because the countries of Western Europe had shrunk from the financial cost of paying teachers a salary high enough to attract the kind of men they wanted from the open market, that they fell back on various enticing devices and on certification. In France, for instance, those who accepted a ten years' teaching engagement with one of the teaching brotherhoods were excused military service, and in Prussia the military service was shortened. In most countries one of the few ways for a poor boy from a state primary school to get any further education was to sign a contract to become a teacher.

[1] The ban on married women was finally removed by statute in England in the 1944 Act.

The moral certificates were, perhaps, the least realistic educational device in history. In the French system they had at least to be signed by someone else—a mayor or a minister of religion—but in many areas of America they took the form of declarations signed by the teacher herself. Neither, of course, could have been of any value unless there had been substantially more applicants than posts in teaching.[1] Edgar Knight quotes one, used as late as the twentieth century in one district of the U.S.A., which is so magnificent in its disregard of reality that it will serve, even as a caricature, to illustrate the futility of the whole system. The declaration which had to be signed by every teacher read as follows:

"I promise to take a vital interest in all phases of Sunday School work, donating of my time, service and money without stint for the uplift and benefit of the community. I promise to abstain from all dancing, immodest dressing and any other conduct unbecoming a teacher and a lady. I promise not to go out with any young men except in so far as it may be necessary to stimulate Sunday School work. I promise not to fall in love, to become engaged or secretly married. I promise to remain in the Dormitory or on the school grounds when not actively engaged in school or Church work elsewhere. I promise not to encourage or tolerate the least familiarity on the part of any of my boy pupils. I promise to sleep at least eight hours a night, to eat carefully and to take every precaution to keep in the best of health and spirits that I may be better able to render efficient service to my pupils."

The thought of one of those poor girls, after going out with a young man (purely in order to stimulate Sunday School work of course) trying to keep simultaneously her promise not to fall in love and her promise to sleep eight hours a night, is the best commentary on the whole system of moral certificates and declarations. Where they were not a device for political supervision, they were simply a face-saving clause for the authorities. Unable to pay enough to be able to reject candidates who were unsuitable, they safeguarded themselves by making the teachers produce certificates which both sides knew to be a farce.

[1] In the same way "probationary years" are not really of much practical value if there is a general shortage of teachers. The average headmaster under whom a young man is doing his probation will, in any case, be very loath to give judgment against him, and even if he does the State will know that it is very unlikely to get anyone better.

The only effective move was the establishment of normal schools (or training colleges). Primarily, of course, these were intended, not to increase the supply of teachers, but to render more valuable by training those who were already prepared to teach. As long as secondary education was strictly limited, however, they did also attract people into the teaching profession, though there was always the problem of the student who, at the end of her training or after her first year or two as a teacher, broke her engagement, like Sue Bridehead, and went off to better herself in some other employment.

Publicly controlled normal schools for the training of elementary teachers were set up in most western countries in the first half of the nineteenth century. France, Holland, Norway, Prussia, Switzerland and Scandinavia all had such normal schools before 1835; we have already seen that the first semi-official one in England dates from 1840, and this had been preceded in 1838 by the first in America. Private and philanthropic institutions for training intending teachers had, of course, existed at earlier times in all these countries, but these publicly provided or sponsored normal schools were the real beginning of a general training system for the new teachers demanded by mass primary education.

In general, the European system in the nineteenth century was to confine the training of the elementary teacher to purely elementary work, with the addition of a growing proportion of pedagogics or educational theory. The more authoritarian the country, the more strictly the elementary teacher was confined to the subjects he was going to teach, and the level at which he would teach them. The tradition that pupils of the state primary schools did not, as a rule, proceed to secondary education, and were destined for "the lower walks of life", meant that no high degree of culture was demanded from their teachers. If a man understood simple grammar and arithmetic and could make the children learn it, he was doing all society required of him; indeed, in many countries such as Prussia, the fear of the dissatisfied and revolutionary primary school teacher was such that they were definitely discouraged from pursuing their own education beyond the elementary stage. This limitation was general throughout Europe. Matthew Arnold found in France under the second Empire, for instance, that none of the teachers in the primary normal school could manage quadratic equations. The French system continued throughout the century to take promising youths from the elementary school, give them two years of sound training in elementary subjects with a year of pedagogics and then send them back to teach in the elementary school again.

In England there was a greater variety, as might have been expected, and in some cases a greater liberality, particularly where colleges were provided by the Church. In the hurry to produce teachers with *some* knowledge of the subjects they would teach, a number of the earliest training schools offered very short, very intensive courses of only a few months. Others provided three-year courses much more nearly of secondary standard. These latter, however, were seriously limited by the regulations introduced in the Revised Code of 1862 which brought English education for a few years much nearer to continental practice, and in particular limited the curriculum of primary teachers in training to the primary subjects. In general pedagogics were not as popular in England as on the Continent, though there was a good deal of "rule of thumb" teaching technique.

In America the private "academies" had long specialised in teacher training. From 1838 publicly provided normal schools began to be common and had been established by most New England states by the middle of the century. These normal schools like those of Europe, suffered from a restriction of their academic curriculum to purely elementary studies, but they carried "professional" training further than it was usually taken in Europe and in them begins the typically American devotion to the science of education. By the end of the century more and more teacher training was beginning to be done in the high schools, which for that purpose maintained courses in methods of teaching, school law, psychology, etc. From this developed the practice of intending primary teachers graduating first from high school (this became compulsory in New York in 1890 and Massachusetts in 1894) and then taking a two-year teachers' course; and finally there grew up the present system of graduation at liberal arts colleges or at the teachers' colleges which form part of the great universities.

In this respect, as in many others, American practice anticipated that of Europe, and England stood more or less half-way between America and the continent.

Supply and Training of Secondary Teachers in the Nineteenth Century

The supply and training of secondary teachers involved no similar problems until nearly the end of the century. As long as secondary education was effectively the privilege of a wealthy class, those who wanted it were prepared to pay the teachers an economic rate and there was therefore no serious shortage. Matthew Arnold, writing in 1864, quotes £800 a year[1] as the salary of an under-master in an English public school. Nor was England alone in this respect. An able professor in a Paris *lycée* might get as much as £400 a year, ten times the salary of a primary headmaster, and was in many ways better off than his English counterpart. The French system of concentrating the big *lycées*, even those with boarding departments, in the big cities and of delegating all "discipline" to the *répétiteurs* meant that a man of real scholarship was often found lecturing four or five hours a day at a *lycée* and combining it with a life of literary and academic research. The English assistant master in a public school, usually exiled to a community in the depths of the country, more often combined his teaching with keeping a lucrative boys' boarding-house, though even in England scholars of international repute have always been found among the staffs of the public schools. In Prussia the top salary for a *Gymnasium* headmaster was £300 and the bottom for an assistant £75 per annum, but Arnold found these not too low in a "frugal society" and compensated for by the high respect which secondary school teachers enjoyed in the community. In any case even they were well over double the salary of a primary teacher. One of the greatest changes in the economic structure of the teaching profession in the last hundred years has been the very large decrease in the differential between secondary and primary teachers and the definite decline in the position of the secondary teacher relative to the rest of society.

In most of the western countries during the nineteenth century secondary teachers were expected to hold a university degree, and no provision for training other than that given by the university was made. The one great exception to this rule was in France where the École Normale Supèrieure, though

---

[1] This sounds very high; but at Shrewsbury, where salaries were not very high, the "under-master" was getting £562 a year and the French master £340 in 1862.

originally established by Napoleon I as part of the University of France, enjoyed a more or less independent life throughout the nineteenth century. The École Normale Supèrieure had a high reputation throughout Europe, not only as the only institution specially designed for the training of secondary teachers, but also for the high standard of its scholarship. In the first part of the century its curriculum was also remarkably wide, wider than that of most universities. From 1830 onwards it was possible to study for the aggregation, or licence to teach, in letters, philosophy, grammar, history, mathematics, physics or natural sciences. To these, German was added in 1841 and English in 1846. In addition to this wide curriculum, teaching practice (six weeks at a *lycée*) was introduced in 1839.

The École Normale was however, like all other educational institutions, suspect to the authoritarian government of Napoleon III and the curriculum was considerably curtailed after 1850. It should be noticed that neither in the old nor in the curtailed curriculum was the theory of education included. The purpose of the École Normale was still overwhelmingly concentrated on teaching the subjects which the intending professor would have to deal with, not on teaching him to teach.

The proposal that secondary teachers should be *trained* as opposed to *educated* was not heard until the spread of state-aided secondary education in the last quarter of the century. It was met by very strong opposition from the established secondary schools and universities throughout Europe. In England those who regarded it as unnecessary were nicknamed the "grace of God" school, because they were held to believe that certain men were born secondary schoolmasters "by the grace of God" and needed no teaching. They included, however, the great majority of those who controlled the public schools. A similar scepticism about the value of training for secondary teachers seems to have existed in France, where M. Coulanges, the Director of the École Normale from 1880 to 1883, stated roundly that it was useless to learn to teach, opposed the introduction of pedagogics and had actually reduced the teaching practice to a purely nominal two weeks—with the result that the École merely duplicated the work of the university colleges such as the Sorbonne.[1]

[1] In 1901, for instance, university students actually won 39 out of the 80 aggregations for *lycée* teachers, while students from the École Normale only won 22.

In Germany secondary teachers had, since 1810, been required to do two years probationary teaching after their university degree, and to submit, before final acceptance as a teacher, to a test not only of their competence in their subject, but also of their ability to teach; but even this system, considered at the time extremely rigorous, was clearly based upon a view of secondary teaching as an art to be acquired empirically and not a science to be learnt in a training school. The final test was a practical demonstration of the teacher's ability with his class, not a written examination in educational theory or history.

Twentieth-Century Developments

. The chief developments in the first half of the twentieth century have been the improvement in the status and training of the primary teacher, the gradual lessening of the dependence on women, the movement towards a unified teaching profession and the problem of staffing secondary education for all.

(a) *The Status of Primary Teachers in America.*—The primary teachers in Europe had still two main causes of complaint in the early years of the twentieth century: they were ill-paid and they were still bound to a purely primary environment. On the other hand, the establishment of universal primary education meant that their power in the State, if once they acted as a united body, was very great. Every State needed a vast body of primary teachers, and no State could afford, in view of their influence in the schools, to antagonise the whole body. Moreover, the gradual opening of other professions to women, and the levelling-up of salaries to something approaching equality, deprived the employing authority, state or locality of one of its economic weapons against the teachers' organisations.

The degree to which the primary teachers have been able to secure their aims has depended chiefly on the political organisation of the different countries. In the United States, with its vast number of different employing authorities and its traditional belief in private bargaining, it has been very difficult to achieve conditions of service as fair and secure as soon prevailed in Europe. It was not merely that salaries were low—which has remained true in all countries. One of the first objectives at which the European teachers aimed was security—security of tenure, security of salary and some sort of pension scheme. By the end of the First

World War they had secured a position in which a teacher was free from the threat of arbitrary dismissal, was assured of a salary graded on an accepted scale, and could look forward with confidence to a pension at the end of his service. None of these things was achieved nearly so easily in America. The traditional method of employment was by annual engagement, which meant that any teacher might find at the end of the year that he was either not re-engaged or offered a quite different and lower salary. Since there was no general Ministry of Education it was very difficult to bring the individual employing agencies to abandon this system, and by 1941 only 40 per cent. of the cities included in a nation-wide survey offered their teachers security of tenure on the European model. A further 13 per cent. used the "continuing contract", but the legal force of this was only that due notice of termination had to be given. In the remaining 47 per cent. of the cities a teacher could still awake on the annual engagement day to find that he was simply not being re-employed.[1] Pensions also varied very widely from one authority to another, although by the end of the Second World War virtually all teachers benefited by some sort of pension scheme.

Salaries, too, varied very much more than in Europe, both from district to district and from year to year. They were particularly hard hit by the slump of 1932—far harder, for instance, than the officially "cut" salaries of English teachers. The position is well summed up by Russell and Judd (*op. cit.*), from whom most of this information is derived: "Salaries of teachers are, in general, lower than those of other groups of workers with comparable preparation. There is no deliberate limitation of the supply of beginning teachers, and with a relatively large supply, particularly in times of economic depression, the basic salary tends to approach the minimum subsistence level." Without the intervention either of a well-organised trade union or of the State, it is clear that this primitive "iron law of wages" will in fact operate in its pure form. W. F. Russell (*Comparative Education*, 1918) calculated that a carpenter in the U.S.A. received an annual salary of $805, a labourer $513 and the average primary school teacher $485.

---

[1] This was not just a theoretical possibility. Edgar Knight records that in one city using this system seventy-six teachers and principals were dismissed without notice or reasons within a month.

On the other hand, the American belief in education and the rapid expansion of secondary schools meant that the primary teachers achieved their second objective, freedom from the purely primary environment, much more quickly. We have seen that by the end of the nineteenth century an increasing number of primary teachers had been coming from the new high schools. As high school education became more and more widespread, the teachers' colleges and liberal arts colleges (nearly half of whose graduates went into teaching) came to draw exclusively on high schools; and this was already common at the beginning of the twentieth century, when German primary teachers were still debarred from a secondary education. Finally, in the last few years there has been an increasing tendency for prospective primary teachers to train at the university education departments on a level of complete equality with those who will later be teaching in secondary schools.

(b) *The Status of Primary Teachers in Europe.*—In Europe salary rates remained low. The average for a man in England was £129 per annum and for a woman £96 in 1914 (a rate which the McNair Report (1944) describes as disgraceful exploitation), but the material conditions of service improved after the First World War, largely as a result of the activity of teachers' organisations and the co-ordination of employing agencies. In Prussia the primary teachers achieved a relatively secure economic position by 1909, but all over Europe there was still much reliance on that teacher's "sense of vocation" which Guizot had maintained should supplement his salary. On the whole, however, the teachers soon recognised that they were getting roughly as much out of the national budget as the nation was prepared to pay. Such economic grievances as were expressed followed one or other of two lines. The first was that women were being paid at an unequal rate for an equal job; and this is neither a purely educational issue nor one which can be briefly discussed. The second was that the importance of the teacher and the technical skill required for the art of teaching were so great that the scales of salary were ludicrously low. This view was supported by much educational writing, but came into strong conflict with the widely, if unconsciously, held view of the teacher as economically on the level of a superior domestic servant. There is an almost ludicrous contrast, for instance, between society's estimate of the average primary teacher, expressed both in status and pay, and this description, by Thomas Dewey, of his functions: "He must survey the capacities and needs of the particular set of individuals with whom he is dealing and must at the same time arrange the conditions which provide the subject-matter or content for experiences that satisfy those needs and develop those capacities. The planning must be flexible enough to permit free play for individuality of experience, and yet firm enough to give direction towards continuous development of power. . . . The educator more than the member of any other profession is concerned to have a long look ahead." It is almost as unrealistic to suppose that society can expect to attract such men in large numbers into a profession paid on the scale of the refuse collector, as it is to suppose that society will so far change its view as to pay all teachers on the level of the doctor or dentist.

The general, even if unenthusiastic, satisfaction with the improved rates of pay and conditions of service meant that there was no permanent shortage of primary teachers in Europe. Such shortages as occurred were due either to temporary dissatisfaction or to political causes such as the introduction of the Nazi regime in Germany or the great wars. But while there have been enough teachers to staff the schools as they stood, there have never been enough to effect a reduction in the size of classes.

The European teachers, on the other hand, have been less successful than the American in securing a unified profession with "parity" of training and status for primary and secondary teachers. The maximum demand of those who sought this as an ideal was that all teachers should receive at least a secondary education, and that the training of primary teachers beyond the secondary phase should be a university course. As in other aspects, progress along "progressive" lines has been least in France, where the training of primary teachers is still a function of the primary normal schools, drawing their students direct from higher primary education at the age of fifteen to sixteen. In Germany the Weimar Republic was, as usual, full of progressive intentions, and the new constitution laid it down that the training of teachers was to be "regulated uniformly throughout the Reich in accordance with the principles valid for higher education". In all the states except Bavaria and Wurttemberg this was honoured by the establishment of systems which ensured the primary teacher a secondary education, but it was only in the most advanced states, Saxony and Brunswick, that their final training took place at the university. The wider and more cultured training given to primary school teachers was naturally somewhat unpopular with the Nazis, and this, combined with a prospective shortage of primary teachers, led them to revert, from 1939 onwards, to the previous system of training primary teachers separately—and, of course, teaching them largely to be good party members. This retrograde step is being reversed by the new government.

In England, as usual, there was great elasticity, but from 1902 onwards it became more and more the normal thing for a primary teacher to have at least a secondary education, and by 1938 four-fifths of all primary teachers had also received two years training at a training college. Although the battle for secondary education and proper training had been won, only very few (nine per cent.) of primary teachers were university graduates; the remainder received their training at colleges established either by the Churches or, after 1904, by local education authorities. Until 1926 the Board of Education was responsible for the examination of candidates from these colleges, but in that year a reform was introduced with the intention of creating some definite link between all training colleges and the universities. The colleges were arranged in regional groups, each centring round a university, and the examination entrusted to Joint Boards on which the university and the colleges were represented. This was clearly a step, if rather a "paper" one, towards university training for primary teachers, and in 1944 the McNair Committee urged the Universities to set up Institutes of Education, responsible for the examinations and also for bringing the curricula of the Training Colleges and provision of further education and training of teachers in service within the purview of the University. Such Institutes are now established in all but one of the Universities.

In the matter of status the English primary teachers secured the essence of the progressive demand in 1945, when the first Burnham Committee on salaries, after the passing of the 1944 Education Act, followed the recommendation of the McNair Committee, and introduced a single basic salary scale for all teachers, with small extra allowances for the additional academic qualifications of the secondary school teacher. The effect of this on the status of the secondary teacher is discussed later.

(c) *The Training and Supply of Secondary Teachers.*—The lack of enthusiasm for training among secondary schoolmasters, and to a lesser extent schoolmistresses, continued well into the inter-war period, and was due chiefly to two causes. In the first place, this well-paid and limited branch of the profession had, up to date, been able to attract a very high quality of teacher in each country. Among such men the "grace of God" theory was very largely valid. The best teachers *are* undoubtedly born, not trained, and, what is more, few of them teach alike. Grundtvig's methods, for instance, could easily have been condemned by a superficial expert as mere "chalk and talk" without the chalk. In a branch of the profession which had so far drawn very largely on such men, the potential value of training, not to the born teacher but to the man who would by nature be no more than mediocre, was not so obvious. In England this feeling was reinforced by the fact that training for graduates was, and still remains, voluntary. This anomalous situation has meant that in England and Wales, alone among fully industrialised countries, the initial position has been preserved, in which the heads of schools and senior teachers may not themselves have been trained and are therefore sceptical of the value of training for the young graduate. It is difficult for a man in a senior position, who may in fact have become a first-class teacher through a process of trial and error, to be convinced of the value to his junior staff of a professional qualification which he himself has not got.

Secondly, the University Departments of Education which undertook the training of Graduates for secondary school teaching, were at first very unsure of themselves. The training of primary teachers had consisted partly of teaching them the subject, history or mathematics, which they in turn proposed to teach; partly in training them, vocationally, as teachers, just as a painter, actor or engineer is trained; and partly in giving them a liberal education. The new graduates already knew their subjects and were supposed to have had a liberal education already. The primary teacher's training had been "concurrent" with his academic education: the secondary teacher's was to be superimposed. It is not surprising that, faced with a completely new form of training and a climate of opinion which was more than a little sceptical of its value, the University Departments were at first in considerable confusion about the nature and purpose of their courses. The result was a good deal of evasion or lip-service. In Germany until the last war the training of secondary teachers consisted, in fact, of little more than the passing on of tried methods by each generation of older teachers to their juniors during their probation years. Educational theory was honoured in theory, but not in practice. In France it was not even honoured in theory, to the extent of being admitted as part of the secondary schoolmaster's training, until 1924; and to this day it is considered of far less importance than distinction in his subject. Even in the U.S.A. Professor Kandel was lamenting as late as 1933 that "despite the extensive popularity of professional subjects in education, the situation found in European countries also prevails in the United States: widespread mistrust, if not contempt, among subject-matter specialists for theory of education and methods of instruction". [1]

A more detailed examination of the English experience may throw some light on how this situation arose. When, at the beginning of the twentieth century, along with the great expansion of secondary education, the university education departments first turned their attention to the training of secondary schoolmasters, they found, as has often happened in English education, that, though they were quite sure that what they were about to do was necessary and important, they were not at all sure how they were going to do it. This hesitation arose partly from a fundamental confusion about the purpose of the course, partly from examination difficulties which affect all University courses and partly from purely temporary causes. The fundamental confusion was between University education and vocational training. Many of those who most strongly urged the necessity of training, using the analogy of medicine and the law, clearly thought of it as primarily the acquisition of a body of practical skill and precedent—what Americans would now call the "know-how" of the profession. This was training and not education. The Universities on the other hand were committed to a far more academic tradition, and envisaged some part at least of the graduate's course in Education as being on the academic level at which the graduate had been accustomed to work. In this view they were supported by two factors. In the first place Education was already beginning to establish itself in many Universities as an academic discipline in its own right. It is true that there was much opposition on the

[1] *Studies in Comparative Education.*

grounds that its field of study was really made up of segments' taken from those already occupied by Philosophy, Psychology and History. But the trend towards mixed disciplines in the sociological field was already strong and it became increasingly difficult for Universities which had accepted as disciplines Economics, Government, Race Relations, Criminology or International Affairs to deny academic status to Education. If, then, advanced work of University level was being done in Education should not some part of this be included in the graduate's course of training? Secondly, the conception of a large body of teachers' "know-how" equivalent to the lawyer's case law or the physician's clinical experience is false. There are, of course, certain general tricks of the trade and certain techniques of teaching specific subjects, but in so far as these can be taught on a purely technical level, they could have been given to the graduate in a non-University course of a few weeks. Such courses might have done something to eliminate the more crass mistakes, but they would not have produced trained or better teachers. No two men teach, or should teach, exactly alike and the Universities were right in seeing that a trained teacher needed not merely to know but to understand his method.

With this in view they devised courses which included something of vocational training, with as much as one third of the year's work devoted to practical teaching under supervision in a school, and something also of the newly developing academic discipline of education. Unfortunately this new discipline was still in a very embryonic stage at this time and the necessity which most Universities found of setting a terminal examination at the end of the course produced at first some examples of unreality which only confirmed the worst suspicions of the opponents of training. It is surely reasonable that those who are ultimately going to be responsible for the administration of schools, either as Headmasters or as teachers in an increasingly self-governing profession, should at some time in their lives study the historical forces which have produced the often very complicated systems of education in which they work. It is less reasonable that they should be expected to answer, as they were thirty years ago, such examination questions as: "Estimate the importance of Roman catholicism on Girls' Schools in Central Wales in the Seventeenth Century." Such academicism was, of course, partly due to the temporary factor that Education was still so new as a discipline that the original work on which the student's course could best be based had not yet been done. But it does much to explain the scepticism of the practical teachers. The University course for secondary teachers is now stabilised as a combination of practical vocational training with no more than an introduction to the way in which Philosophy, Psychology, History and Sociology can illuminate not only the relationship between learner and teacher but the purpose and place of the School in the social structure. Such an understanding is surely necessary for every teacher who is going to do more than merely repeat what he was taught himself. It can, of course, be achieved by autodidactic methods and the English system still allows this, but in that case the raw material of the autodidact's trial and error is the pupils who pass through his hands in the first three years.

The confusion between professional training and University education seems also, if conversely, to have been responsible for the distrust amounting to bitterness between Faculties of Education and the rest of the University in America. To some extent this was probably due to the customary tendency of a new discipline to seek academic respectability by developing as quickly as possible its own "mystery", couched in what friends call a terminology and foes a jargon. There is, however, a continuing danger both of unreality and of distrust wherever the bulk of primary teachers receive their further education in the form of a University course leading to a degree in Education, which is claimed as equivalent to a degree in one of the specific academic disciplines. Unreality comes in because the main quality needed in a good teacher of children below the age of eleven is not that she should be a person of high academic ability. Nor could any country afford to staff its primary schools with such rare people. The faculty of education, however, will be tempted to meet the criticisms of other faculties by producing a course which superficially at least is of degree level. From this arises the distrust of other faculties for the whole business of "education", at least in the more traditional Universities, since a degree course which is adapted to the intellectual level of the average primary teacher appears to debase the academic level of degrees in general. To a lesser extent the same natural forces operate where the training of teachers for non-selective secondary schools culminates in a degree in Education.

In many western countries this question is bound up with the movement for a unified teaching profession. This is as much a social as an educational movement and it seems important to ensure that if it is successful it achieves success by levelling up and not by levelling down. It is, of course, very largely a matter of salaries. "Finally there are at last signs," wrote M. L. Jacks in 1950, "that the unification of the teaching profession may come about. New influences are at work, fostered partly by the equalisation of salary scales and conditions of service, and in part by the recognition that it is idle to demand "parity of status" among schools while there is "imparity of teachers". But whatever views one may have about parity or equality in status and salary for teachers of all types of children, it is mere humbug to pretend that the intellectual level of the average primary teacher is the same as that of the Sixth Form Master.

It is surely questionable too whether the whole concept of a unified teaching profession has not gone seriously astray. A unified profession is not necessarily one in which there are no significant differentials in pay or qualifications. Indeed, it might well be argued that such equalitarianism and neglect of the operations of the market would themselves make the unification of any profession impossible. A unified profession is surely one in which there is a common minimum qualification, leading to a common minimum salary; a common code of professional conduct; and a common concern for those elements of life with which the profession is concerned. Within such a profession it is perfectly natural that there should be differentials in pay and status and that the higher pay and status should be commanded by those who, in addition to the common qualifications, possess the rarer intellectual skills. One of the legitimate causes of dissatisfaction in the 1950's was the conviction of the able specialist secondary schoolmasters that the "unification of the profession" was proceeding by a process of levelling down and that the differential which his ability would command in any other sphere of life, was being whittled away.

As far as I see it, the truth about a unified profession is this. Any fully developed country will need to employ a very large proportion of its adult workers as teachers. Ideally all these will need to have certain personal qualities of sympathy, responsibility, intellectual honesty and moral conviction. It is above all important that the younger the children they are going to teach, the more genuine should be their love of children, and the more intellectually advanced the children they are going to teach the more genuine should be their love of learning. A nation will gladly accept as much of these qualities as it can get from all its teachers. As well as having these qualities a good teacher must understand children and must understand what he is teaching. Both are important, but the level at which the subject needs to be understood is much simpler when young children are being taught. These then are the requirements. Let us now look at the prospective teachers. Like entrants to all other mass professions they will vary considerably in intelligence: the average training college entrant would not have been capable of securing admission to a University; many girls training for primary work would find it equally hard to pass the academic examinations taken by abler students who are training for secondary work. Fortunately this does not matter. The less able intellectually can become admirable teachers of younger children provided they have the personal qualities outlined and that they have learnt to understand children. There is no reason of course why some of the intellectually ablest should not choose to teach the very young. Indeed there is every reason, from an experimental point of view, why they should. But since they are a limited asset in the profession and their place in the Sixth Form cannot be taken by the girl of limited ability, however devoted, no society could afford to use more than a limited number of them in this way. So far the structure of the profession looks just like that of any other. Good nursing may be as important to the patient's recovery as a skilfully conducted operation, but it is not so difficult and it does not therefore command equal pay or status. I suspect that the supposed difference is connected with "understanding children". The primary trained teacher deserves "parity" with the honours graduate because one understands children while the other understands mathematics. But this is not so. First, we have no reason to suppose that this is true. Understanding of children comes either through intuition and experience (which is a good reason for excusing married women from some of the academic requirements for qualification); or through the application of a knowledge of psychology academically acquired. In the latter process the abler student will outdistance the less able and the fact that the student who has trained for primary work has spent longer on child psychology does not mean that she has reached an intellectual level comparable to that of an Honours degree. *Both* should understand their pupils and society is only acting as it always acts when it accords higher pay and status to the fortunate possessor of rare and valuable skills.

CHAPTER ELEVEN

EXAMINATIONS

EXAMINATIONS have long played a very important part in education; but since one of their chief functions is to act as a link, both between different stages of education and between formal education itself and active employment, they belong to no particular chapter of this book and are best treated separately.

In considering their history it is important to remember that they have at least three different functions and that these three cannot be separated in practice, however much that might be desirable in theory. The first of these in point of time was certification: the certifying examination is a way of ensuring that a prospective priest, doctor or engineer is competent to discharge his duties. This was the purpose of the first examinations in history, the entrance examinations for the Chinese civil service, inaugurated at least fifteen hundred years ago; it is still the purpose of professional examinations, such as those of an engineer or doctor to-day.

An examination of this type cannot, however, avoid being also selective, on a competitive basis, and regulative; for, in the first place, the standard demanded must depend in practice, not on any abstract ideal, but on the prevailing standards of knowledge and the supply of adequately skilled candidates; and, secondly, competition for success in the examination must inevitably affect the course of training of those who intend to take it. Clearly, for instance, the same degree of medical knowledge would not, and should not, be required to qualify as a doctor in Central Borneo as in America: and if the Chinese civil service examinations demanded the memorisation of the Confucian classics, it was inevitable that ambitious young Chinese would spend years of their lives memorising them. These characteristics are inherent in the nature of examinations, in spite of occasional pious resolutions that examinations "must not dictate the

247

curriculum". They can only avoid doing that if nobody wants to pass them.

Such a situation is not entirely to be deplored; the secondary functions of examinations, those of regulating and inspiring, can be very valuable. Once it is recognised that the regulative effect of examinations is inevitable, the surest way of securing that a certain course of training or syllabus is followed in the schools is to frame the crucial examination in such a way that those who have pursued it will pass and those who have not will fail. But examinations will do more than that. Everyone who has ever learnt any skill or taught it to a child will recognise the added incentive which is gained by breaking up the task into manageable units, so that progress is obvious and measurable by periodic tests. Such tests are examinations, and nearly all good teachers use them.

Of the three functions of examinations—certification, regulation and incentive—it was the last that particularly attracted attention at the beginning of our period. In England, at least, men had before them the report of the Oxford University Commission of 1850 which stated that it was the introduction of properly conducted examinations which "first raised the studies of the university from their abject state". It seemed obvious that the next step was to introduce a similar reform in the secondary schools. It is so common nowadays to hear educators inveighing against examinations as a menace to true education, that the enthusiasm for them shown in the mid-nineteenth century seems to us very unfamiliar. To our greatgrandfathers the introduction of more and more rigorous examinations was one of the most promising of all purely educational reforms—quite apart from any value they might have for certification or testing.

Testing, which is the main consideration of modern educations when they speak of examinations, is a special form of certification in which the examiner is trying to find out, not what the candidate already knows, but what are his capabilities for learning. His purpose is not to select those most fitted by previous training or achievement for a certain type of employment or even course of study, but to decide what kind of education will be most suitable to each child. Thus the tester might well select a certain child for technical education on adequate psychological grounds, although he had no previous technical experience at all, and could not be certified as capable of the simplest technical operation.

Secondary Leaving Examinations in the Nineteenth Century

We have seen in a preceding chapter that the close of the eighteenth century found the European universities in a state of unparalleled decadence. From that decadence all of them, not merely Oxford, were rescued very largely by the introduction of genuinely conducted examinations on the lines which persist to-day. It was not only that insistence on written papers and theses meant that a degree could only be gained after a real course of study, but the introduction of honours lists produced among the students a spirit of emulation and competition. From that time onwards the anxiety to get "a first" has undoubtedly been one of the great incentives to work, at the undergraduate levels, at least in the English universities. It may be a sad commentary on human nature, but it is a fact.

By the middle of the nineteenth century, then, the main public interest in the sphere of examinations lay in the extension of such a system to secondary schools. Except in England, under the Revised Code of 1862, examinations in primary schools were not an issue of any importance, until the "scholarship" system of entry to secondary schools developed at the end of the century.

The extension of secondary examinations was promoted by a belief in their value for two different purposes, certification and incentive. It was encouraged also by the high reputation of the German secondary schools, which, as we have seen, were taken as a model for both Europe and America at this time, and in which a regular leaving examination had already been established. The early experience of the German *Gymnasien* is a good example of the confusion which can be caused by the two purposes for which such examinations can be used. As early as 1788 a university entrance examination had been imposed, largely in order to prevent young men flocking to the universities as a way of avoiding military service, and though this fell into desuetude, it was revived and made obligatory in 1812. Co-ordination was poor at first, however, and examinations were held both by the schools and the universities: the universities, who were interested only in certification, tended to lower the standard if they were short of students, or if they wanted to admit students on other grounds; and the schools which were interested mainly in incentive, tended to raise the standard too high. As a result

Matthew Arnold records that of 139 students entering the University of Bonn in 1822, only one had passed the *Abitur* (leaving examination) as fully qualified and 122 held certificates declaring that they had failed to qualify for a university.

By the middle of the century state intervention had regularised the position of the *Abitur*, and the principles laid down in 1856 have remained valid to this day. In the first place, it was a state examination, held only at the school and conducted by the teachers of the school with the assistance of representatives of the Ministry of Education. Not only did the universities not control the examination, as they tended to in England, but they were not even represented on the examining body. This was in line with the prominent part played by the state in university examinations also, for it must be remembered that the majority of German university students were taking the state "finals", and not the university degree, at the end of their university career. Secondly, although intended to act as a certification examination for the universities also, it was clearly designed as an incentive examination for the schools; it was, much more than nineteenth-century English examinations, internal—that is to say, each school conducted its own examination; candidates were required to have passed at least two years in the sixth form, and a rubric was attached dealing with the candidate's "conduct, diligence and attainment". It was these latter requirements which enabled Matthew Arnold to say that the criterion was not the candidate's performance in the examination, but his whole school career.

In France and England it was not until the middle of the century that secondary school leaving examinations took definite form at all. The French *baccalauréat* had been revived by Napoleon I, but remained what it had been under the *ancien régime*—an oral "disputation" with no serious content. Its real importance dates from the introduction of written papers in 1852. The *baccalauréat* was, and remains, a completely external state examination open to anyone, whether attending a school or not, in which the same papers are taken by candidates all over the French world. The typically French uniformity with which it has been conducted led, in fact, to an ingenious fraud, when the time difference between Saigon and Paris enabled students who had left the hall in Saigon to telegraph advance information about the questions to Paris before the examination there had begun.

In England the year 1858 marks the beginning of the examination era. In this year the Universities of Oxford and Cambridge, in response to requests from local committees, agreed to organise local examining centres for what was called the "Examination of Students not members of the University". These were, therefore, originally extensions of the universities and the standard of the examination intended to be roughly the same as the *baccalauréat* or *Abitur*; indeed, the first criticism of them made by the Taunton Commissioners in the report of 1868 was that they were too difficult to test the work of the majority of the students. They were in origin completely external, and they did not qualify the successful candidate for entrance to the university, or indeed for anything. Their value therefore was entirely as an incentive, both to schools and pupils. The establishment in the same year, however, of a most important certifying examination, that for the Civil Service, undoubtedly helped to establish in the public mind the value of an examination record as a certificate of competence. The fact that these Oxford and Cambridge "Locals" were often held in school buildings and taken predominantly by pupils from the school led to a short-lived system of internal examinations, in which the university provided the papers and criticised the results for individual schools separately, often including in this an inspection of the school premises. Out of this there might have developed a system of internal examinations and "accredited" schools, such as grew up in America, but the function of inspection was taken over by the Board of Education and the prestige of the external examination ensured its general acceptance.

One certifying examination in England soon began to assume an importance out of all proportion to its original intentions. The University of London, by opening its degree examinations to students who were not, in any other sense, members of the University, had already provided England at that level with the most "external" of all possible forms of examination; for the colleges or institutes at which the students prepared for the examination had no say whatever in the setting or correcting of the papers. As employers and professional bodies began to feel the necessity of a certifying examination for those leaving secondary schools, they began to use more and more the matriculation examination of London University for this purpose, so that by the end of the century only a minority of those taking the matriculation had any intention of proceeding with university studies.

The last quarter of the century, therefore, saw the European secondary leaving examinations established essentially in the forms which they have since retained: in France external and in Germany internal state examinations, and in England a variety of examinations, conducted by the universities, with differing standards and purposes. In America the diversity of educational authorities was so great that, except by the New York Board of Regents and the Joint Board of the Eastern Universities, no general external leaving examinations were established.

One reason why other authorities in America preferred the accrediting system was that by the time the question of examinations and college entrance was seriously tackled in the 1890's the first attack on examinations in Europe had already gathered force. This attack was directed, not, like the twentieth-century attack, against their validity, but against their educational value. It was a constantly reiterated cry of the liberal and humanist scholar in the nineteenth century that examinations were killing the real spirit of scholarship, and later that they were stifling all freedom in the curriculum. The first point of view was vigorously expressed by Grundtvig, during his struggle to keep the folk high schools free of the state examination system: "All examinations as we know them are repellent to me, and examinations in anything which is dear to our hearts are appalling." The two limiting phrases in this sentence are important. Grundtvig, like most of the critics, was attacking examinations *as we know them*; and he was concerned with their evil effect on the true love of learning. He was supported in this attack by Thring in England, who objected most strongly to examinations in English literature, which he stigmatised as "cramming". It is difficult not to have great sympathy with this view, and with those who hold that the whole development of "Eng. Lit." as a school subject has been of questionable value. The opposition has so far triumphed, however—at least in Europe; and the force of their view must be admitted. It is, in brief, that the true love of learning is not sufficiently widely spread to form the sole incentive for secondary school work, nor teachers of the inspiring quality of Thring and Grundtvig sufficiently common. With the average pupil and the average teacher the incentive of the examination is a valuable stimulus, and with the exceptional teacher it does no harm, since he can almost invariably teach without any reference to it, and still produce pupils who do brilliantly. As to examinations in things we love, they say, quite as many pupils have come to love a subject through starting it with an examination in view, as have lost an initial love of it through having to take an examination.

The second part of the liberal attack was to some extent confused with an attack on the curriculum; the objection to the pressure exerted by the *Abitur* in Prussia, for instance, was really not so much an attack on examinations, as on an educational system which demanded too much from the secondary schoolboy and used the examination as a weapon for extracting it. Nevertheless, there was some justification in the complaint that an examination syllabus, too rigidly conceived, forced all schools into a single mould. On the other hand, when the English examining bodies tried to meet this complaint by allowing any school to submit a special syllabus of its own, it was surprising, in view of the prevalence of the complaint, how few schools took advantage of it.

Primary Leaving Examinations in the Nineteenth Century

By the end of the century primary leaving examinations were just beginning to present some of those problems which have deeply concerned educationists in the last few years. In countries with a rigidly supervised system, such as France, the *certificat d'études primaires* was purely a certifying and incentive examination and served a useful and unquestioned purpose. In England the use of examinations under the Revised Code to establish the amount of grant payable to the school was condemned, as we have seen, from the start, and in its indirect effect on teaching methods was probably the least satisfactory system ever devised. It was only a temporary phase, however, and the real problems arose with the spread of free places in the secondary schools for which pupils from the primary schools competed by examination.

These "scholarship" examinations exhibited many of the faults that arise from a confusion of functions. The scholarships, which were eagerly coveted, inevitably had a strong regulative effect on the teaching of the whole school, since primary schools were often judged by the number of their successes in the scholarship examination. They had been designed, however, not as regulative or inspiring examinations for primary schools, but as selective examinations for entry to academic secondary schools. In practice, therefore, the curriculum of the primary school began to be governed by an examination which should have concerned only a small minority, just as the secondary school had been over-influenced by the requirements for entry to universities, to which most of its pupils had no intention of going.

Another feature of public selective examinations rendered their influence on the general curriculum even more pernicious. Where entry to a limited and coveted form of secondary education, provided out of public funds, depended on the result of an examination, there was an insistent demand that the examination should be, above all things, demonstrably fair and impartial. It is a feature of all examining that the wider and deeper the range of knowledge or capacity that is examined, the less certain the examiners can be of the accuracy of their marks and the greater will be the effect of general "social background". In their anxiety to set questions which could be marked with complete accuracy and to give everyone an equal chance, the examiners rigidly limited their syllabus, and employed questions of the type which educationists of their period parodied as: "Who chased whom how many times round the walls of what?"

Raymont, writing at the beginning of the twentieth century, drew attention to the evil effects of these examinations as:

(a) The regard of examinations as ends rather than means.
(b) The occasional over-pressure on pupils, producing a harmful precocity.
(c) The over-estimation, in judging schools, of examination success.
(d) The influence of bad examinations on teaching. (In this respect he particularly quotes the concentration of examiners on easily markable lists.)

Twentieth-Century Developments

The two most notable developments in the field of examinations in this century have been the attack on the reliability of traditional examinations and the growing popularity of the "mental test". The two are clearly interrelated, because the mental test owes much of its favour to the view that it at least produces more accurately verifiable results than the old-fashioned examination. Any question of the value of a process must start from a consideration of its purpose, and the attack on traditional examinations is bound up with a changed view of the purpose of examination. We have seen that almost up to the end of the nineteenth century the primary purpose of examination was regulative and inspiring. With the increased use of examination, rather than capacity to pay fees, as the test for entry to the next stage of education, the primary purpose of examination became selection or testing. In the first case the designers of examinations were primarily concerned with their effect on the teaching in the schools which took the examination, and in the second with the accurate selection, by means of examination, of the right pupils for the subsequent stage. It does not follow that the same sort of examinations will be the most suitable for both functions. Before going on to consider the result of this changed emphasis, however, we must glance at the answer produced in America, about the turn of the century, to the first, or educational, attack on the traditional external examination.

At the beginning of the century it was still assumed that the traditional examination of the "college entrance" type was, in fact, the most suitable way of choosing college entrants. The objection to it was that it was completely unsuitable as a regulative or inspiring examination for secondary schools, whose main function was no longer to prepare for college entrance. In the European selective secondary schools this problem was not so acute as in the comprehensive high schools of America, and something was done to solve it in England by the creation of Joint Examining Boards on which the secondary school teachers were represented. In America the much more radical solution of internal examinations, conducted at accredited schools, was adopted for all secondary leaving examinations except entrance to a few eastern universities.

The accrediting system started in Michigan, where we have already seen that the State University played an unusually large part in the organisation of secondary education. Instead of demanding that candidates for entry to the State University should pass its own entry examinations, the University organised a system of inspecting and "accrediting" secondary schools in

R   255

the State, and then admitting, without any further examination, any graduate from an accredited school. The system spread outside the State, and in 1895 the leading universities of the North Central States formed a North Central Association of Colleges and Schools. This Association kept a list of accredited schools, whose graduates were automatically acceptable to any member university. There are now National and Regional Accrediting Agencies throughout the U.S.A., and this is the normal method of securing entry to a college or university.

The great advantage of the accrediting system is that it allows the examinations to be conducted by the schools, in accordance with each school's individual character and curriculum, and, if desired, over a considerable period of time. This eliminates two ways in which "luck" affects normal examinations—the lucky choice of questions and the unlucky choice of examination day. At the same time the universities are able to satisfy themselves that the schools which they accredit are maintaining the standard of education required. The disadvantages are: first, that the system can only apply to the larger city high schools, while other arrangements have to be made for the graduate from an unaccredited rural school; and, second, that the more highly organised the accrediting system becomes, the more likely it is to concentrate attention on easily measurable externals rather than the less calculable values of true education. In a nation-wide accrediting system, for instance, it is almost inevitable that some fixed standards of the buildings, equipment, etc. required in an accredited school will be laid down. This tends to increase an already dangerous tendency to devote a larger and larger proportion of educational funds to equipment rather than to teachers. Even if the accrediting agency has the sense to realise that the most important thing in any school seeking accreditation is the quality of its teachers, administrative convenience will lead them to gauge this on paper qualifications rather than first-hand knowledge. What happens in fact is that the accrediting agency demands that a certain proportion of the teaching staff should hold Ph.D.s or M.A.s in education, and though this may be more realistic than concentrating on the number of washbowls, it is still far from touching the heart of the matter. And its influence in encouraging unnecessary or semi-spurious research work has been recently brought into question.

In general, however, the twentieth century has been more concerned with the selective than with the regulative function of examinations. Two factors led to this transfer of attention. We have seen that one was the increasing use of examinations for the selection of pupils to benefit from state-aided education. The other was the extension, mentioned in Chapter Four, of the statistical method to problems of education. P. B. Ballard pointed out in *The New Examiner* (1923) that whereas in the first issue of the *Journal of Educational Psychology*, issued in 1910, there was only one reference to problems of mental measurement, in the current issue it was difficult to find references to any other problems at all. The educationists in search of a genuinely scientific form of examination which should be able to select children with a degree of proved reliability were first attracted by the work of Binet in France. Binet had started in 1895 on researches designed to provide an accurate method of determining mental deficiency. In order to do this he was led to work out, by a method of random sampling, a standard scale of attainment against which any child could be measured. This scale was published in 1908 and formed the basis of many subsequent scales for measuring mental age. A logical development, based on the psychology of Spearman (see Chapter Four), was the development of special tests to measure first the quality of "g" or general intelligence, and then the various specific factors. Since Spearman identified "g" as the ability to "educe" relations, most of the questions in general intelligence tests are designed to test this faculty. Tests of this kind were given to the U.S. Army recruits in large batches in 1917 in order to grade them in respect not of achievement but of capacity to learn, and the success of the operation made a great impression on educationists all over the world. The use of the correlation technique and the possibility of standardising such tests by trying them on large numbers of pupils made it possible to prove that they had a high degree of reliability—that is to say, that the candidate's score remained more or less constant if an equivalent test was repeated after a short interval. Moreover, the nature of tests—a large number of questions demanding single right or wrong answers—meant that variations due to the *examiner's* unreliability were avoided altogether.

Naturally it was not long before the believers in the new type of test or examination turned their attention to a detailed and accurate attack on the old. The new techniques of statistical measurement and interpretation made it much easier to do so, and it was soon proved that the old-fashioned type of examination, consisting largely of a number of essay questions, was highly unreliable, in two ways. In the first place, controlled experiments with a number of different examiners marking the same papers showed that they varied immensely in the mark that each one gave to the same answer. Professor Valentine quotes an experiment where the teachers were marking seventeen essays and using particular care, since they knew that they were being tested: yet one of the essays was marked second by one examiner, third by two others, thirteenth by a fourth, and actually sixteenth out of seventeen by a fifth.[1] Perhaps the most staggering example of this unreliability occurred by mistake in an American university and has often been quoted since. A number of professors were examining in history and, having fixed sixty per cent. as the "pass mark", took the precaution of circulating to each other for re-marking any paper which came just on this "border-line". One of the examiners, in order to give himself a clear standard of judgment, had written out a set of model answers, and this set got mixed up with the "border-line" papers and circulated to his colleagues. At least one of them actually failed his colleague's model paper, and the marks it received varied from forty to eighty per cent. Since 1920 many devices have been introduced to make the marking of essay questions more reliable, but there is no doubt that it is still a very chancy business compared with the marking of an intelligence test.

Secondly, a statistical survey of the subsequent careers of those who had entered schools or universities as the result of examinations showed that in a significant number of cases they were no true guide in the selection of suitable candidates. This was particularly true in the selection of children at an early age, as in the English eleven-year-old "scholarship" examination.

The advantages of the new type of examination over the old were argued forcibly in England by Ballard and may be summarised as follows:

(a) Accuracy in marking. Variations due to the examiner are entirely eliminated.

---

[1] C. W. Valentine, *The Reliability of Examinations*.

(*b*) Standardisation.

(*c*) Economy. They can be set to hundreds and marked by clerks.

(*d*) Specificity. It was objected that in the old type of examination English composition entered into every paper. In the new type, based on one word answers or underlining, a geography paper tests knowledge of geographical fact and nothing else. (It will be noted that this is a return to "Who chased whom how many times round the walls of what?")

(*e*) The elimination of "cramming". (It was at first believed that it was impossible to coach for intelligence tests, or that if coaching was done it would prove ineffective. Recent experience has shown that this is not so.)

As a method of selection the statistically controlled test has to a very considerable degree superseded the examination, particularly in America. There have been constant objections to it, largely on the score that, like most processes derived from a technique of measurement, it concentrates attention solely on those qualities which it is capable of measuring, to the exclusion of those which are possibly more important but less measurable. It is, the opponents say, as if the educational authorities were to say: "Your old-fashioned way of measuring a child's capacity for an academic course is very inaccurate and unfair. We cannot measure this capacity by our new methods, but we can measure, with extreme accuracy and fairness, the length of their ears. We therefore propose to make this the criterion of selection, and thus eliminate all inaccuracy at a blow." This is, of course, an extreme parody, but there is possibly some truth in the epigrammatic definition of "intelligence" as "the quality measured in intelligence tests". Nevertheless, experiment has proved that as a prognostication of future success in education, except where specific "ground work" is necessary, the scientific intelligence test is just about as reliable as the old-fashioned examination—and much easier to administer.

The more serious objection to replacing examinations entirely by such tests is that, from the regulative point of view, they are positively harmful. So much attention has been concentrated on the selective function of examinations that it has been almost overlooked that the new ones can no more escape their regulative function than the old. If English composition is eliminated from geography papers, pupils will inevitably begin to treat English composition as a special sort of art, to be practised for passing

English composition tests, but for no other purpose. If the only technique required for passing the vital examinations is a knowledge of more or less disjointed facts and the ability to underline in pencil, then these are the techniques which will be practised in the schools. It is useless, as education authorities in England have found out, to fulminate against coaching in intelligence tests, if performance in intelligence tests is to decide a child's future. Whatever the regulations say, the nature of the examination inevitably controls the methods of teaching; and from this point of view the warnings of the nineteenth-century educationists against "easily markable lists" are as relevant to-day as when they were given.

Finally, the unreliability of all external examinations, either new style or old, when it comes to selecting the most suitable candidates for the more advanced stages of education has led to a growing interest in other means of selection—either by means of recommendation from accredited schools, by far greater attention to school records, by easy transfer from one type of school to another, or by probationary periods in the university.

EPILOGUE

HAVING kept as closely as possible in the preceding chapters to a historical brief, I propose in this short epilogue to grant myself the indulgence of pursuing a few personal hares—or, if the reader prefers to think of it that way, of expelling a few personal bees from my bonnet. An epilogue, I suppose, should sum up what has gone before, and most people would agree, in summing up, that the great change in education over the last hundred years has been the gradual assumption by society of duties which were previously carried out or neglected by the individual or the parish.

Universal primary education first took all children from the home to ensure that they learnt the elements of literacy and calculation; more recently, universal secondary education has taken out of the parents' hands much of their further training. Beyond the schools stand the publicly sponsored youth services and adult education, and the rapidly expanding universities. All this has been provided out of central or local taxation for the normal citizen, and at the same time, particularly in the twentieth century, there has been a great increase in the variety of special educational services supplied by public authority to the handicapped, the maladjusted or the delinquent. An immense effort has been made, in fact, to perfect the organisation of education so that every child or youth should receive at some sort of school the type of education for which he is fitted.

All this surely represents a very great social advance, and in the most valuable of all spheres, the development of individual worth and character. No sane person could wish that it had not happened; but the process has not been without flaws, and those flaws arise, I believe, from tendencies inherent in the control of education by the State. "Society" is a pleasant term with which to play in the literature of sociology; but, in practice, when we say that this duty has been assumed by "society" we mean that it has been assumed by public authority and ultimately by the

261

State. And the State, as an educator, has an inevitable tendency towards certain specific failings.

Let me hasten to say, first, that I wish neither to blame nor deplore the concern of the State for education. Once grant the positive theory of the State's functions, which is now almost everywhere accepted, and it is clear that the State *must* control education—either through a central or local administration. Moreover, no other agency could ever have brought about the magnificent results which have come from State education. Through no other means than public control and finance could educational opportunities have been offered anything like as widely as they have been in the last hundred years. If, in this personal summing up, I concentrate on the defects that have arisen from State action, it is because I accept the public control of education as a necessity. Its defects, I believe, arise very largely from the nature of the administrative mind.

It is the nature of administrators—and the State in practice is composed of administrators—to love two kinds of thing, the measurable and the complicated. They love the measurable because those who deal with the measurable can see on paper the record of their achieved results and answer criticism by means of unimpeachable figures. In this predilection they are at present aided and abetted by those experts on whom public officials rely in the daily administration of their business. The progress of the physical sciences, which are based on a technique of measurement, has been so great in the last hundred years that experts in education, as in every other sphere, have tended to concentrate on those aspects of education which can be brought within the scope of measurable scales.

That administrators should love the complicated would seem at first paradoxical: surely one would expect that they would seek above all things to simplify their task. Human nature, however, does not seem to work this way. Administrators are usually very intelligent people, with a talent for organisation; and very intelligent people with a talent for organisation like building up in their own department an elaborate and complicated mechanism.[1] This may seem so trivial and personal an argument as to be out of place in discussing a great subject like education; but even education is the product of a vast number of personal and individual human beings, and if it is indeed a trait of human

[1] This sentence was written before the publication of *Parkinson's Law*, which of course operates in Education as surely as in other forms of Administration.

nature, then it cannot be irrelevant to the way in which education is administered. Whether it *is* such a trait the reader must judge for himself; certainly the experience which many temporary administrators had in the war of what was vulgarly known as "empire building" seems to bear it out; the "empire builder" was not always consciously intriguing for promotion; he actually believed that in expanding and complicating the organisation under him he was improving the administration.

Now if these two facts are true, that administrators love the measurable and the complicated, education is a dangerous subject for them. For the true needs of education are immeasurable and simple.

"The essential principle of education is not teaching; it is love", said Pestalozzi, probably the greatest of all primary teachers; and Thring, certainly one of the greatest of all secondary teachers, only went so far as to qualify it by adding one word— "a thinking love". From the practice of some educational administrators one might easily assume—wrongly, I believe— that they thought it was not love, but sanitation. My contention is not that they do think this, but that they act as if they thought it, and that they do so because the number of wash-bowls in a school is so much more easily measurable than the amount of love. In general, the experts are not very helpful to the administrators here. A very few of them have cheerfully settled down to the thankless task of making love measurable. Ballard, in *The New Examiner*,[1] for instance, seems to assume that it must be because degrees of it exist, and Raymond Cattell in *A Guide to Mental Testing*[2] talks of "resolving the attitude of affection into primary ergic components", which seems to me about as practical a proposal as the system, drawn from an American degree thesis, of measuring human happiness in "euphor units". On the whole, however, experts have very reasonably turned their attention to those other, and less important, facets of education where their technique can be usefully employed.

I believe, then, that the first dangerous tendency of public administration over the last hundred years has been that the important thing in education—love—has been overlooked and

---

[1] P. B. Ballard, *The New Examiner*, p. 39.
[2] Raymond Cattell, *A Guide to Mental Testing*. It is only fair to say that he mentions the process only as possible, not desirable.

even crowded out of the schools in favour of less important things, mainly because it is not measurable.

I can well imagine that the reader is beginning to suspect at this point that all this talk about "love" is just some more of that sentimental and vaporous jargon from which so much educational writing suffers. Clearly you cannot train teachers in love, pay special responsibility allowances for love on the Burnham scale, or calculate a school's eligibility for "grant" or "accreditation" on the amount of love that goes on in it; but that does not mean that love is unimportant, and it is just because you cannot do these things that it is treated as if it were.

There are three ways in which the public administration of education tends to neglect the more important for the less—in the proportion of funds and energy devoted to buildings and equipment, in the qualifications demanded from teachers, and in the expansion of administrative and "advisory" services. In each case the important thing in education, the relationship between the individual teacher and pupil, which should be based on love, and therefore immeasurable, has been sacrificed to something else which is less important but measurable.

The rapid rise in standards of "required" accommodation and equipment needs no more evidence than that of our own eyes. The number of wash-bowls, the acres of vita-glass, the gymnasium apparatus are there for everyone to see; the classroom of the future exhibited at the Festival of Britain, with its noiseless floor, its built-in radio and "visual aids", was only the culmination of a tendency which can be observed all over the country. In America the expenditure on educational building and equipment is said to have doubled every decade since 1900. All this, of course, is in itself very good, or would be very good in a community where the funds available for education were unlimited. But the expenditure on teachers has not doubled every decade, nor was there any exhibit at the Festival of Britain to suggest that a teacher with a real love of children or of learning is worth all the equipment in the catalogue. The extent to which this diversion of resources to tangible and measurable equipment is a specific failing of public administration as opposed to private may be partly gauged by the contrast between the publicly maintained schools and the independent schools in England. The standards of accommodation and equipment in the independent public schools are often far behind those of the new maintained schools: the staffing ratio and staff salaries are far ahead.

It may be objected that many of our schools are still badly equipped, cheerless and out of date, and that it is churlish, particularly in any one who claims an interest in education, to express anything but enthusiasm for the beautiful new schools which are being built to take their place. But this is actually the fallacy which derives from the administrative outlook. The new schools are physically there and everyone can see them; what they cannot see is that every shilling spent on them has to come out of the one budget, and that we have been concentrating on buildings and equipment to the detriment of men and women. I, for one, would rather have my son well taught in a small class by a good teacher in an old-fashioned, cold, dreary schoolroom, than see him one of a huge throng conducted by a harassed drudge, but living in a palace. And this is one reason at least why many parents spend large sums to send their children to the "public schools".

Here someone may object that what I am asking for is merely a redistribution of money—less for equipment and more for teachers—and that this is a strange result of maintaining that the essential principle of education is love. Love, surely, is not bought for money. The answer to that is bound up with the second dangerous tendency of public administration.

There are two kinds of love which make all the difference to education, love of children and love of learning. The first makes the difference between the good and the bad primary teacher; in the secondary stage it is almost as important, but as the work becomes more advanced its importance dwindles and that of the second increases. Obviously the ideal teacher has both. Of course neither type of love can be bought, in the sense that people will not develop it as the result of being paid extra for it; but the amount of it that the nation's children will get is affected by the proportion of the educational budget which is devoted to men rather than buildings, in two ways.

In the first place, love is stifled by too great numbers. It is, at its best, a personal relation between the teacher and the individual pupil, and though it does work to some extent with a class, it has very little chance if the class is too big. Teachers know this, and for the last fifty years they have been putting a reduction in the size of classes at the very head of their proposals for reform. The State has answered by giving them almost everything else. The buildings, the equipment, the special schools of different types have changed almost unrecognisably since Matthew Arnold's time, but the one simple important thing has not been done. The size of classes remains much the same, or worse.

Secondly, although you cannot inspire the kind of love that teaching demands by offering rewards in money, you can keep a number of people who have it out of the profession by paying teaching on a lower level than comparable trades—particularly those married men and women whose love of children makes them want to bring up, in reasonable conditions, a family of their own.

These, then, are two reasons why a diversion of financial resources from the tangible and measurable to the intangible and important might give us schools which were less obvious civic monuments, but better places of education.

It is not only in the proportion of its funds that it devotes to teachers that public administration tends to seek a wrong balance of values. Its second weakness is that, by its very nature, it places more and more reliance on paper qualifications. Public administration has not been blind to the importance of getting good teachers into the schools. But whereas an individual or parish board can appoint a teacher because they know his virtue as a teacher, the impersonal public administrator can only go on certificates and training courses. It is not possible to teach the kind of love that is required or to grant certificates for it, and so the most important factor in selecting teachers is quietly ignored, and a totally false value put on what should be secondary considerations, simply because they are certifiable. Teachers themselves seem to me to have been at fault on this issue. In their anxiety to "raise the status of the profession"—and so, they clearly hoped, to raise its pay—they have tended to press for the employment of more and more university graduates in primary schools. But it is not the intellectual qualities, the qualities easily certifiable by university degrees, that matter most in primary teaching. Moreover, since the kind of love that we have been talking about commonly goes with a vigorous personality, it is not likely that primary teaching could ever attract many of that small minority who combine it with high intellectual ability and are, in fact, the leaders of any nation. A country is lucky if it gets a reasonable proportion of those in secondary schools. The result of demanding higher and higher intellectual qualifications, of the sort which are easily measurable, from primary teachers has been, in fact, to exclude from the primary schools many possible teachers who have far more important qualifications of character, and to replace them with those who have a certain intellectual facility and very little else. And this is largely the fault of public administration with its demand for something visible and measurable in the way of certificates.

Nor has much of the training which public authority has demanded from "qualified" teachers been entirely realistic. William James pointed out, as many as fifty years ago, that it would be fatal if the new interest in educational psychology which he was stimulating led the ordinary teacher to think any the less of herself as a teacher because she was not a conscious psychologist. Yet the tendency since his time has been to demand more and more in the way of theoretical knowledge about psychology, and to care less and less for the type of wisdom which comes from a practical love of children, simply because the one is certifiable and the other is not. The medical profession—very close, surely, in its aims to the teaching profession—and psychiatrists in particular, are insistent about the danger of amateur or superficial psychological treatment, but educationists are becoming more and more prone to write as if every teacher is or should be something of a theoretical psychologist. The danger of this is not only that it may encourage a form of superficiality, but that it may discourage those whose minds are not of a theoretical type, and sow among the thinking public a distrust for educational theory as a whole. There is already a divergence of opinion between the great majority of practising teachers, in secondary schools at least, and the general corpus of "educational thought" which should be very disquieting. To see how disquieting, one has only to imagine a situation where the great majority of practising doctors regarded with scepticism the theories of medicine taught at the universities.

Again, the remedy does not seem to lie with any positive action that public administration could take. The practical love of children, which is, I believe, the best qualification for primary teaching, is not a thing which could be taught or for which certificates could be issued. Two suggestions do seem worth considering, however: the first is that the intellectual and theoretical qualifications demanded for primary teachers should be lowered, so that those who have the more important qualification, uncombined with any great capacity for theoretical work, should no longer be kept out of the profession; the other is that, both in the training of teachers and in the publicising of educational research, much more attention should be paid to the difference between theory and practice, particularly in the sphere of secondary education where the theory seems often to be a somewhat uncritical adaptation of that evolved for primary schools.

Thirdly, the administrative mind has led to a considerable waste of educational resources on administrative and "advisory" or "consultative" work. Here again the proposition is difficult to prove. Every reader will probably know of some educational authority in his own country or neighbourhood, which in the past operated with a staff of ten or twelve and now employs hundreds. Many will have experienced under war conditions the tendency which all central administrations seem to have, to duplicate the staff who are actually doing the job "in the field" with other officials at headquarters who are trying to do it for them, or tell them how to do it. A common result was that those in the field felt irritated and those at the centre frustrated. In the same sort of way education authorities in England now appoint "advisers" in every subject from carpentry to religious instruction. They are presumably men of such quality that they would make outstandingly good teachers, but instead of following their vocation they travel round the area "advising" the practising teachers on how to do their work. This sounds good in theory, but in practice it overlooks one almost universal human trait, the tendency to reject advice—particularly advice from the "expert" who "looks in from the head office and doesn't have to tackle the difficulties himself". If the advice of such officials is rejected, then they are good teachers wasted—and good teachers are far too rare to waste. There is in all central administrations an understandable desire to supervise as closely as possible the work for which the administration is ultimately responsible, but teaching is not an activity which can be treated like this. That delegation of authority, which is essential in any organisation if it is not to be encumbered by divided responsibility and duplicated staffs, is inevitable in education; for in education the thing that matters most is a personal relationship which would escape the trammels of any administrative system. The objection to the spread of administrators and advisers in education is not therefore that they are effectively doing something pernicious, but that, far too often, they are wasted. It would be a fascinating, but alas improbable, development, if some education authority in England were suddenly, for one school term, to reduce its office staff to a skeleton, and send the officials out to teach in the schools of its area. A lot of records would go uncompiled, a lot of letters would go unanswered—many of them such as need never have been written—a lot of silly questions would get no reply, but I find it hard to believe that for that term the children would not be better educated.

Finally, it is possible that the fondness of all administrators for the complicated often leads to the diversion of educational resources from a very few simple reforms to a multitude of ingenious and divergent experiments which are very interesting but less essential. It is at least arguable, for instance, that the educational system of England would be better to-day if it had been decided in 1946 that one single and simple reform, the rebuilding and restaffing of primary schools, should have precedence for the next five years over everything else. Administrators would have been saved endless work on development plans which were obsolete before they were finished, we should not have had a sprinkling of secondary modern schools here and there, with an occasional technical school and the germs of a county college; but we should have had the one thing upon which everything else can be built and without which it can hardly be built right—enough primary schools, with small classes and good teachers. It is, of course, only a very tentative personal opinion that the simple decision was also the right decision; it may be that some of the other developments really were a more valuable use of the limited resources we had; but, for all that, the administrator's love of complication would have made the simple decision a difficult one to take, even if it had been right, for it would have rendered unnecessary so much ingenuity and argument and committee work; and it is the danger of administrators that many of them actually get to like ingenuity and argument and committee work for its own sake.

Looking back over the last hundred years, then, we can surely see that the intervention of the State to promote and control education has brought about a social change of immense value to mankind; but in bringing about this change the State has inevitably increased the strength of those tendencies in bureaucracy which are dangerous to any sort of social activity and particularly dangerous to education. Up to now the result of this blindness has been nothing more serious than a wrong balance in the distribution of her resources. Whether things get better or worse must depend on the view that administrators take of their own function and capacities. The best hope for the future lies in the fact that many administrators, in this country at least, are themselves aware of these dangerous tendencies. On April 11, 1951, the Permanent Secretary to the Ministry of Education addressed the Royal Society of Arts on the very subject we have been considering—"A Century of British Education"—and I can think of no more fitting conclusion to this epilogue than to quote the closing words of Sir John Maud's address:

"If I may, for the first time this afternoon, now speak not only for myself but for my colleagues in the Ministry of Education, I swear that, as best we may, we will resist the occupational disease of self importance. The chief end of education, I believe, is individual personality, and the chief means to that end is the teacher. And so, as the service that civil servants like myself owe the public is to promote education, I declare myself unreservedly a servant of the teacher—sometimes a disobedient humble servant, perforce, but never his master."

O si sic omnes!

Postscript.

I have made no change in this epilogue for the second edition. I should now regard it as rather extreme in places but I would not wish to recant on any major issue. I could not really support, for instance, a lowering of the academic standards required from primary teachers; but I would not wish to see them raised except in proportion as their course is lengthened; and I would hope that much use would be made of the special provisions for admitting married women to shortened courses of training. I am not as sceptical about administrators, advisors and educationists as I was before I became one; but I still feel rather guiltily that we all ought to come off the sidelines more often and teach in schools. Unfortunately it is not very easy to arrange.

INDEX

272